Ewing Reviewing

2020

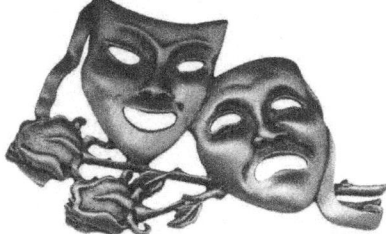

Jan Ewing
William J. Cataldi

**Major Works Off- & Off-Off-Broadway & Online in New York City
as Reviewed on HI! DRAMA**

PUP'S BOOKS ● NEW YORK CITY

Photojournalism by DLW Photography NYC ● Standard B&W Edition

ISBN: 979-8-596-88948-2
Printed by CreateSpace, an Amazon.com Company
Available at **http://bit.ly/EwingReviewing2020-Standard**

Cover Photo & Photo Plates 1–39 © 2021 by Dan Lane Williams
DLW Photography NYC
https://www.dlwphotographynyc.com/

Published by
pupsbooks.com
New York, New York

Table of Contents

Performances appear in the order in which they were seen.
This Table of Contents has been alphabetized for convenience.

Introduction

As I write this, *Corona Virus-19* is the single most discussed issue in the world, and the thought of discussing it again makes my toes curl. It's painfully clear how (and how *much*) it impacted the performing arts. Our hyperactive culture screeched to a halt, leaving creatives of all sorts stuck at home in front of their computers, brain cells twitching, inexorably coaxing a substantial new art form into existence. spite of the misery, pain, chaos and death that marked 2020 as a year few of us want to remember, something positive did take place.

"Hundreds of plays are being performed Off- and Off-Off Broadway every day." That's a quote from the back of **Ewing Reviewing 2019**. At the time, a bewildering variety of live performances were taking place in NYC, almost around the clock. Right after I wrote that, however, at the beginning of March, it stopped … abruptly and completely. Our embarassment of riches turned into desolation and poverty. Not only was there noplace to be seen, everybody was suddenly broke and stuck at home with nothing to do.

OUR COLLEAGUES

How that turned into the *Zoom Revolution* is the subject of William J. Cataldi's informative essay, "Lessons Learned from the Pandemic" (p. 175). This is only one of the many insightful pieces William has contributed to this year's volume. His reviews, both live and online, bring a unique, intellectual perspective to cultural events. Sometimes, he's controversial, but his comments are cogent and intelligent. They always provoke thought, which is exactly what they're supposed to do.

I want to thank Jen Bush for contributing her review of the Zoom version of my own play, *Nursery Rhymes* (p. 113). It appeared on the **Arts Independent** site in January. Jen is a writer for **PassionPit Publications** covering *theatre, film,* and *literature.* Eva Heinemann of **HI! DRAMA** is also with us again (see below). She and I both adore Victorian slapstick, so we cowrite many reviews of that sort. Her viewpoint is always fresh and welcome.

We are also delighted to introduce Dan Lane Williams of **DLW Photography NYC** who has contributed an essay and a set of stunning photographs entitled *Bright Lights, Covid City: Broadway in the Dark.*

An ode to the city that (almost) never sleeps; a photographer turns his lens on New York City's majestic theatre district during COVID.

Dan's work (printed in full color or black and white, depending upon the edition), is a profound statement on the grandeur of the Great White Way, shining, as ever into the heavens of the world, with no one there to see it. The photographs are at once stunning and heartbreaking.

Mr. Williams is an actor and photographer residing in New York City. He serves the northeast and tri-state area shooting weddings, family and other events, headshots, portraiture, film and theatre stills as well as personal projects and fine art. He is available for bookings and has special safety protocols in place during the pandemic. To purchase prints, click *http://bit.ly/DLWBroadwayPrints.*

Those of you who have seen and read earlier volumes of **Ewing Reviewing** will notice that some of the following information remains the same. This is general information that has not changed.

HI! DRAMA

This excellent site, which has been constantly active during the Pandemic shutdown, consistently covers more new experimental plays and musicals than anyone else in New York City. In order to see their almost daily postings, including reviews and announcements of coming events on social media, check out **Facebook.com/hidramas** or watch the television show on alternate Saturdays at 1:30pm EST on Spectrum Ch. 56, RCN Ch. 83, Fios Ch. 34, or streamed live on *www.mnn.org* (click on MNN#2).

A word about the "FACES" placed at the end of most reviews. This is a longstanding **HI! DRAMA** tradition that sums up the reviewer's opinion. The best is **HAPPY FACE PLUS**, the worst is **UNHAPPY FACE MINUS**. The other "FACES" are self-explanatory.

UNION ASSOCIATION

Actors' Equity Association (AEA), *founded in 1913, represents more than 50,000 actors and stage managers in the United States. Equity seeks to advance, promote* 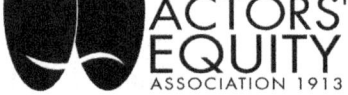 *and foster the art of live theatre as an essential component of our society. Equity negotiates wages and working conditions, providing a wide range of benefits, including health and pension plans. **AEA** is a member of the **AFLCIO**, and is affiliated with the **FIA**, an international organization of performing arts unions. The Equity emblem is our mark of excellence.*   — Actors' Equity Policy Statement

On Broadway, cast and crew members must belong to an appropriate union. In this book, Broadway productions are identified and union membership is assumed. For Off- and Off-Off Broadway, wherever that might be, Equity members can appear only if an **AEA** waiver has been obtained by the producer. An asterisk (*) indicates the name of each **AEA** member appearing under this waiver.

Similarly, this symbol (°) appears next to the names of members of the **Stage Directors and Choreographers Society**. Other professional organizations are credited when they appear in individual reviews. All information in this book has been provided by the producer or the press agent.

EWING REVIEWING 2020

This book is the third in a series to be published yearly, providing exposure for, and historical information on, a cross-section of *Independent Theater* performances, drawn at random from the previous calendar year in New York City, and, now, thanks to Zoom, from online sources all over the United States and the world.

The Index (see p. 179) is a reference index, not a subject index. It provides an easy guide for connecting companies and individuals to their productions. It is designed to access a participant once in each event. If a name has three page numbers listed, that person is involved in three different plays, not listed three times in one play. *Note:* If their specialty is noted, assistants are listed under that specialty (i.e., "Assistant Directors" appear under **DIRECTORS**). *Everyone* who appears onstage is listed under **ACTORS**.

ACKNOWLEDGMENTS

First, many thanks to Eva Heinemann, **Outer Critics Circle** member and founder of **HI! DRAMA**. Not only is her knowledge of today's theater remarkably deep, but she also seems to know everybody in the business. The Theater is her life and nothing makes her happier than finding and supporting a new talent.

Thanks, as well, to the intrepid Jay Michaels, who has put his downtime to good use by creating **Channel i – the independent arts channel** (*JayMichaelsArts.com*), a new media platform designed to house a wide variety of independent disciplines. Bless him for his energy and optimism.

I'm also grateful to my partner, William J. Cataldi, not only for his fine literary contributions, but also for his heroic proofreading and unstinting moral support. He keeps me writing, and I can hardly say anything better than that.

Finally, thank you to the uncountable production artists who have continued working throughout this dark year, developing and using the new online media to enrich our lives. Their creations are remarkable. Almost everything we see is worth remembering, which is why, in the final analysis, I wanted to create this book.

— Jan Ewing, NYC (February 2020)

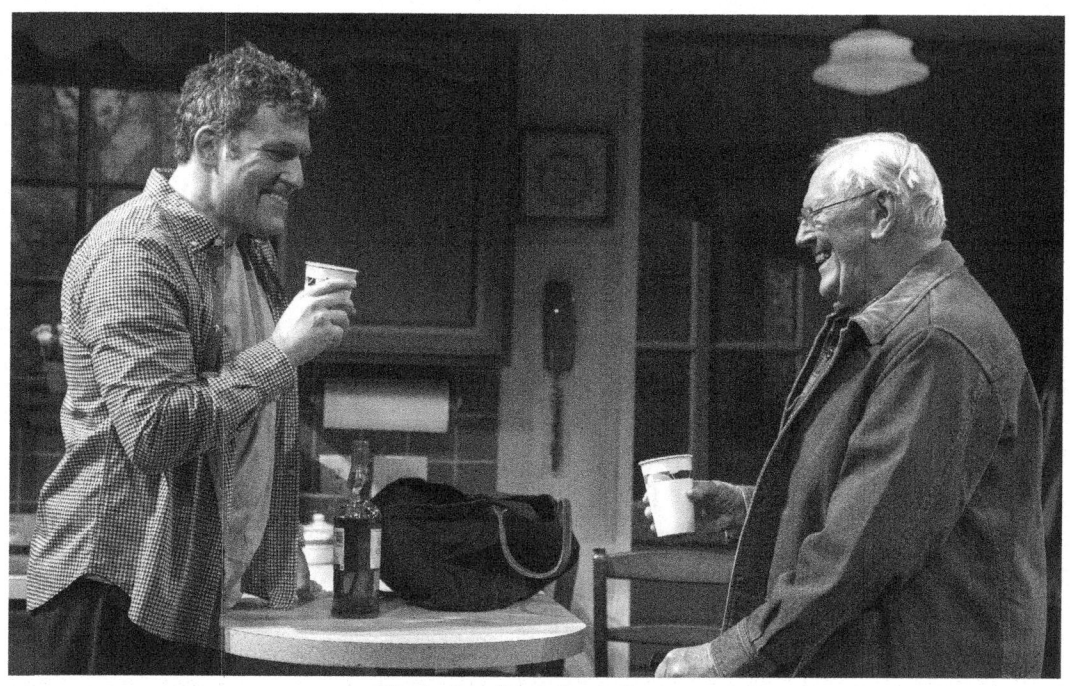

Craig Bierko & Lou Cariou

Harry Townsend's Last Stand

- Presented by Dennis Grimaldi
- Play by George Eastman
- Directed by Karen Carpenter
- Production Stage Manager: Alan Fox
- Assistant Stage Manager: Nathan K. Claus
- Scenic Designer: Lauren Helpern
- Costume Designer: David C. Woolard
- Lighting Designer: Jeff Davis
- Sound Designer: John Gromada
- Advertising: Hofstetter & Partners
- Marketing: Leanne Schanzer Promotions
- Production Manager: Mary Duffe
- General Management: Brierpatch Productions
- Press: Keith Sherman & Associates
- Photo: Maria Baranova

THE CAST

- Harry Townsend: Len Cariou
- Alan Townsend: Craig Bierko

1

BACKGROUND

Most of us have no idea how to deal with old age. We're so obsessed with youth that we deny we're old until we *are* old. Then, it's too late. Things fall off. Joints wear out. Eyes get blurry. People begin to act like we're made out of glass, too fragile to live on our own, forgetful and decrepit whether we are or not. The only *good* thing about it is that young people start giving up their subway seats. A dubious distinction at best.

THE PLAY

George Eastman's *Harry Townsend's Last Stand* knowingly explores that ongoing process on two fronts; the elderly man who insists that nothing has changed, and the unfortunate caretaker who has to deal with his inevitable decline. I'll never forget the day I had to tell my mother she could no longer drive. She looked at me and said, "So, my life is over?" I felt like a criminal.

But, eventually, one has to ask, "What do we do with dad?" None of us wants to send a parent to "the home," but almost always there comes a time when he or she needs more care than can be given on a casual basis, and it's going to get worse, never better. In spite of having promised about a million times over the years never to do that, we have no choice. It's an awful decision to have to make, but one almost all of us are forced to consider if we live long enough.

THE PERFORMANCE

As Harry Townsend, Len Cariou is spot-on that elderly parent. He's an octogenarian himself, a theatrical treasure, as great a Broadway legend as anyone can ever become. From his first appearance, he radiates charm and intelligence, unerringly playing the confident, masculine man Harry has always been, only occasionally falling into confusion. There's no suggestion that he might be suffering from Alzheimer's, or any problem that cannot be explained by simple old age, and Mr. Cariou's performance is so fine that he doesn't seem to be acting at all. Under the circumstances, he may *not* be acting, but it must be observed that the play requires Harry to dominate the stage for two hours, and Mr. Cariou's delivery was robust and unerring. I've seen actors half his age stumble over that much material.

As Alan, Craig Bierko was suitably tentative when it came to convincing his father that he could no longer live on his own. As I said, it's extraordinarily hard to deal with an aging parent, particularly when they have strong opinions, and Alan approaches that difficult task at a time when he must redefine his own middle-age anxieties. He is also a fine actor, and played Alan with sympathy and more than a little understanding.

CONCLUSION

Director Karen Carpenter has put together a handsome production, with an attractive, practical set by Lauren Helpern, and effective lighting and sound effects by Jeff

Davis and John Gromada. Frankly, it was a great pleasure to see a play not centered around adolescent angst. Old age is not a hopeless wasteland. It is another stage in life, as valid as any other. It can be a time of intelligent reflection and profound accomplishment, encouraged by the sort of wisdom that can only come from many years of experience. Len Cariou is a perfect example; active, able, and as powerful as ever. See this play before it closes. You won't find better acting anywhere. **HAPPY FACE**

PERFORMANCE INFORMATION

- November 18 – March 15th, 2020
- City Center Stage II
- 131 W. 55th Street, NYC
- (212) 581-1212
- https://www.harrytownsendslaststand.com/

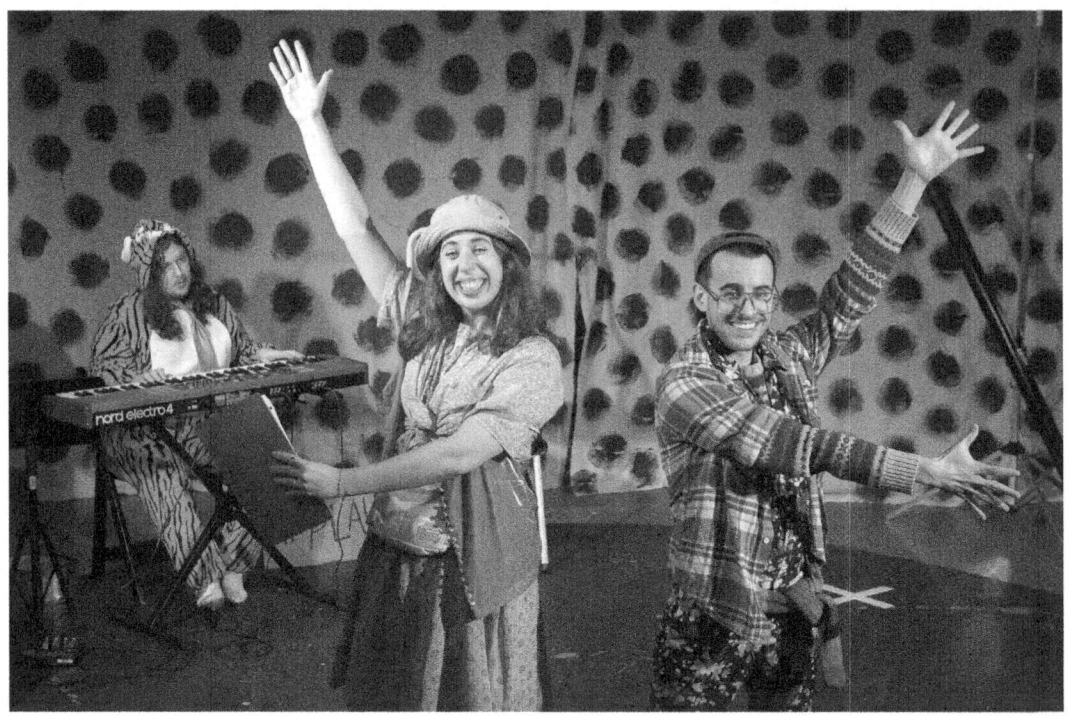

(L–R) Ben Pagano, Mallory Muratore & Remy Germinario

Caveman Play

- Presented as part of the **Exponential Festival**
- Play by Savannah Reich
- Director: Alex Tobey
- Assistant Director/Stage Manager: Jack Dentinger
- Scenic/Lighting Designer: Christina Tang
- Press: Alex Tobey

THE CAST

- Rocky: Remy Germinario*
- Chicken Feathers: Mark Mauriello
- Dandelion: Mallory Muratore
- Douglas: Ben Pagano

BACKGROUND

In *Caveman Play,* Savannah Reich has written a light, funny script about a very serious subject. The term "totalitarian agriculture" was coined by philosopher Daniel Quinn in his thought-provoking 1996 novel *The Story of B.* To paraphrase Mr. Quinn slightly, "Totalitarian agriculture subordinates all life forms to the relentless, single minded production of human food. It is the belief that the whole world is ours by right, and that *all* the land should be used by human beings for their own purposes."

Not only is that the most laborious possible way to live, it provides a rationale for our relentless subordination of every other life form on the planet. For 10,000 years, since agriculture replaced hunting and gathering, it's been the source of greed, oppression, and the reckless destruction of wildlife habitats. I'm not sure where Ms. Reich got the inspiration for her excellent comedy (there's no specific mention of totalitarian agriculture in it), but it's certainly the right time to bring up the subject. Australia is on fire and the polar ice caps are melting. It looks like we're getting what we deserve, and we did it all to ourselves.

THE PLAY

It's 10,000 years ago. Cave dwellers Rocky and Dandelion, have decided that staying put and growing food (agriculture) is preferable to hunting and gathering (living off the land). It will allow them to build a house, wear clothes, and work for twelve hours a day (as Rocky wryly observes). For the past year, the two of them and their pet tiger, Douglas (who just happens to play a mean synthesizer) have lived this way. Now, the hunters and gatherers (the audience) have returned, and the pair has brought them together for a presentation on the "marvels" of agriculture.

It starts with a bang and goes very well until the shaman, Chicken Feathers, suggests that agriculture might not be the best way forward. It's downhill from there, and the discussion that ensues is remarkably pertinent. Dandelion speaks *for* agriculture, Chicken Feathers speaks *against* it, and the audience is then asked to vote. Throughout, the action is delightfully inclusive. The actors involve the audience with skill and humor (I found a tomato under my seat) and the laughter never stops.

THE PERFORMANCE

Ms. Reich has written an hilarious script, and director Alex Tobey and his cast milk every line for its humor. Ben Pagano plays Douglas the tiger with a dry wit, never cracking a smile as he punctuates the action with subtle music and sound effects from his synthesizer. He offers a great deal of common sense, always saying what he thinks. As Dandelion and Rocky, Mallory Muratore and Remy Germinario are a stitch. They are natural comedians. Ms. Muratore's smile lights up the stage, and Mr. Germinario's impish quality is totally engaging.

Chicken Feathers, archly played by Mark Mauriello, is the snake in the garden. He believes agriculture is too much work, time consuming and ultimately bad for the community. When he and Dandelion debate the pros and cons of the matter, and the audience finally votes on which road to take, the cast members must improvise their reaction, depending upon the outcome. They do this with skill and a great deal of charm.

I don't want to say how we voted the night I saw the play, but sometime, somewhere, back in some dark cave, it seems a bad decision was made, one that has resulted in 10,000 years of murder and war. That certainly says a great deal about those who voted. Considering what's going on in our world today, we can't afford to make that mistake again.

CONCLUSION

I didn't mean to bring down the off-the-wall joy of this play with my remarks about totalitarian agriculture. But, the playwright presents intelligent arguments on both sides of this subject, and she couldn't have done a better job if she'd read Mr. Quinn's book. Maybe she did. Whatever, *Caveman Play* is a delight from beginning to end. It's a festival play, so the sets and lighting are somewhat perfunctory. But, it's funny and entertaining, and its run as part of the **Exponential Festival** was too short. It discusses an incredibly important subject in a remarkably accessible way. I hope to see more of Savannah Reich's work very soon. **HAPPY FACE**

PERFORMANCE INFORMATION

- January 8th – 11th, 2020
- Patch Works
- 98 Moore Street, Brooklyn, NY
- https://www.theexponentialfestival.org/cavemanplay

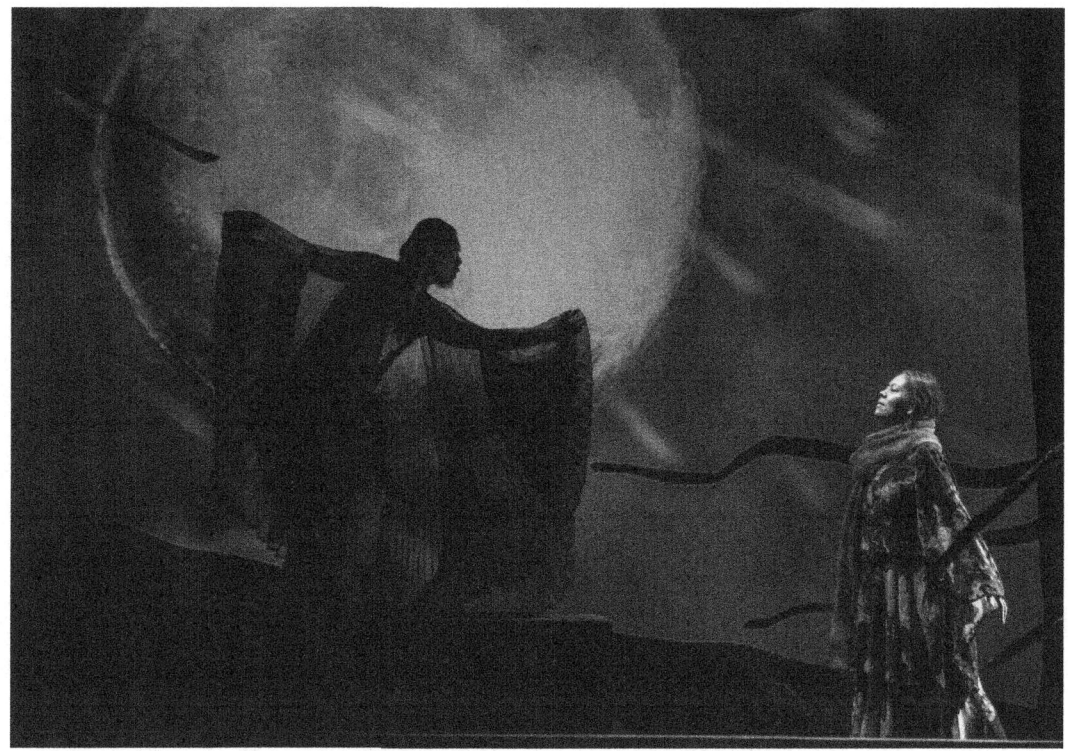

Ju-Eh/Juecheng Chen & Nina Yoshida Nelsen

Blood Moon An Opera

- Commissioned and Produced by **Beth Morrison Projects**
- Co-presented with **Baruch Performing Arts Center**
  in partnership with **Japan Society**
- Presented as part of the **Prototype Festival**
- Composed by Garrett Fisher
- Libretto by Ellen McLaughlin
- Directed by Rachel Dickstein
- Musical Direction: Steven Osgood
- Scenic Design: Susan Zeeman Rogers
- Lighting Design: Yuki Nakase Link
- Sound Design: Daniel Neumann
- Costume Design: Maiko Matsushima
- Puppet Design: Erik Sanko
- Media Design: Katherine Freer
- Video Engineer: Moe Sharooz
- Makeup Design: Liv Swenson
- Choreography: Takemi Kitamura & Rachel Dickstein

- Stage Manager: Lissy Barnes-Flint
- Scenic Assistant: Yu-Hsuan Chen
- Assistant Lighting Design: Qi'er Luo
- Video Assistant: Kelly Colburn
- Assistant Director: Kiyo Kamisawa
- Assistant Stage Manager: Tim Love
- Dance Associate: Akiko Aizawa
- Press: Calliope PR
- Photo: Maria Baranova

THE CAST (in order of appearance)

- Moon: Ju-Eh/Juecheng Chen
- Puppeteer/Dancer: Takemi Kitamura
- Aunt: Nina Yoshida Nelsen
- Nephew: Wei Wu

INSTRUMENTALISTS

- Harmonium: Kamala Sankaram
- Viola de Gamba/Cello: Adam Young
- Flutes: Isabel Lepanto Gleicher
- Piano/Keyboard: William Hobbs
- Taiko/Bamboo Flute: Fumi Tanakadate
- Taiko: Barbara Merjan
- Rehearsal Pianist: Emily Goldman

THE PLAY

Japanese Noh theater is a form of classical dance/drama dating back to the 14th-century. Traditionally, it retells an event, frequently using spiritual manifestations of natural objects (in this case, the Moon) to present and analyze moral issues in the Buddhist tradition. In *Blood Moon,* composer Garrett Fisher and librettist Ellen McLaughlin have drawn on a six-hundred year old Noh drama concerning a man who destroyed his own life by committing an unspeakable act. As a young man, he abandoned the aunt who raised him and left her to die.

Forty years have passed. The Nephew, having come to the end of his own life, has returned to the scene of his crime to seek forgiveness. The Moon is full, impatient for this episode to end. The Aunt still haunts the mountaintop where she died. Is atonement possible?

THE PRODUCTION

Let there be no mistake, *Blood Moon* is a full blown, modern opera, atonal, intense, and extremely difficult to perform. Director Rachel Dickstein and her fine cast have created a visually stunning manifestation of an otherworldly event. Clever projections and constantly evolving lighting effects designed by Yuki Nakase Link combine to bring the performance space to life. The moon waxes and wanes, the trees close in and out around Susan Zeeman Rogers' simple, but elegant set. The overall impression is that the environment is breathing in concert with the singers. Add to that Daniel Neumann's carefully thought-out sound effects, projected into and around the audience space, and you have a living ambiance that almost demands the suspension of disbelief.

THE MUSIC

Musical Director Steven Osgood and his fine orchestral ensemble do a splendid job bringing this haunting score to life. Garrett Fisher's music is *academic* in the best sense of that word. Revolving around the Taiko, a Japanese barrel drum that comes in various sizes (usually played in ensemble), it is heavily rhythmic and thoroughly serialistic in concept, highly reminiscent of the twelve-tone-system developed by Arnold Schoenberg in the 20th-century. There *are* many Indian and Japanese motifs included, particularly in the ensemble use of the Taiko, so whether or not the Schoenberg reference actually applies would require an examination of the score. But, that's the overall impression, and I can't imagine the performing artists didn't have a difficult time putting it together.

THE PERFORMANCE

Everyone in the cast is a splendid, trained singer. They perform this extraordinarily difficult music with great skill. As Moon, Ju-Eh/Juecheng Chen is aloof and condescending. Moon narrates the events. Everything seems to indicate that she's done this countless times in the past and is getting annoyed at the inability of Nephew, the protagonist, to deal with his angst. Ms. Chen moves effortlessly about the stage, flowing like liquid in a diaphanous gown created by the costume designer Maiko Matsushima.

As Nephew, Wei Wu is a remarkably fine baritone. With ringing highs and substantial, mellow lows, he wears his anguish on his sleeve. Whether Nephew achieves his goal is open to interpretation (very Buddhist like), but the fact that he has asked the question is what matters. Both Moon and Aunt are annoyed with him. But, at least, he is trying.

Aunt is represented by two entities. She is stunningly voiced by mezzo-soprano Nina Yoshida Nelsen, elegantly danced by puppeteer Takemi Kitamura. Ms. Kitamura's choreography, designed with input from the director, is fluid and ethereal. She moves Erik Sanko's exquisite "Aunt" (a life-size puppet) like the wind, moving in and out of the narrative as Nephew, at first able to see only the "shade," gradually begins to speak directly to Ms. Nelsen. It is an intriguing device, drawn heavily, I understand, from Noh theater.

CONCLUSION

I enjoyed this opera immensely. It is musically sophisticated and dovetails brilliantly with Ellen McLaughlin's intelligent libretto. But, it is not an "Off-Broadway" offering in the usual sense of the word. It is intellectual and demanding, innovative and complex, extremely difficult to perform, and not in a style easily embraced by any but the most knowledgeable musical aficionados.

I think (hope) that it will be performed many times. It should have a prolonged life in music schools, conservatories, opera companies, and any venue where "serious" music is performed and enjoyed. But, it's a bit of a stretch for Off-Broadway Regardless, thanks to the **HERE Arts Center** and the **Prototype Festival** for bringing it to us. In every way, it's an absolute stunner. **HAPPY FACE PLUS**

PERFORMANCE INFORMATION

- January 9th – 17th, 2020
- Baruch Performing Arts Center
- 55 Lexington Ave, NYC
- www.prototypefestival.org

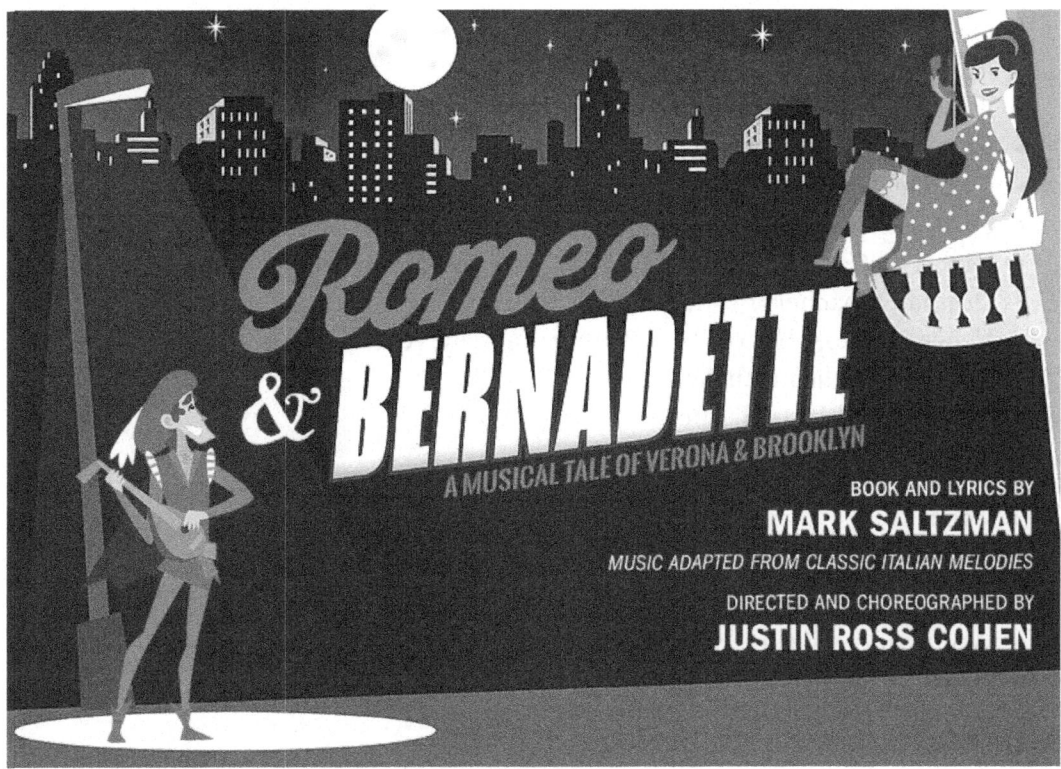

Romeo & Bernadette
A Musical Tale of Verona & Brooklyn

- Presented by **Amas Musical Theatre** in association with Eric Krebs
- Book & Lyrics by Mark Saltzman
- Music adapted from 18th-century Italian melodies
- Music Supervision, Arrangements & Orchestrations by Steve Orich
- Directed & Choreographed by Justin Ross Cohen
- Musical Director: Aaron Gandy
- Set Design: Walt Spangler
- Sound Design: One Dream Sound
- Costume Design: Fabio Toblini, Joseph Shrope
- Production Manager: Mike Schulz
- Lighting Design: Ken Billington
- Production Stage Manager: Christine Viega
- Casting Director: Carol Hanzel
- Press Representative: Richard Hillman PR
- Associate Producer: Robert Becker
- Photos: Russ Rowland

THE CAST (In order of appearance)

- Romeo: Nikita Burshteyn
- Bernadette: Anna Kostakis
- Sal Penza: Carlos Lopez
- Don Del Canto: Michael Marotta
- Camille Penza: Judy McLane
- Dino Del Canto/Brooklyn Guy: Michael Notardonato
- Donna Dubachek/Brooklyn Girl: Ari Raskin
- Usher, Bellhop, Enzo Aliria, Father Keneely, Arden, Viola, Roz: Troy Valjean Rucker
- Tito Titone: Zach Hanne
- Lips: Viet Vo

ORCHESTRA

- Music Director/Keyboard #1: Aaron Gandy
- Associate Music Director/Keyboard #2: Jason Loffredo
- Woodwinds: Simon Hutchins
- Drums: Jon Berger

THE PLOT

"Romeo — yes, *that* Romeo — finds himself in 1960s Brooklyn, chasing a girl he believes is his beloved Juliet. But no, it's Bernadette, the beautiful, foul-mouthed daughter of a crime family in this wild spoof of Shakespeare's timeless tale." That succinct, clear statement, taken from the company's press release, sums up the plot of this musical so well that I don't think I can improve upon it. Besides, if I use it, I'll have more room to write about the work itself, which is exactly what I want to do.

BACKGROUND

One thing about reviewing theater in New York City is the incredibly high standard we see in practically every performance. Producing a play here is impossibly expensive. Fully 80% of the productions that reach Broadway lose money, and it's only the exceptional Off-Broadway offering that can even pay its actors. A number of years ago, I produced a play Off-Off-Broadway myself. As it happened, our entire budget (outside theater rent) was consumed by *parking*. What this means is that substandard work seldom gets on a stage. When it does, it disappears quickly.

So, there's something good to say about practically everything, even if a play or production itself is bad. Given the difficulty and expense of getting anything onstage, I feel it's my responsibility to mention those things that work even when there are things that don't, hoping that companies will be encouraged to make improvements as they move down the road. As a result, I'm sometimes accused of being too nice. I don't want that to happen here, because this time, I have to praise everything. What I wrote below makes me sound like the show's press agent, but it can't be helped.

THE PLAY

Mark Saltzman's *Romeo & Bernadette* is absolutely thrilling, with a brilliant concept and script, truly stunning music, and a performance that literally made the hearts of the audience sing. The book is first rate. Getting Romeo to 1960s Brooklyn is worked out logically, the suspension of disbelief made almost effortless. The dialogue is consistently hysterical from beginning to end, with remarkably apt lyrics; clever, witty, and adapted to the music with extraordinary intelligence and skill.

THE MUSIC

About the music, I could write an essay. Everything in this "almost" modern love story (1960 is not *that* long ago) is drawn from the 18th-century Italian Baroque. The score is breathtaking, with romantic waltzes and unforgettable love songs. Musical Supervisor, Steve Orich, has done an incredible job with the vocal arrangements and orchestrations, masterfully adapting all those lovely melodies and spirited dances into the pop music and theater styles of the 1960s.

Mr. Orich's keyboard work, exquisitely realized by Musical Director Aaron Gandy and his associate, Jason Loffredo, is positively rhapsodic, with the single woodwind player, Simon Hutchins, seeming to draw flutes, clarinets, and bassoons out of thin air. Add to that Jon Berger's well timed percussion (*not* the same as banging a drum) and you have a musical ensemble that can hold it's own anytime, anywhere.

Mr. Orich's vocal arrangements are equally as fine. Duets, trios, quartets, and sextets, with fine voices singing in harmony, while Director/Choreographer Justin Ross Cohen uses chachas, foxtrots, and exhilarating theater choreography to establish an ambiance of excitement and timeless beauty.

THE PRODUCTION

Walt Spangler's set is simple and adaptable. It consists of a series of open frames and white spaces which change shape to move smoothly, without pause, from scene to scene. Ken Billington's excellent lighting uses color and shade to alter the set and establish the mood, while Fabio Toblinim and Joseph Shrope created costumes that are not only beautiful and appropriate (Romeo's leather codpiece could not be more Italian) but can also be changed quickly. See below for more on that.

THE PERFORMANCE

I got the impression that everyone in the audience fell in love with Romeo. Nikita Burshteyn is a newcomer to New York City, and we're lucky to have him. He's a fine, comic actor: young and good looking, with a lovely trained tenor. When he sang to Bernadette of the *angels in your voice* in the haunting "O, for a Song," a good part of the audience wept. How often does that happen in cynical New York City? As Bernadette, Anna Kostakis was as much in love with Romeo as we were. She moved effortlessly from spoiled mob daughter to smitten baroque heroine. Her rendition of "One Tender Word," something she wished she could get from her mob-wannabe fianceé, Tito, was warm and sympathetic.

Michael Notardonato, who opens the show as Brooklyn Guy, with the extraordinarily funny "Die, Already" and the hilarious expository chorus number "There's More," morphs into Dino, mob-kid and Romeo's Bensonhurst sidekick, with engaging charm. His accent is perfect, his dialogue slick and cleverly delivered, his singing and dancing top-notch; a joy to watch every time he comes onstage. As Donna Dubachek, Ari Raskin is a stitch, milking every line for its humor. She more than holds her own as the only other young woman in the show.

As Bernadette's mother, Camille, Judy McLane is every inch a star when she sings "Hail the Contessa." Her soaring high notes and magnetic stage presence are fully in keeping with her remarkable Broadway credits. Troy Valjean Rucker, as Usher, Bellhop, Enzo Aliria, Father Keneely, Arden, Viola, and Roz, moves flawlessly through all seven roles with enormous skill. He's a talented actor, floating between genders without a pause. He changes costumes so quickly, and so many times that I lost count (kudos to the costume designers mentioned above). He has a fine, well-trained baritone voice, singing opera, and the first Italian iteration of the lovely "Caro, Mio Ben" ("Dearest, my Beloved") before Mr. Orich turns it into a smashing wedding ensemble later in the show.

As Tito Titone, Bernadette's fianceé (until she meets Romeo, anyway), Zach Hanne is determined to become a "made man." His reaction when Romeo appears is perfectly in keeping with a murderous punk. He's a hoot when Bernadette insists he learn to chacha, and surprisingly sympathetic when he sings "To Be Tito Titone," after finally giving up. Last, but by no means least, we have Carlos Lopez, Michael Marotta, and Viet Vo, as confused mob-boss fathers Sal Penza, Don Del Canto, and the very funny Lips, a mob-man of all works. Everyone in the cast was polished and professional, and everyone had his or her moment.

CONCLUSION

Romeo & Bernadette has everything a great musical needs, terrific music, glorious singing, block-busting ensembles, and love. Director/Choreographer Justin Ross Cohen and his cast have put together what I can say without hesitation is the best, fully staged *new* musical I've seen since I began reviewing. If it doesn't move on to Broadway, I'm not sure anything can. Every moment is sheer magic. See it now, while you can afford it. It's truly a work of genius. **HAPPY FACE PLUS**

PERFORMANCE INFORMATION

- January 14th – February 16th, 2020 (click below for times & dates)
- Mezzanine Theatre
- A.R.T./New York Theatres
- 502 West 53rd Street, NYC
- (866) 811-4111
- www.amasmusical.org

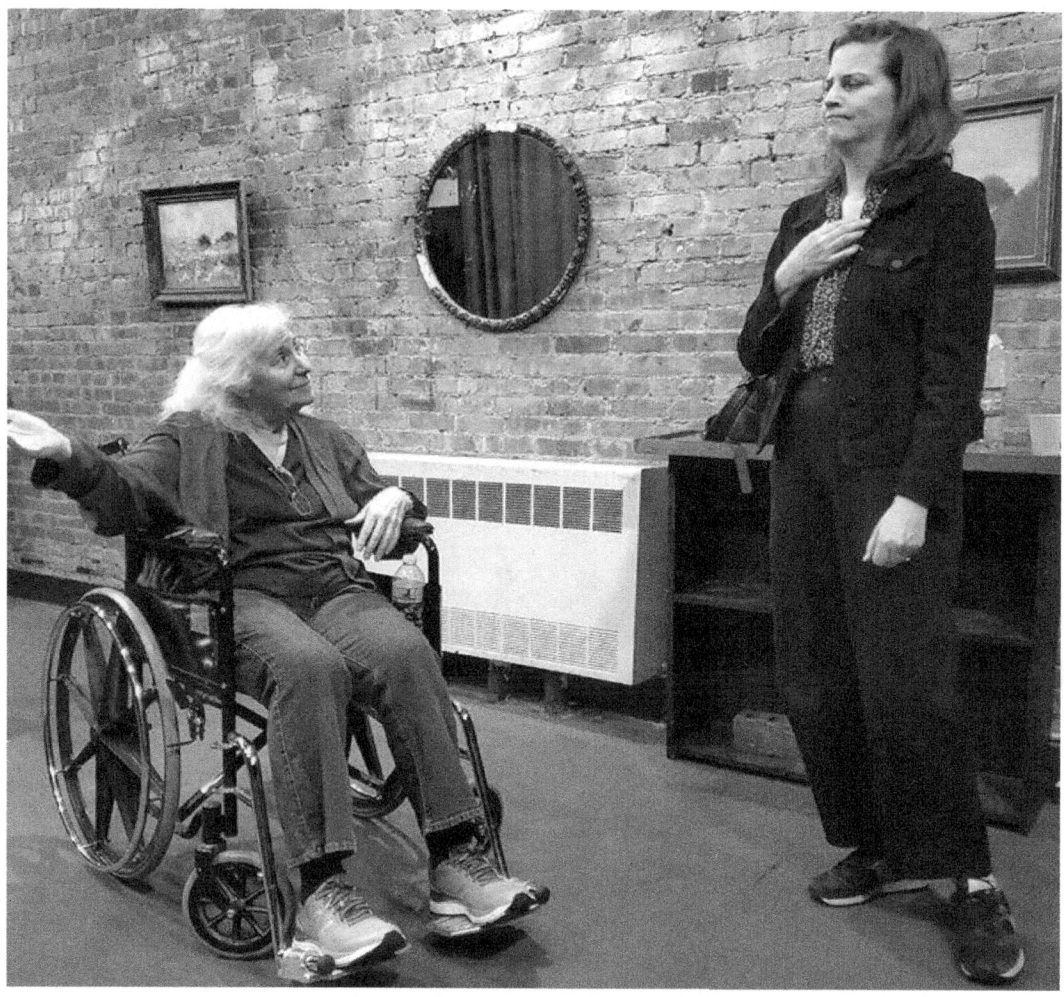

Valerie O'Hara & Meredith Rust

Moves and Countermoves
Reviewed for HI! DRAMA by William J. Cataldi

- A night of new works by James Crafford
- Produced by **The American Theatre of Actors**, et al.
- ATA Artistic Director: James Jennings
- Playwright: James Crafford
- Director: Michael Bordwell
- Light/Sound Design: Ken Coughlin
- Press: Jay Michaels Arts & Entertainment

Moves and Countermoves encompasses two short plays by James Crafford, *This Game is Not Over,* and *After the Hanging.*

The Game is Not Over (Play #1)
- Joel: Thomas J. Kane
- Donna: Meredith Rust
- Joyce: Valerie O'Hara

After the Hanging (Play #2)
- Jed: Alan Hasnas
- Tobie: Laurie Rae Waugh
- Lila: Tzena Nicole

This Game is Not Over opens with Donna and Joel playing a game of chess in Joel's comfortable, upper-class home, which he shares with his wife, Joyce. Donna and Joel were lovers briefly, before he married Joyce twenty-odd years previously. Wheelchair bound Joyce enters and asks Joel to run an errand. While he is away, Donna and Joyce converse about romantic love and sex.

In *After the Hanging,* the KKK has lynched a black man in the late-1920s Deep South. Alone in Jed's bar, Jed and Tobie discuss the lynching as though it were an afternoon sporting event. There is a knock at the back door. The black man's wife, Lila, enters and confronts the white pair.

Playwright James Crafford links the two plays, which at first glance have nothing to do with one another, with certain themes which he considers important. They include the playing of games (chess in Play #1, and baseball in Play #2), patience, the penis, and death by hanging. Mr. Crafford constructs his plays well, and the themes bring them together with clever coherence, but it's difficult to understand what the themes mean in the playwright's vision. As the second play progressed, I began to feel that the two plays would have been better served in longer, stand-alone forms. Both plays were certainly good ideas — just underdeveloped here.

In Play #1, Meredith Rust as Donna and Thomas J. Kane as Joel offer up stiff and formal dialogue for no apparent reason. They have, after all, had sex with one another, albeit a long time ago. Wealthy people can be casual too. I suspected faulty direction, until I saw Play #2 (more on that below). Ms. Rust and Mr. Kane may need more practice. Ev-er-y sin-gle word doesn't have to be so dis-tinct-ly enunciated. Valerie O'Hara as Joyce seemed formal too, but not so stiff. She infused her lines with far more nuance and emotion. Her *Penis Speech* was moving and beautiful. I refer to that speech in italics, because Mr. Crafford's composition was the second best part of the evening. The *Penis Speech* should go down in history. Play #1, however, lacked depth, and might best be thought of as a play "treatment."

Play #2 was a completely different story. Alan Hasnas as Jed, Laurie Rae Waugh as Tobie, and Tzena Nicole as Lila gave stunning performances in flawless, early 20th-century southern vernacular, filled with emotion and focused humanity. It must be difficult for white actors to use the term "nigger" currently, but the actors here did so without any hesitation whatsoever, which is a testament to their commitment. Any questions I had about director Michael Bordwell's skill evaporated when I saw this gem of a piece. Again, it was short, but it had a clear meaning. I'm not going to reveal what the play was about, because I want readers to see it for themselves, and any description wouldn't do it justice. Suffice it to say, Jed is the main character here. This is his play, and the ending, with him alone, was the best part of the evening. I wept.

Moves and Countermoves is definitely worth a look. I enjoyed it. As long as my readers don't expect Shakespeare, Mr. Crafford won't disappoint. Remember, this is experimental theater, and needs to be appreciated as such. I'll leave it to readers who go to decide if the experiment paid off. **HAPPY FACE MINUS**

PERFORMANCE INFORMATION

- January 22 – February 2, 2020 (click below for times & dates)
- The B.E.T. (Beckmann Experimental Theatre)
- 314 West 54th Street, NYC
- (212) 581-3044
- http://americantheatreofactors.com/

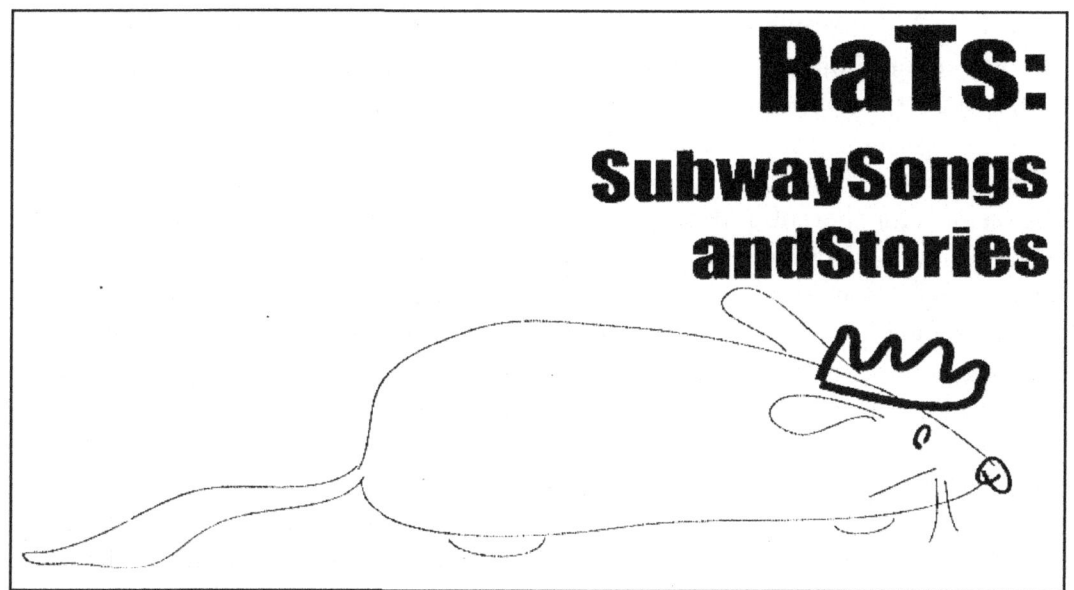

RaTs: Subway Songs & Stories A report

- Play by Maguire Wilder
- Music: Gavin Knittle, Lo Williams, Kiara Negroni, Natalie Thomas, Kyle Best & Lucas Saur
- Director: Kyle Best
- Producer: Maya Singer
- Production Designer: Lucas DeGirolamo
- Associate Production Designers: Amelia Kassing & Kiara Negroni-Martinez
- Stage Manager: Sarah Samonte
- Assistant Stage Manager: Lee Monahan
- Press: Jay Michaels Arts & Entertainment

THE CAST

- Rat Princess: Fara Faiszan
- Tabby Cat the Sewer Rat: Maiya Pascouche
- Rat Chorus: Claire-Frances Sullivan, Markesa McLamb, John Knipsel

BACKGROUND

At first glance, Maguire Wilder's musical play *RaTs* seems like a clever idea. Rat Princess and Tabby Cat the Sewer Rat live in a subway tunnel. Their lives are centered on two things, food and sex. But, life is hard. The MTA wants them dead, their "pack" is just as mean and class conscious as that of any human high-schooler, and their life is short. It's a gold mine of material, ripe for satire, which could be funny or sad. Unfortunately, the best thing about it are the names of the characters. As a workshop project, it is simply not ready for production. Because of that, I am writing a progress report, not a review.

THE PLAY

The script is incoherent. It purports to be a love story between two female rats, but nothing new is said about female relationships of any kind. The characters aren't "rat" like, not that such a characterization is required, but it would at least have provided a joke or two. As it is, I'm not sure whether the play was supposed to be funny or not. It ends on a dark note, as we hear a dialogue between MTA employees that provides the only cogent exchange in the presentation.

The music, composed by five different people, all sounded exactly alike; the same three chords, repetitive and monotonic. All the songs were about either sex or food, which makes sense, they are *rats,* after all. But, there was nothing memorable about any of them. The musicians seemed skilled, but they weren't given much to do. They did double as the Rat Chorus, but that didn't make the music any more interesting.

THE PERFORMANCE

As Rat Princess, Fara Faizan shrieked and ran around the stage a lot. Most of the time, I couldn't understand her at all. I wish I could be more kind, but I can't. Maiya Pascouche played Tabby Cat the Sewer Rat with a bit more style. She sang one or two nice notes, but the music, itself, was not engaging, so it's hard for me to recall how well she sang it.

CONCLUSION

RaTs is a funny concept, but it needs to be completely reworked if it's going to go anywhere. There were thirteen people involved in this production. It's surprising that so many people came up with such a mundane, uninspiring performance. *RaTs* closed on January 26th.

PERFORMANCE INFORMATION

- January 23rd – 26th, 2020
- TheaterLab
- 357 West 36th Street, NYC
- (212) 929-2545
- www.theaterlabnyc.com

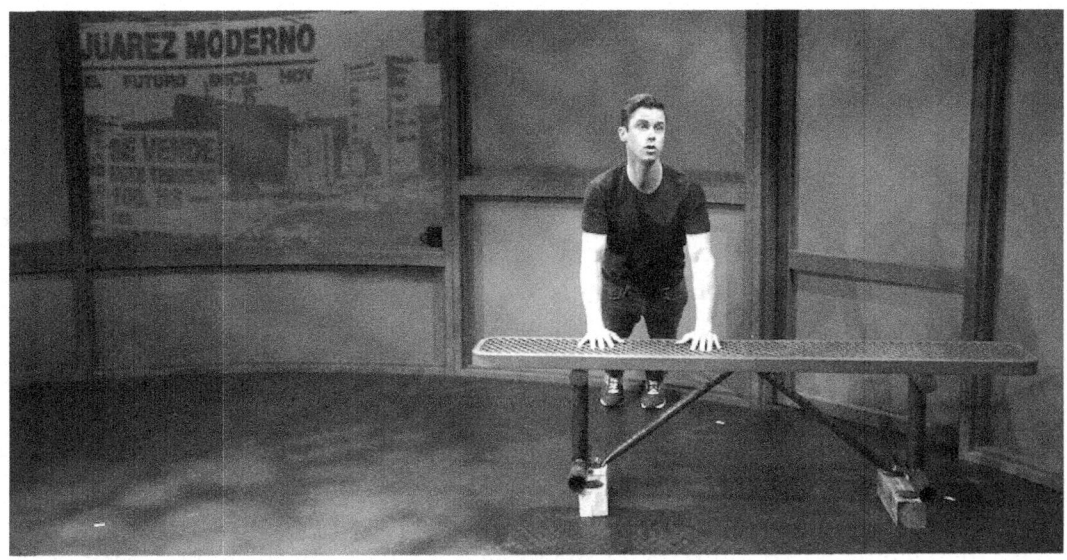

Dan Hoyle

Border People
Reviewed for HI! DRAMA by William J. Cataldi

- Produced by **Working Theater**
- Producing Artistic Director: Mark Plesent
- Managing Director: Laura Carbonell Monarque
- Written and Performed by Dan Hoyle
- Directed by Nicole A. Watson
- Scenic Design: Frank Oliva
- Lighting Design: Jimmy Lawlor
- Sound Design: Jorge Olivo
- Video Design: Yana Birÿkova
- Stage Manager: Kara Kaufman
- Press: Mendiola Arts Management
- Graphic Design: The Watsons
- Photo: Carol Rosseag
- Originally developed with and directed by Charlie Varon

THE CONCEPT

Dan Hoyle is a journalist educated in theater. He traveled all over North America, seeking out and interviewing mostly people of color, focusing on folks who had no home. Theater serves him as a means to share his journalistic insights by turning them into art. In *Border People*, Dan (somehow it seems appropriate to refer to him by his first name) portrays some of his interviewees by becoming them in short vignettes.

When I write that the folks he portrays have no home, I do not mean they necessarily have no place to live. They are not, strictly speaking, homeless. Instead, Dan explores the rarely mentioned topic of existential homelessness — the lack of any kind of coherent group inclusion. One interviewee complains early on that he grew up in a middle-class home in New Jersey. Despite his education, he lacks white credentials, because he is black. In the projects, where he lives now, he lacks black credentials, because he didn't grow up on the streets of New York. His life is an endless struggle to keep out of trouble, trouble brought on by his lack of credentials, his lack of belonging.

Plenty of the folks Dan portrays are asylum seekers in the US and Canada, usually fleeing persecution in their country of origin. We hear the details of their stories. "My brothers and father were killed in Honduras by the cartels." "I love God, but that's not enough for the Saudi government. I face imprisonment or death if I return. Will Canada accept me?" Dan's interviewees illustrate these stories far better than would be appropriate for me to do here. Some of the folks are gay. Too poor, too isolated, too black, too foreign, too weird; they don't even register as relevant to the bourgeois, post-Obergefell LGBTQ community in the US, which is busy enjoying its place at the table. For all of these interviewees, death is right there at their side; but amazingly they want to live. They keep struggling for survival. A lot of these stories are bone-crushingly heartbreaking.

Existential homelessness means you live in a world where you are welcomed nowhere. You are always viewed with suspicion. You are an alien from another planet. It turns out that skin color, education, citizenship, passports, permanent residency cards, family, money, occupation, sexual preference, street credentials, the way you walk, the way you talk; *none* of it makes a difference for most people. Whether you are alienated from the groups you aspire to because you are unwilling to compromise your integrity, or whether the groups you aspire to want you dead outright, nothing you do will ever include you, because you are different. People don't like people who are different. The world is about strict conformity. Period.

THE PERFORMANCE AND PRODUCTION

As a white man, Dan takes a great risk portraying people of color. I doubt, judging from what I could tell about him, that he has a lot of street cred. He risks being seen as a modern version of a minstrel singer, and therefore racist. Or, he risks being insufficiently authentic, creating racial caricatures. The only way he could avoid those dangers is with impeccable journalism, and profoundly sincere acting. And that's what we got.

In an era when journalism has sunk to its nadir, Dan's journalism has all the qualities one would have expected in an earlier, better age: actual transcriptions of interviews, attention to detail, selective use of the interviews that doesn't skew to false conclusions, honesty, authentic reporting. Dan would never make it in most newsrooms today. Then he takes his journalism and does something miraculous with it. He turns it into art. "Border People" is not a documentary. It would have been if he had filmed the interviewees (at great risk to them), and created a film of them talking. This is art. Dan has taken the interviews and carefully transformed them, through the medium of his own mind and heart (adding himself to the mix in the process), and depicted the interviewees with his body and voice, so they become something beyond what the journalistic process can ever hope to yield. "Border People," for its deliberate inclusion of Dan, is larger than the sum of the interviews, even with documentary commentary.

For one thing, the art made me, as an audience member, feel like I was Dan, interviewing these people. I wasn't just Bill watching Dan interview these people on film. The process involved me — a brilliant stroke of genius on Dan's part. It was impossible to run away, or change the channel. The confrontation was immediate.

Dan infused these vignettes with jokes and humor. Many audience members laughed; I did not. For me personally, the humor didn't have the intended function. I didn't think these stories were funny at all. "Border People" made me suffer. That's not a bad thing. That's not a negative criticism. On the contrary, when art makes the viewer suffer — that's great art.

Dan is a fine actor. He's young. He doesn't offer entirely natural performances which reflect the original interviewee like a perfect mirror. He's had to work very hard to give us what he's given us. His sincerity and commitment make up for anything missing. His work is outstanding. Any criticisms of him as a white man for doing this would be thoughtless and crass.

I have to extend an apology to the folks who worked with Dan on this project, the people behind the scenes. The stage, video and lighting were impeccable. Nicole A. Watson's direction must have been arduous. I sense many, many hours of working with Dan on every nuance. I apologize because I'm too worn out dealing with Dan to offer up the individual praise everyone involved deserves. I'm especially grateful to the folks at Working Theater for bringing this to New York. Bravi one and all. **HAPPY FACE PLUS**

PERFORMANCE INFORMATION

- January 25th – February 22nd, 2020
- A.R.T./New York Theatre
- Jeffrey and Paula Gural Theatre
- 502 West 53rd Street, NYC
- (866) 811-4111
- https://theworkingtheater.org/events/border-people/

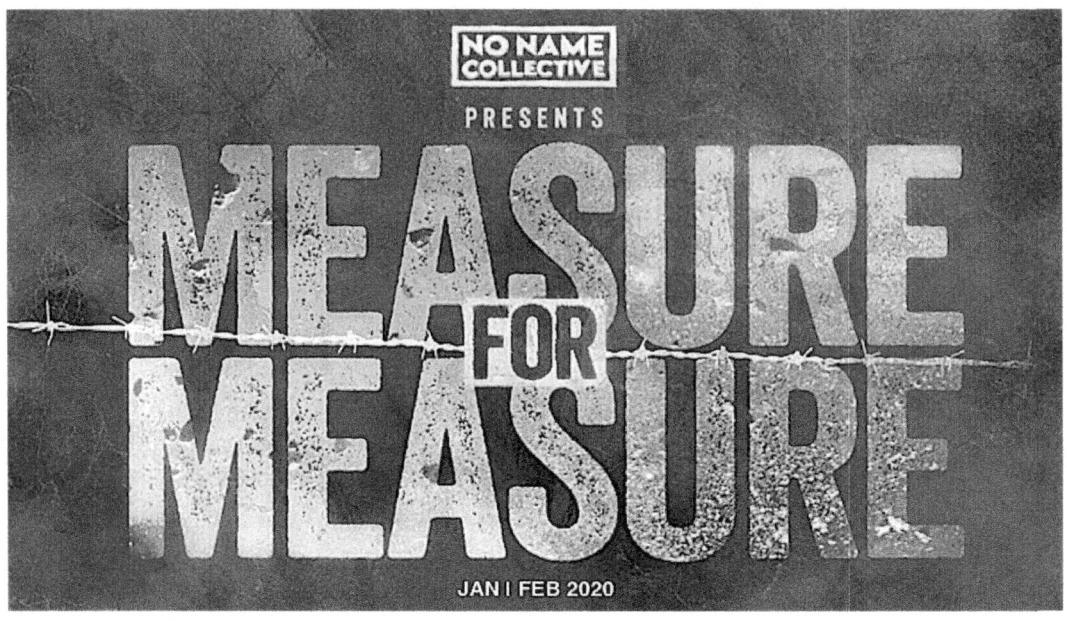

NO NAME COLLECTIVE

PRESENTS

MEASURE FOR MEASURE

JAN I FEB 2020

Measure for Measure

- Play by William Shakespeare
- Presented by the **No Name Collective**
- Producer: Annallese Kirby
- Associate Producer: Melanie Thompson
- Producing Partner: Alie Pyne
- Director: Michael Fleischer
- Stage Manager: Rebecca (Bex) Hoi
- Scenic Designer: Jennilee Aromando
- Costume Designer: Ellie Gossage
- Assistant Costume Designer: Lauren Slakter
- Lighting Designer: Kenzie Carpenter
- Sound Designer: Melissa Farinelli
- Graphic Designer: Nicasio Andrade
- Fight Choreography/Intimacy Directors: Dispatch Combat Collective, Madeleine Emerick, Conor D. Mullen
- Fight/Intimacy Captain: Greg Pragel*

THE CAST (in alphabetical order)

- Juliet/Servant/Officer: Shannon Cabbell
- Angelo: Danny Crawford*
- Mariana/Pompey: Marisa Gold

- Duke: Nolan Hennelly*
- Isabella: Maggie Hood
- Escalus/Abhorson: Anuj Parikh
- Claudio: Greg Pragel*
- Friar/Barnardine/Officer: Rikin Shah
- Lucio: CJ Stewart
- Provost: Amy Stringer
- Mistress Overdone/Francisca/Officer: Gareth Tidball

BACKGROUND

Although it is quite "dark" in it's subject matter, Shakespeare's *Measure for Measure* was originally classified as a comedy. Because moral justice prevails over civic justice, compassion takes precedence over the law. Thus, it has always been considered a problem play. Elizabethan culture demanded that criminals, even fictional criminals, be punished. But, that doesn't happen here. Although the hypocritical Angelo is given a life sentence some might consider harsh, the play ends more or less happily, and no one dies.

As is so often the case with Shakespeare, the argument is still quite relevant. It could have been drawn directly from **#MeToo**. Isabella, a young novitiate, learns that her brother Claudio has been sentenced to death for engaging in extramarital sex with his fianceé, Juliet. When Isabella approaches Angelo, the city's magistrate, to beg for Claudio's life, Angelo conditions his help on her willingness to surrender her virginity. What she does, and how she does it, is the subject of this powerful play, first produced in 1604.

THE PLAY

I very much appreciate the mission of this young company, founded in 2017 to pay (in their own words) "homage to the great William Shakespeare and his contemporaries by focusing our performances on cuts of classical texts." With energy and imagination, thay have updated *Measure for Measure* by using music and choreography in clever and interesting ways, while mostly adhering to the Bard's language and intent. It's a fascinating concept, and I look forward to watching it develop.

On the other hand, I'm not sure I can agree with the substantial cuts they've made. In order to focus on the core concept — Angelo's sexual harassment of the innocent Isabella — almost everything that originally made this play a comedy has been removed. The part of Lucio, a soldier of fortune, whom I have described in the past as this play's Bottom, has been severely truncated. The hilarious opening scenes where he first interacts with the bawdy Mistress Overdone (except for those parts dealing directly with Claudio's arrest), have been replaced with pantomime and dance. This *does* focus the play on sexual misconduct, which I'm sure is the intent, but it *is* Shakespeare, after all. Regardless of the intent, editing his plays is a questionable enterprise at best. They are subtle and speak to us on many levels. How much can they be changed and still be Shakespeare?

THE PRODUCTION

The company made good use of the simple PIT Loft theater space. Scenic designer Jennilee Aromando created some interesting, abstract, set pieces, in a transparent, spider-web style, that were effectively used to change the shape of the stage. Kenzie Carpenter's lighting was colorful, and skillfully used, while the sound, designed by Melissa Farinelli, set the mood with appropriate sound effects and recorded works from a remarkably wide variety of musical genres. I did find the music somewhat disorienting at times. Moving from Vivaldi to Rock 'n Roll, with much of it ending abruptly, was not always effective when morphing from scene to scene. But, this is a small caveat. The music was well-suited to the spirited choreography.

THE PERFORMANCE

As Isabella, Maggie Hood was gentle and sympathetic while still displaying a great deal of strength and resolve. Her speeches were clear and well delivered, an absolute requirement when doing Shakespeare. As Claudio, Greg Pragel was the most accomplished Shakespearean actor in the play. His language was positively elegant, and the understanding he brought to Claudio's predicament, intelligent and moving. Above all, he was totally believable as a human being in despair.

Nolan Hennelly, as the Duke, had a tendency to rush his lines. He improved as the play progressed, but never seemed completely at ease with the Elizabethan vernacular. Because of that, the Duke lacked a certain aristocratic gravitas, something that I'm sure Mr. Hennelly could correct with practice and strong direction.

As Lucio, CJ Stewart did his best with what was left of his part. He danced well, and his erotic interchange with Gareth Tidball who played Mistress Overdone — virtually all presented in pantomime — was as effective as it could be. At times, however, he seemed more a stand-up comic than a soldier of fortune.

As Angelo, Danny Crawford seemed almost casual. He was quite sure of himself, secure in his ability to wield life and death. But, his qualms about approaching Isabella lacked depth, which did not allow him to be as powerful as the part requires. As Juliet, Shannon Cabbell was effective in a relatively small part, as were Marisa Gold as Mariana and Anuj Parikh as Escalus. How they would have fared in a more complete version of Shakespeare's play is an interesting question.

CONCLUSION

Director Michael Fleischer and his cast have created a fast moving and effective condemnation of sexual harassment. On that basis, it has a lot going for it and is well worth seeing. That Shakespeare would probably not have approved of the cuts, and their effect on the rest of the play, is why I'm giving it a **MIXED FACE PLUS**.

PERFORMANCE INFORMATION

- January 30th – February 2nd, February 6th – 9th, 2020
- The PIT Loft
- 154 West 29th Street, NYC
- (212) 563-7488
- https://www.wearethenoname.com/

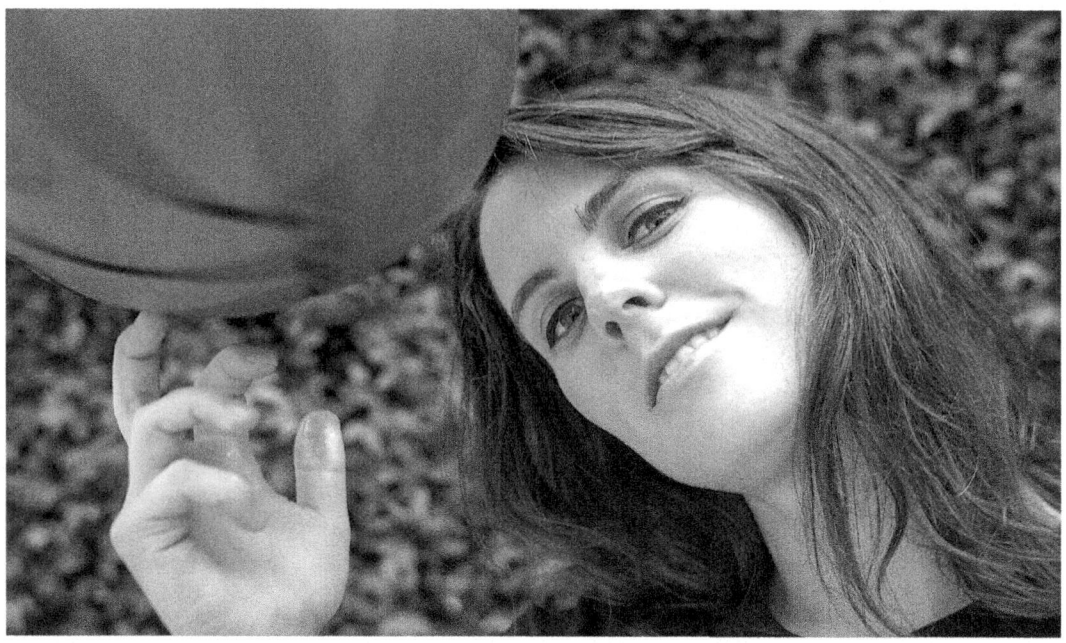
Olivia Levine

Unstuck

- Written & Performed by Olivia Levine
- Directed by Molly Rose Heller
- Press: Alton PR
- Photo: Josephine Bradlee

OCD (paraphrased from the Web)

Obsessive-Compulsive Disorder is an anxiety disorder characterized by uncontrollable thoughts and ritualized, repetitive behaviors. If you have OCD, you probably realize that your compulsions are irrational — but even so, you are unable to resist.

BACKGROUND

Like most of us, I've known a number of people who, in retrospect, I now realize were affected by OCD. I have to confess, I'm no longer a kid, and a good part of my life had already gone by before it was even recognized as a disorder. Back in the day, compulsive behavior was misunderstood and ridiculed. This wasn't always done openly. Most often, in my immediate cohort, anyway, it was done quietly, behind the sufferer's back. It was caused by ignorance, not malice. But, that's no excuse. I'm extremely happy that we now understand OCD as a medical disorder, just as I'm happy that being gay, the other major element in Ms. Levine's presentation, is now recognized as a natural condition.

THE PERFORMANCE

Olivia Levine's fascinating take on OCD, as it affected her life as a lesbian, was more like stand-up comedy than a play. This is not a criticism. She is quite talented and very experienced in that regard, and her presentation was intelligent and extremely informative as well as being funny. We all learned a great deal as she spoke about growing up while having to repeat everything three times and not knowing why, and that was one of the smaller difficulties she mentioned.

Her offering was a delight, repleat with humor and affection as she described what must have been a very difficult childhood. From what she says, it seems her condition was not diagnosed properly until recently. It wasn't until she was an adult, in college, that she began to ask the questions that finally led to successful treatment.

Growing up gay is, of course, another subject entirely. Coming out stories are all over the place these days, and they've begun to sound a lot alike. I'm happy to say that's not the case this time. The addition of the OCD element made the narrative fresh and entertaining, and I did learn something very significant. As a queer man, who grew up in the 50s, who thought of himself as a criminal until he was twenty-two years old, I couldn't get over how much we have in common; the hiding, the lying, the yearning for impossible relationships, the entirely inappropriate heterosexual expectations forced upon us until we are finally able, with great disruption and difficulty, to break free.

Lesbians and queer men are almost always lumped together in our culture, but we are not the same. Male and female paradigms differ in any number of ways, regardless of sexual preference. Ms. Levine and I grew up in very different times, but she has made it clear that we were both surrounded by exactly the same sort of stupidity and ignorance, and she suffered the same way I did. Growing up as an outlier is just as fraught with pain as it has always been. In spite of the acceptance we think we have achieved, we need to remember that as we move forward. For making that clear, Ms. Levine deserves a very **HAPPY FACE**.

PERFORMANCE INFORMATION

- January 30th – February 23rd, 2020
- The Tank
- 312 West 36th Street, NYC
- (212) 563-6269
- www.olivia-levine.com
- https://thetanknyc.org/

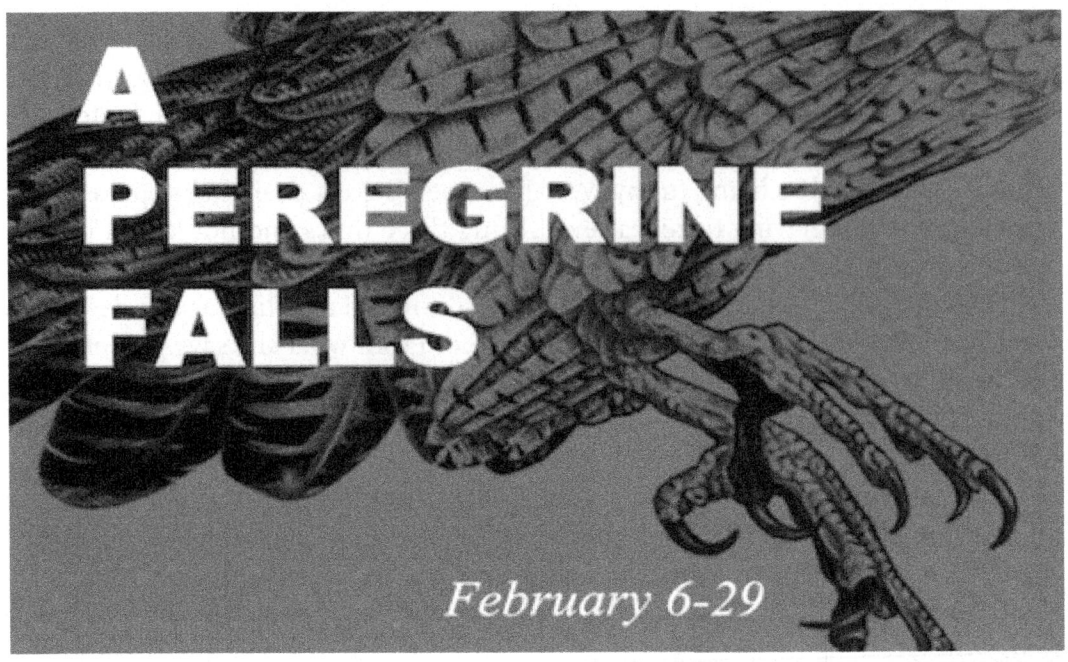

A
PEREGRINE
FALLS

February 6-29

A Peregrine Falls

- Produced by **Loading Dock Theatre**
- Presented in association with **The Workshop Theater**
- Executive Producer: Taphat Tawil
- Play by Leegrid Stevens
- Directed by Padraic Lillis
- Scenic Design: Zoë Hurwitz
- Lighting Design: Simon Cleveland
- Costume Design: Jevyn Nelms
- Sound Design: Leegrid Stevens
- Technical Direction: Eli Reid
- Stage Manager: Lisa R. Stafford
- Production Manager: Elizabeth Sarkady
- Fight Director: Austin Lucas
- Original Music: David Handler
- Press: Rain or Shine PR
- Photos: Clinton Brandhagen

THE CAST (members of Actor's Equity Association in order of appearance)

- Taylor: Kevin Cristaldi
- Charlie: Sidney Williams

- Kailey: Erin Treadway
- Leece: Julia Brothers
- Randy: Mason Walker

THE PLAY

When Kailey comes home after a long absence and announces she's pregnant, her parents, Charlie and Leece, are ecstatic. She's been living with her husband in Montana for several years and not often been in touch. Since childhood, she has suffered from Schizoaffective Disorder, a chronic mental condition characterized by hallucinations, mania and depression. Their relationship has always been difficult, and they hope her sudden appearance means she will again be part of their lives.

Leece, Kailey's mother, is a devout Mormon. Charlie, a recovering alcoholic, has recently returned to the church after a crisis of faith. Taylor, his brother, who also serves as the narrator, is the family success story. His two daughters, who appear only through the original music played throughout, are world-class violinists just beginning their rise to fame. But, something's wrong. Kailey's inability to communicate raises questions that need to be answered, and the resulting plot twist at the end of the play took most of the audience by surprise.

THE PRODUCTION

Everything about Leegrid Stevens' *A Peregrine Falls* was beautifully conceived and executed. Zoë Hurwitz has created an effective, transparent set, built of aluminum frames inset with LED lighting strips. The sound effects, designed by the author — particularly those representing storms and bad weather — are well conceived and remarkably subtle, while the original music by David Handler is world class; classically based violin duets representing two unseen members of the cast.

The lighting, designed by Simon Cleveland, was subtle, and effective, reflecting coming storms and emotional anxiety with changing colors and shifting patterns. Padriac Lillis and the excellent cast make fine use of the compact Wild Project theater space, moving into and around the set with an efficiency that allows the action to proceed smoothly, without a pause, from beginning to end. I also appreciated the ten-minute intermission between the two acts. It gave the audience some time to consider the direction of the narrative. In this day of shortened attention spans, intermissions have fallen out of fashion.

THE PERFORMANCE

This is a well-written play, and every actor had his or her moment. As Kailey, Erin Treadway portrayed the symptoms of Schizoaffective Disorder with remarkable understanding. Her erratic behavior and reactions were spot-on believable. Sidney Williams, who played her father, Charlie, gave us a nuanced portrayal of a modern-day everyman. In some ways, his performance was the most impressive in the play.

Particularly, when he fell off the wagon in Act Two, his inebriation was subtle and real. He played a gentle, loving father, totally overwhelmed by a problem he had either not considered or had been unwilling to acknowledge. When he broke down at the end of the play, it was extraordinarily moving.

Kevin Cristaldi plays a number of roles, including the narrator and Kailey's Uncle Taylor. His initial enthusiasm is quite engaging, but there's something demonic in his manner whenever he appears that suggests elements in his character that might not be so attractive. As Leece, Kailey's mother, Julia Brothers is more than sympathetic. All she wants is to communicate with her daughter. When the world around her collapses, her faith is shattered forever. Her pain is unforgettable. Mason Walker, who plays Randy, Charlie's employee, is also effective, but his part is small and he isn't given a great deal to do.

CONCLUSION

A Peregrins Falls is intensely personal and very beautifully constructed. The sets are handsome, the music stunning, and the acting first rate. This extremely touching play runs at the Wild Project through February 29th. **HAPPY FACE**

PERFORMANCE INFORMATION

- February 6th – 29th, 2020
- The Wild Project
- 195 East 3rd Street, NYC
- (212) 228-1195
- http://thewildproject.com/
- http://loadingdocktheatre.org/peregrine-falls/

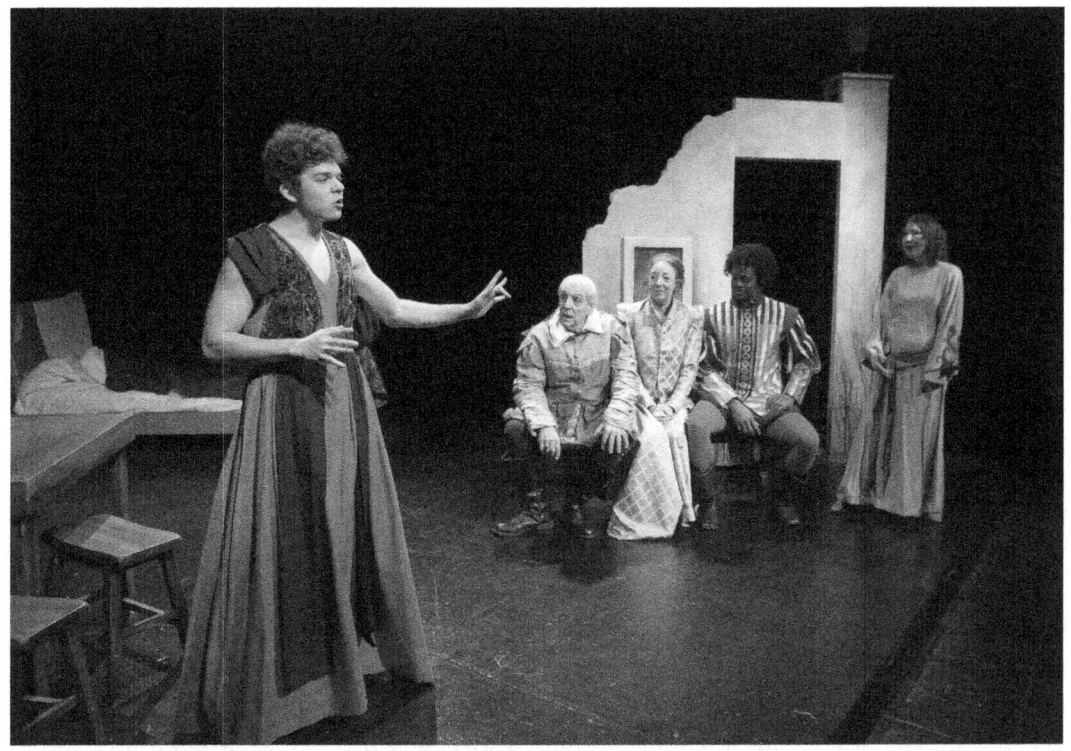

(L–R) Bennett Saltzman, Gene Santarelli, Ethelyn Friend, Jacob Silburn & Carla Lewis

Brocade

- Produced by the **Xoregos Performing Company**
- Play by Robert E. DiNardo
- Directed by Shela Xoregos
- Composer/Lyricist: Barbara Rottman
- Music Director/Violinist: Laura Zawarski
- Costumes: Sara Decker
- Sets: Vincent Gunn
- Lighting: Gabrielle Button
- Stage Manager: Nikki Reed
- Press: Off Off PR
- Photos: Hunter Canning

THE CAST (in order of appearance)

- The Novice: Sarah Kebede-Fiedler
- Countess Felicita Bonini: Carla Lewis*
- Orazio: Bennett Saltzman
- Countess Bianca Bonini: Ethelyn Friend*

- Agostino Amadi: Gene Santarelli*
- Mustat: Jacob Silburn

THE PLAY

Set in Venice in 1615, Robert E. DiNardo's *Brocade* is a charming comedy that's not only funny, but also provides a great deal of fascinating information on the life of the seventeenth-century Italian underclass. Orazio is a talented young orphan raised in a convent by Mother Superior Benigno, formerly the Countess Felicita Bonini, who fell out of the ruling class when her family went broke. During his upbringing, he took up embroidery in order to help the nuns repair their habits. As a result, he grew up sewing and eventually developed into a first class dress designer, a "cutter" as such people were known at the time. But, as an orphan, with no family connections, Orazio was unable to become a member of the Cutter's Guild, meaning that he was prevented from designing and making clothing for people of "quality."

But, talent will out. When the play begins, Orazio has already become the favorite dress maker of the 11,000 legal prostitutes in Venice, a profitable if dubious distinction. He has gone into business with the Countess Bianca Bonini, Mother Benigno's sister, who now runs a boarding house in order to survive. Will Orazio ever be able to break into a world that will appreciate his remarkable talent? What about Felicita's mysterious old lover, Agostino, who returns and confesses that he always loved Bianca? The answers are wonderfully entertaining.

THE PERFORMANCE

Brocade is deliriously funny from beginning to end. Mr. DiNardo has written a witty, well-researched play about sex, class conflict, and religion in the 1600s. The sets, designed by Vincent Gunn, are modest but well built, with an eye to period Italian styling. Sara Decker's costumes are really stunning, as one would expect in a play about haute couture. There is also some fine music, composed by Barbara Rottman, with some increasingly proficient violin work (the Novice in the play, well played by Sarah Kebede-Fiedler, is studying violin and improves as the play progresses) provided by Music Director Laura Zawarski.

As Orazio, Bennett Saltzman was quite engaging. Energetic and masculine, even when he makes his first entrance wearing one of his own dresses. He gives us an intriguing picture of what it must have been like to grow up an orphan in a place like Venice. With good humor and an unshakable belief in his talent, as well as encouragement from all those prostitutes, he is determined to make his mark.

As Contessas Felicita and Bianca Bonini, Carla Lewis and Ethelyn Friend are more than sympathetic. When their family went broke, Contessa Felicita became Mother Superior in a convent noted throughout Europe as a brothel for traveling salesmen. Unwilling to let that continue, and pregnant herself, she rededicated her religious order to the care of orphans. Contessa Bianca, of the other hand, a much more lady-like lady, opened the last piece of property belonging to the Bonini family as a boarding house. Orazio is living there when the play begins.

As Mustat, Orazio's (slightly) older lover, Jacob Silburn tries to bring a bit of common sense into the narrative. Mostly, he succeeds, but when a man he recognizes from the past, Agostino Amadi, appears unexpectedly, he isn't sure how to react. As Agostino, Gene Santarelli is an absolute stitch. A former Venetian stud, once considered the most beautiful man in italy, he is now old and lonely. That won't last long, of course. He's very rich, and, in the final analysis, we discover that he's the father of Mother Benigno's illegitimate child.

CONCLUSION

Brocade is a clever, intelligent take on life in a time and place we can hardly imagine. It's a handsome production, with a fine set, stunning costumes, lovely music, and first class acting. It even has an intermission, which means it's a real play. See it if you can. It more than deserves a very **HAPPY FACE**.

PERFORMANCE INFORMATION

- January 30th – 16th, 2020
- Theater for the New City
- 155 First Avenue, NYC
- (212) 254-1109
- https://xoregoscompany.com/
- https://theaterforthenewcity.net/wp-tnc/

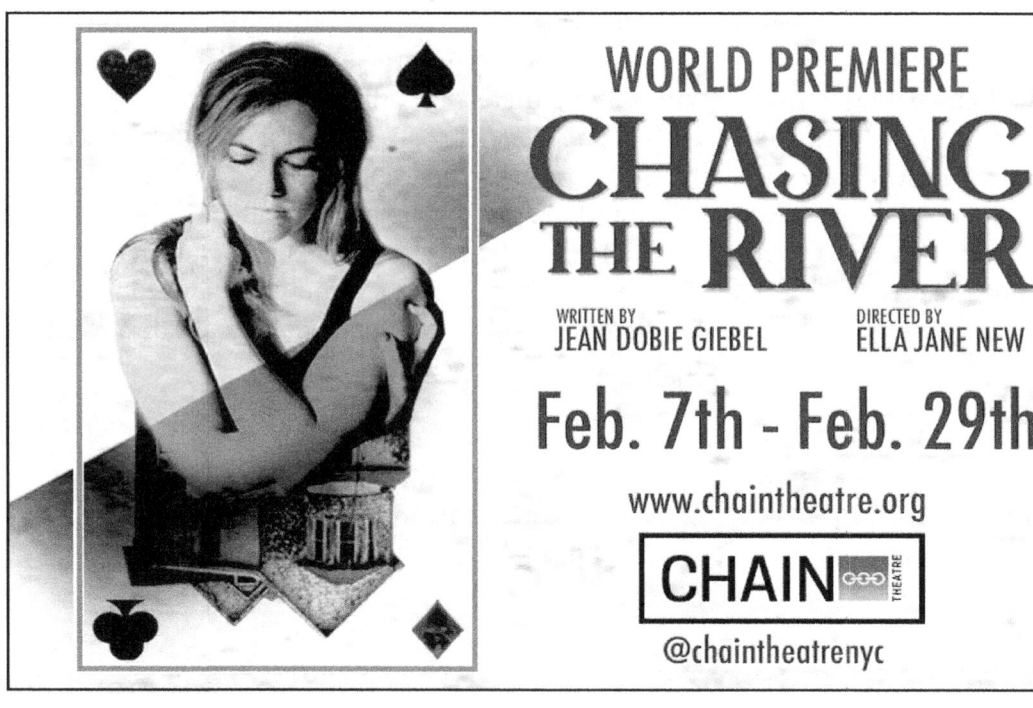

Chasing the River

- Presented by **The Chain Theatre**
- Play by Jean Dobie Giebel
- Directed by Ella Jane New
- Set Design: Raye Levine Spielberg
- Stage Manager: Ericka Lee Conklin
- Lighting Design: Michael Abrams
- Sound Design: Greg Russ
- Artistic Director: Kirk Gostkowski
- Managing Director: Rick Hamilton
- Production Assistants: Mo Bono, Blaire O'Leary, Andrew Dobbie
- Technical Directors: Karim Ahmed, Dionisio Cortes
- Graphic Design: Adrienne Lovette
- Executive Producers: Ray & Lori Palomaa
- Press: Kampfire PR
- Photos: Matt Wells

THE CAST

- Kat: Christina Elise Perry*
- Sam: David Rey

- Nathaniel: David Wenzel
- Adelaide: Sara Thigpen*
- Margaret: Robyne Parrish*
- Beth: Caroline Orlando

THE PLAY

Jean Dobie Giebel's intense *Chasing the River* concerns a young woman who returns to her childhood home after serving a prison sentence for a widely misunderstood crime. Because of severe domestic abuse, Kat desperately needs to come to grips with her actions. But, such things are never easy, and, almost immediately, she is haunted by ghosts from her past. Like so many people, Kat soon learns it isn't easy to judge those who have wronged us, that our long-held beliefs are often determined by our own behavior.

THE PRODUCTION

With time shifting, aided by Michael Abrams' well-considered lighting and subtle sound effects by Greg Russ, Director Ella Jane New and her excellent cast have given us a detailed picture of Post Traumatic Stress Disorder. The company makes fine use of the Chain Theatre space. Raye Levine Spielberg's set is simple and effective, the action aptly staged and skillfully executed.

THE PERFORMANCE

As Kat, the focus of this drama, Christine Elise Perry adapts to the time shifts almost effortlessly. She plays a child, an adult, a teen-ager, with dexterity and focus, moving smoothly from scene to scene in ways that ensure the narrative is uninterrupted and coherent. David Wenzel portrays Nathanial, Kat's father, an abusive alcoholic, with an intelligent understanding of his condition. When sober, he is kindness itself. When drunk, he is brutal and implacable. The violence in the second act, when he runs amok, is as realistic as anything I've ever seen onstage.

As Sam, Kat's childhood sweetheart, David Rey also adapts skillfully to the time-shifts. Sam is never quite sure what's wrong with Kat, or he doesn't want to know. He's sympathetic, and obviously devoted, but given her underlying condition and his youthful inexperience he has no idea how to react. Robyne Parrish, as Margaret, Kat's mother, is hopelessly conflicted. As a victim of her husband's abuse, she's desperate to remove both her daughters, Kat and Beth (well-played by Caroline Orlando), from his influence. But, Kat will not listen, and Beth is still a child when she suddenly vanishes. Ms. Parrish's performance is strong and nuanced, her despair at not being able to communicate with Kat painfully evident.

As Aunt Adelaide, Sara Thigpen is well-aware of Nathanial's mercurial nature. Although she is not able to directly influence Nathanial's actions, she's the only one who seems able (reluctantly) to provide help, mostly money and practical advice.

Ms. Thigpen presents a complicated character with skill; another fine performance in a fine play.

CONCLUSION

Chasing the River is another well-written take on the seemingly unending trauma experienced at the hands of family members. The dialogue is excellent, the concept consistently addressed, and domestic abuse absolutely a subject that needs to be discussed. Unfortunately, with the rise of **#MeToo** and the feminist imperative now so prevalent in our culture, the subject is suffering from narrative inflation. This play is intelligent and engaging, but the details are distressingly familiar.

I very much enjoyed this performance. See it if you can. But, fresh ways to present this important subject need to be found if it's to remain relevant. For this reason, I have to give *Chasing the River* a **HAPPY FACE MINUS**.

PERFORMANCE INFORMATION

- February 7th – 29th, 2020
- The Chain Theater
- 312 West 36th Street, 4th Floor, NYC
- (646) 580-6003
- http://www.chaintheatre.org/

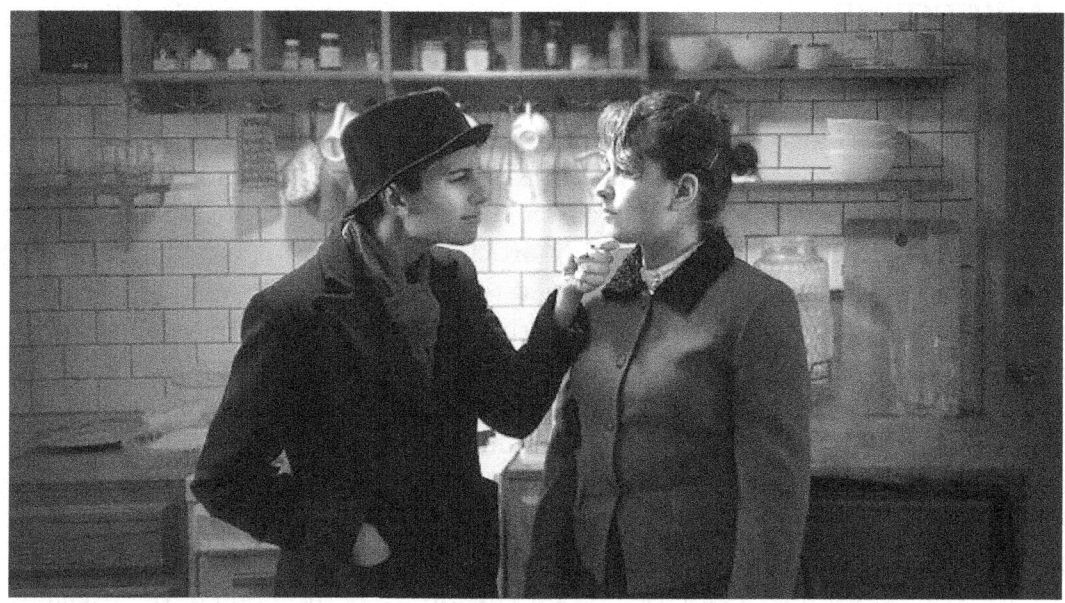

Ashley Adelman & Kate Szekely

Nellie and the Women of Blackwell

- Co-produced by **Wildrence** and **Infinite Variety Productions**
- Production support from Bree O'Connor
- Written by Ashley Adelman
- Directed by Jessica Schechter
- Stage Manager: Hadley Todoran
- House Manager: Cassie Neals
- Assistant House Managers: Alexandria Thomas & Lucie Bhisitkul
- Costume Design: Bree O'Connor
- Experiential, Scenic & Lighting Design: Wildrence
- Sets & Sound Design: Andrew Dunn
- Press: Jay Michaels Arts & Entertainment
- Photo: Ashley Adelman

THE CAST

- Nellie Bly: Kate Szekely
- Tillie/Mrs. Stanard: Ashley Adelman
- Editor/Carrie/Roommate/Nurse Scott/Policeman: Nicole Orabona
- Mrs. Caine/Mrs. Grupe/Woman on Rope: Janessa Floyd
- Sarah Fishbaum: Jan Ewing (2/14/2020)
- Asylum Doctor (VO): Joe Helmreich
- Hospital Doctor/Judge/Attorney (VOs): Andrew Dunn

BACKGROUND

The Blackwell Lunatic Asylum was the first municipal mental hospital in the United States. Opened in New York City in 1839 on what is now Roosevelt Island, it housed both men and women, although many more women than men were "treated" there. In 1887, the remarkable Elizabeth Cochran Seaman, known to the world as Nellie Bly (a woman far ahead of her time), had herself committed (undercover) at Blackwell in order to write a series of articles for the New York Globe, a daily newspaper that enjoyed wide circulation at the time. The result was "Ten Days in a Mad House," a searing exposé of the horrific medical practices she observed and personally experienced during the time she spent at the hospital.

The year 2020 marks the 100th anniversary of women's suffrage in the United States. Suffrage means "the right to vote in political elections." It stems from Latin and French, but it wasn't defined politically until it came to the United States in the late 18th-century. I found myself thinking of that quite a few times while I participated in Ashley Adelman's excellent *Nellie and the Women of Blackwell.*

The play was primarily focused on the dreadful way the women were treated, which was, indeed, inhuman. What struck me the most, however, was the absolute right men had to deal any way they saw fit with the women in their lives. This went on until the 1920s, which was only two lifetimes ago, not so long when one thinks about it. For any reason at all, a woman could be incarcerated at Blackwell: talking back, reading too much, refusing sex, wanting sex; being annoying or too expensive to maintain, which was the case for many "spinster" aunts or other unconnected female relatives. Frequently, they were committed by civil authorities, with no medical input whatsoever. They might not even see a doctor until it was too late, which hardly mattered. The ignorance of the medical profession as to the nature of "lunacy" was astonishing. And, they were men, after all. They almost always gave credence to the opinions and demands of misguided fathers and alcoholic husbands. As a man myself, I was absolutely horrified.

THE PLAY

The Wildrence Company works in a basement space cleverly partioned into four playing areas connected by short halls and "secret" passages. There were roughly twenty participants the night I was there, about as many as could be accommodated. As the play began, we gathered in the office of The Globe's Managing Editor where we met Nellie Bly, were given hospital robes, and assigned our roles. I played the part of Sarah Fishbaum, an elderly woman who had simply been discarded by her family   .

Following Nellie from room to room, we were led into the dystopian world of 19th-century medical confinement. We were starved, humiliated, frozen, made to bathe in cold water (in public), scrub the floor, and make beds while secretly communicating with patients who were locked into tiny spaces under the floor, all the while being kept mostly in the dark, not allowed to exercise or even experience sunlight. It was a frightening reminder of how quickly people can become monsters when they're told others are less than human. Yes, 1887 was a long time ago. So was the Holocaust, it might seem, but the incarceration of children at our borders is going on as I write this, and our current government is telling us their parents are criminals. It's despotic and wrong, and something we *cannot* allow ourselves to overlook.

THE PERFORMANCE

The play was skillfully done, the immersion remarkably effective. Andrew Dunn's sets were simple but creative, his sound effects well-designed and coordinated. The lighting was a marvel given that the spots and illumination in four different rooms (with two playing areas frequently in use at the same time), seemed flawless. Even the heat was manipulated, warm one moment, freezing the next. Everything that happened was intelligently conceived and executed. Kudos to Wildrence for the care they took with every element of this fascinating experience.

The acting was first rate. There were only four performers involved (discounting me and the other extras). Everyone but Kate Szekely, stalwart and inspiring as Nellie Bly, played multiple roles. The author, Ashley Adelman, as Mrs. Stanard, a boarding house keeper, and Tillie, a desperate patient, was differentiated so well, I didn't realize she'd played both parts until I later read the program. Nicole Orabona and Janessa Floyd were miraculous, rotating constantly between eight different characters, unerringly facilitated by Costume Designer Bree O'Connor.

CONCLUSION

When you get right down to it, the issues discussed in Ms. Adelman's play are so current they're terrifying; otherwise decent people rationalizing incredibly indecent acts; things happening today that were unthinkable last year. The narrative is incredibly thought-provoking, with the immersion bringing it home in a way that's impossible to appreciate if one is just sitting in a chair and observing. There's nothing happy about any of this. Nonetheless, the play and the performance certainly deserve a very **HAPPY FACE**.

THE PERFORMANCE

- January 30th – March 7th, 2020
- Wildrence
- 59 Canal Street, NYC
- (646) 657-0630
- https://www.wildrence.com/
- www.infinitevarietynyc.org

Animal Farm

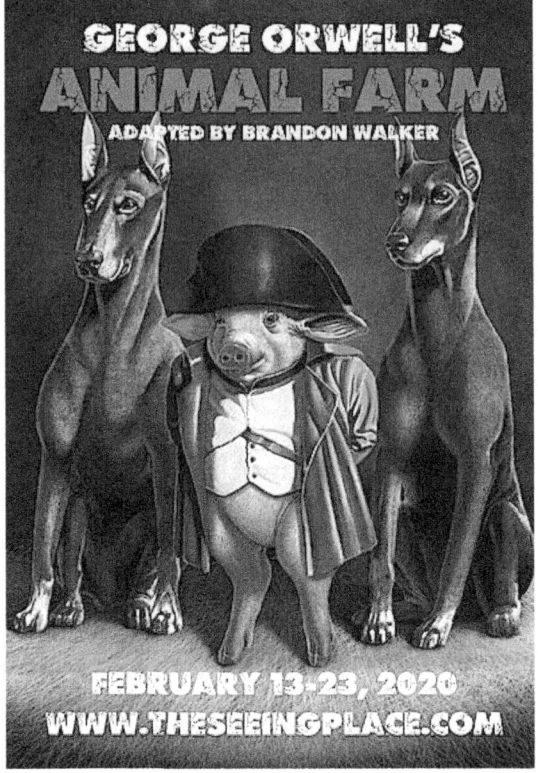

- Presented by **The Seeing Place Theater**
- Based on the novel *Animal Farm* by George Orwell
- Adapted by Brandon Walker
- Co-Producers/Directors: Brandon Walker & Erin Cronican
- Stage Management/Board Operation: Leeanna Tolanda Rivas
- Lighting Design: Lorena Ndokaj
- Scenic & Costume Design: Erin Cronican
- Sound Design: Brandon Walker
- Technical Direction: Robin Friend
- Set Construction: Ellinor DiLorenzo, Louis Kim, Dom Martello, Jon L. Peacock
- Marketing Support: Laura Clare Browne, Barbara Haas, Sabrina Schlegel-Mejia, Sandra Trullinger, Hailey Vest, Weronika Helena Wozniak
- Photos: Russ Rowland

THE CAST

- Squealer/Mollie/Frederick & others: Laura Clare Browne
- Snowball/Clover/Whymper & others: Erin Cronican*
- Old Major/Benjamen/Pilkington & others: William Ketter
- Napoleon/Boxer/Jones & others: Brandon Walker*

BACKGROUND

This is the most disturbing play I've seen in the past year. George Owell's brilliant novel, Animal Farm, published in 1945, is a study of authoritarianism. Loosely based on the Russian Revolution, it concerns farm animals who decide they can no longer wait for their human "masters" to act in their best interest. Starving and cold, they chase away their thoughtless owner, Mr. Jones, and set up Animal Farm; a republic of the animals, by the animals, for the animals. Then, reality sets in.

THE PRODUCTION

Closely following Orwell's original narrative, Brandon Walker's brilliant adaptation of Animal Farm flawlessly morphs four remarkable actors through twenty-six, mostly non-human, incarnations — squeaking, squawking, mooing, chirping, grunting, neighing, quacking, croaking common sense and crying in despair — almost two hours on all fours. They are more than skilled. They are miraculous. As soon as you enter the farm yard, you are welcomed as a comrade. There are three corrals for the audience; sheep, cows, and hens, grouped around the playing area. I was a hen.

The set is simple and rustic, with hay and water pales on the floor. The mostly wooden props, small fences, boxes, are moved around the stage to make corrals and podiums as needed. The lighting is as good as it can be in a medium-sized, black box theater, and the space is well utilized. Thus, is the scene set for a fascinating rendition of this distressing scenario. But, it's better seen than described, so I encourage you to take your children and see it.

THE PERFORMANCE

The actors were splendid, textbook examples of "method" acting. Stanislavski would have cheered as they "become" chickens, dogs, and pigs. Their characterizations were extremely realistic, which suggests good direction and hours spent observing the attributes of each animal. William Ketter, playing a victimized chicken, laid an egg. He flapped his arms, darted his head back and forth, and looked under his squatting body to find it. It was one of the funniest things I've ever seen. At that moment, I do believe he was a bird. Great work, Mr. Ketter. Extraordinarily skillful, remarkably funny.

As Boxer, an overworked horse, and Napoleon, a power-hungry pig, playwright Brandon Walker sets a high standard from the beginning. Trying hard to believe in animal-equality, Boxer is as thoughtlessly used by his comrades as he was by his masters. Mr. Walker, a very gifted man, was extremely moving in the one instance, entirely hateful in the other.

As Snowball, the gentle martyred hero, and Squealer, the slimy collaborator, Erin Cronican and Laura Clare Browne were consistent and entertaining every time they appeared. Not that their splendid performances were in any way limited to those specific characters. Indeed, the examples I've given above, of small bits here are there, are only hints as to the high level of the acting. The play was riveting from beginning to end, and it's still a frightful warning as to what might be happening to us now.

CONCLUSION

Every justification used by Pig Napoleon and his toady, Squealer, as they usurped the inalienable rights of their comrades, corresponds with something the "president" and his toadies have tried on us recently. That's horrifying. Brandon Walker and his superb cast have made that very clear, which is why I found the play so disturbing. It's 2020. Fascism is screaming lies every day. It's insidious and iniquitous. This incredibly inventive play reminds us why. **HAPPY FACE PLUS**

PERFORMANCE INFORMATION

- February 13th – 23rd, 2020
- **The Seeing Place @ The Paradise Factory**
- 64 East 4th Street, Basement, NYC
- www.theseeingplace.com

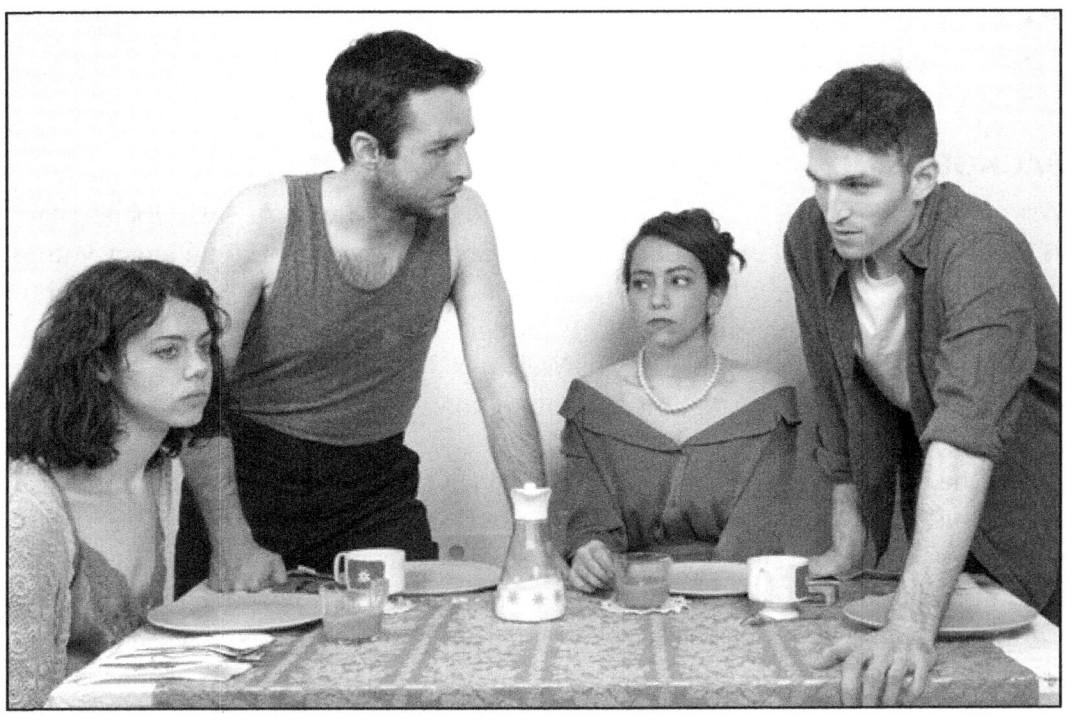

(L–R) Elizabeth Scopel, Tim Creavin, Caroline Aimetti & Ryan Welsh

Look Back in Anger

- Presented by **Celtic Lion Productions** in association with Ryan Welsh & Joy Donze
- Play by John Osborne
- Directed by Aimee Fortier
- Lighting Design: Gilbert "Lucky" Pearto
- Fight Direction: Christopher J. Payseur
- Dialect Coaching: Amy Jo Jackson
- Dramaturgy: Danya Martin
- Wardrobe & Prop Assistant: Emily Tripp
- Carpenter: Daniel Nelson
- House Manager: Samantha Squatrito
- Production-, Graphic-, Costume-Design/Props Master: Mary Marxen
- Production Stage Manager/Sound Programmer: Margaret Baughman
- Press: SpinCycleNYC

THE CAST (in alphabetical order)
- Helena: Caroline Aimetti*
- Colonel Redfern: Stan Buturla*

- Cliff: Tim Creavin
- Alison: Elizabeth Scopel
- Jimmy: Ryan Welsh

BACKGROUND

Written in 1956, the New York Times described John Osborne's *Look Back in Anger* as "the most vivid play of the decade." Mr. Osborne was the original angry young man, the first playwright to directly confront the class war that was developing in Great Britain at the time, and his play is thought to have been largely biographical. Jimmy, played here by producer Ryan Welsh, is an intelligent, working class man who has managed to educate himself, hoping to escape the shabby world in which he was raised. But, that hasn't happened.

As the play begins, Jimmy has been living for three years in a single room with Alison, his upper-class wife, played by Elizabeth Scopel, and Cliff, his college friend and "mate," played by Tim Creavin (also his partner in a small business that's barely keeping them alive). Into this mix comes Helena, Alison's posh friend, played by Caroline Aimetti, and thus begins what the program describes as "a searing look at class, sex, politics and the angry, alienated youth living on the margins."

THE PERFORMANCE

I have to be honest. Had I not already known a great deal about this play, I wouldn't have gotten any of that from the production I saw last week. Whatever it was that won *Look Back in Anger* so many accolades in London and New York in the late 1950s (the subsequent film starred Richard Burton and Claire Bloom) was simply missing. Mr. Welsh's Jimmy was so angry there wasn't a trace of the intelligent young man the other characters were said to have adored. He raved and screamed from beginning to end, in a Scottish dialect so thick that at least half his dialogue was unintelligible. It goes without saying that this is the fault of the director. With some strong guidance, I believe Mr. Welsh has a decent Jimmy in him. But, an actor needs to be three-dimensional, not just pissed off. Otherwise, his character will never be able to engage the audience. That said, I note that Mr. Welsh is also the producer. Director Aimee Fortier may have found herself in a difficult position.

With the lead character more or less inaccessible, the other actors were also put in a difficult position. Generally, they were weak and unconvincing. The British accents were badly done and inconsistent. It would have been far better to ignore the accents and just say the lines. As Alison, Jimmy's wife, Elizabeth Scopel seemed barely there. Alison *is* described as being somewhat withdrawn, but Ms. Scopel seemed vague. Indeed, the only time I actually learned anything about the underlying motivations of the other characters was when Colonel Redfern, a small role sympathetically played by Stan Buturla, came to take Alison home. He spoke clearly and with intelligence. A moment of clarity in a mostly muddy broth.

On the one hand, **Celtic Lion Productions** was brave to take on a play of this magnitude. On the other, they are in no way ready to give it its due, not in NYC anyway. A lot of the problems I saw could have been fixed with strong direction. Even anger requires subtlety. If Mr. Welsh could have mitigated his rage occasionally, maybe shown a little sympathy for Cliff, not badly played by Tim Creavin, it would have made the other characters more believable. As it was, it was next to impossible to understand why they loved him.

CONCLUSION

In the end, all I learned from this performance is that British class conflicts of the 1950s are a dead issue. They have nothing in common with the social conflicts we're facing at the moment. It would seem that *Look Back in Anger* is no longer relevant. I don't like being so negative. But, I feel I must. **UNHAPPY FACE**

PERFORMANCE INFORMATION

- February 15th – 29th, 2020
- Gene Frankel Theater
- 24 Bond Street, NYC
- https://www.genefrankeltheatre.com/

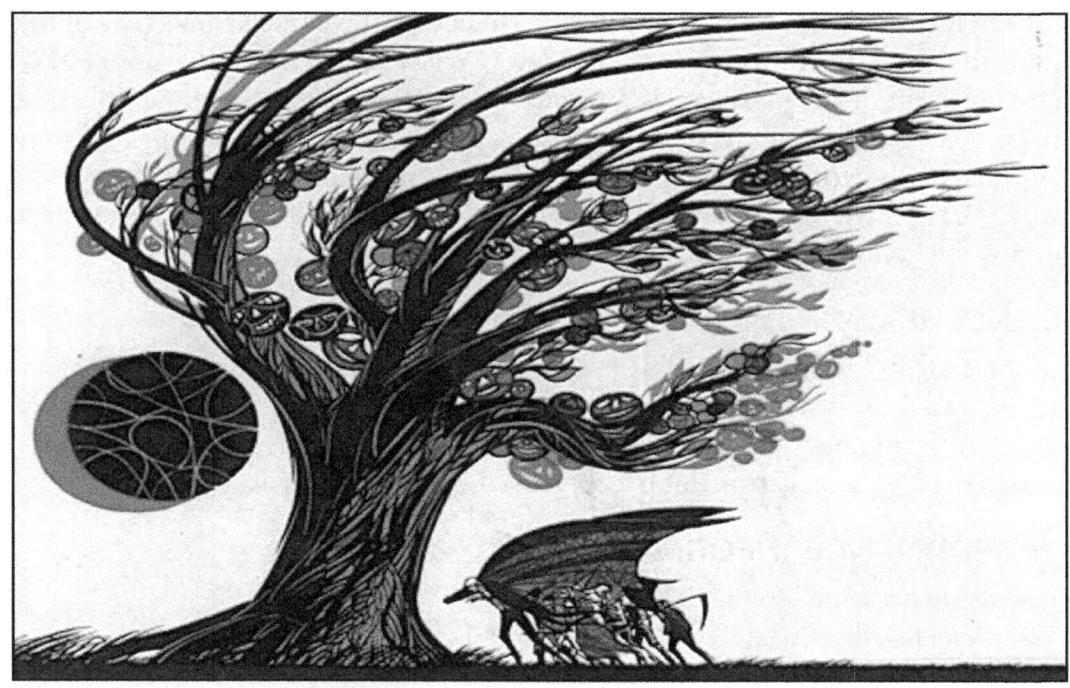

Original Book Cover by Joseph Mugnaini

The Halloween Tree An Opera

- Report on an orchestral reading presented as part of the **Insight.Alt Festival**
- Music by Theo Popov
- Libretto by Tony Asaro
- Based on the novel by Ray Bradbury
- Commissioned by **American Lyric Theater**
- Conductor: Geoffrey McDonald
- Workshop coach & pianist: Gloria Kim
- Stage Manager: Tim Love
- Dramaturg Apprentices: Hannah McDermott, Katherine Pitt
- Videographer: Asaf Blasberg
- Photos: Matt Madison Clark

THE CAST (in order of appearance)

- Lenny: Zackery Morris
- Lynn: Rachel Mikol
- J.J.: Connor McDonald
- Kelly: Kimberly Sogioka
- Tom: Benjamin Taylor
- Pipkin: Christian Sanders

- Carapace Clavicle Moundshroud: Matt Boehler
- A Cloaked Woman: Rachel Rosales

THE ENSEMBLE (Mastervoices)

- **SOPRANOS:** Nicole Coffaro, Becca Hare, Manami Hattori, Sandy MacDonald, Rachel Rosales, Elizabeth van Os
- **MEZZO SOPRANOS:** Katherine Eberenz, Mary Fan, Erica Koehring, Luisa Lyons, Vivianne Potter, Laurie Rios
- **TENORS:** Jack Cotterell, Mark Filatov, Ethan Fran, Cathy Friedman, John Sabatos, Helen Shin, Tommy Wazelle
- **BASSES:** Blake Burroughs, Jonathan Guss, Mikhail Pontenila, Robert Reichstein, Michael Riley, Daniel Rios, Edsel Romero

ALT-CO (American Lyric Theater Chamber Orchestra)

- **CONCERTMASTER:** Adela Peña; **VIOLIN:** Josh Henderson, Nikita Morozov, Tom Chiu, Mioi Takeda; **VIOLA:** Kim Foster, Leah Asher; **cello:** Mitch Lyon, Amanda Gookin; **CONTRABASS:** Scott Ritchie, Dara Bloom; **FLUTE/PICCOLO/ALTO FLUTE:** Jessica Han; **OBOE/ENGLISH HORN:** Michelle Farah; **CLARINET/BASS CLARINET:** Nuno Antunes; **BASSOON:** Nanci Belmont; **FRENCH HORN:** Nicolee Kuester; **TRUMPET/PICCOLO TRUMPET:** Evan Honse; **TROMBONE:** Jen Baker; **TUBA:** Kyle Turner; **PERCUSSION:** Chihiro Shibayama; **HARP:** Tomina Parvanova; **GUITARS:** Brendon Randall-Myers

BACKGROUND

First published as a novel in 1972, Robert Heinlein's fantasy *The Halloween Tree* was originally written as a screenplay for an animated film. It concerns a group of youngsters who embark on a thrilling trick-or-treat adventure. Pipkin, their friend, is seen entering a house thought to be haunted. When they enter the house themselves, to provide support, they find he has fallen foul of a dark force that will take his life unless they are able to complete a series of magical tasks demanded by the house's proprietor, a demonic, un-human creature named Carapace Clavicle Moundshroud.

Encountering mummies, druids, witches, gargoyles, mourners, and skeletons along the way, the small troupe (five in this operatic version) follow Pipkin into the distant past, through Egypt, Greece, Rome, Ireland, Medieval France, and Mexico, where they learn the genesis of All Hallows' Eve and the role it has played in the shaping of western civilization.

THE OPERA

Librettist Tony Asaro and composer Theo Popov have created an entertaining theater piece suitable for both children and adults. Mr. Asaro's adaptation of Robert

Heinlein's book is first-rate, with intelligent, informative lyrics (in English), and a well constructed narrative framework that can easily be staged in any number of creative ways. Mr. Popov's music is skillfully through-composed, cinematic rather than academic. Often rhapsodic, it underlies the narrative with the sort of interaction found in the best operatic scores, not just *accompanying*, but also *partnering* with the soloists and vocal ensemble, thus allowing the plot to flow flawlessly, without pause, from beginning to end.

THE PERFORMANCE

Since this is a work in progress, this presentation was an orchestral reading, a concert presentation with the performers singing from music desks arranged in front of the orchestra. It is an important step in the development a new opera, designed to detect musical and/or dramatic elements that might need correction before undertaking the expense of a staged production. As such, it is the work, itself, that needs to be considered, rather than the individual characterizations or performances.

Be that as it may, this was a fine presentation throughout. The soloists (see above) were excellent, very well trained, and seemed to having a grand time, with Matt Boehler giving us a particularly dark, subtly monstrous, Carapace Clavicle Moundshroud. The ensemble, all members of **Masterworks** (originally formed as **The Collegiate Chorale** by Robert Shaw in 1942), sang the mummies, druids, witches, gargoyles, mourners, and skeletons, with great subtlety.

The orchestra was thoroughly professional, as we have come to expect in New York City. Except for an occasional intonation problem in the strings, something to be expected when any ensemble is navigating a totally new work, it played with riveting skill and exceptional beauty.

The Halloween Tree is a delight. The music (and language) are accessible and frequently funny, the orchestrations ravishing and uplifting, with many ghostly tropes along the way. Considering that it takes place during one of our most glamorous holidays — the great tree being a metaphor for the commonality of our cultural development — it is an educational work that can be staged with color, magic and panache. This excellent opera is a winner. It if doesn't bring some new (young) fans into the fold, I'll be very surprised.

PERFORMANCE INFORMATION

- February 23rd, 2020 @ 7:30pm
- Ailey Citigroup Theater
- 405 West 55th Street, NYC
- (646) 216-8298
- https://www.altnyc.org/the-halloween-tree

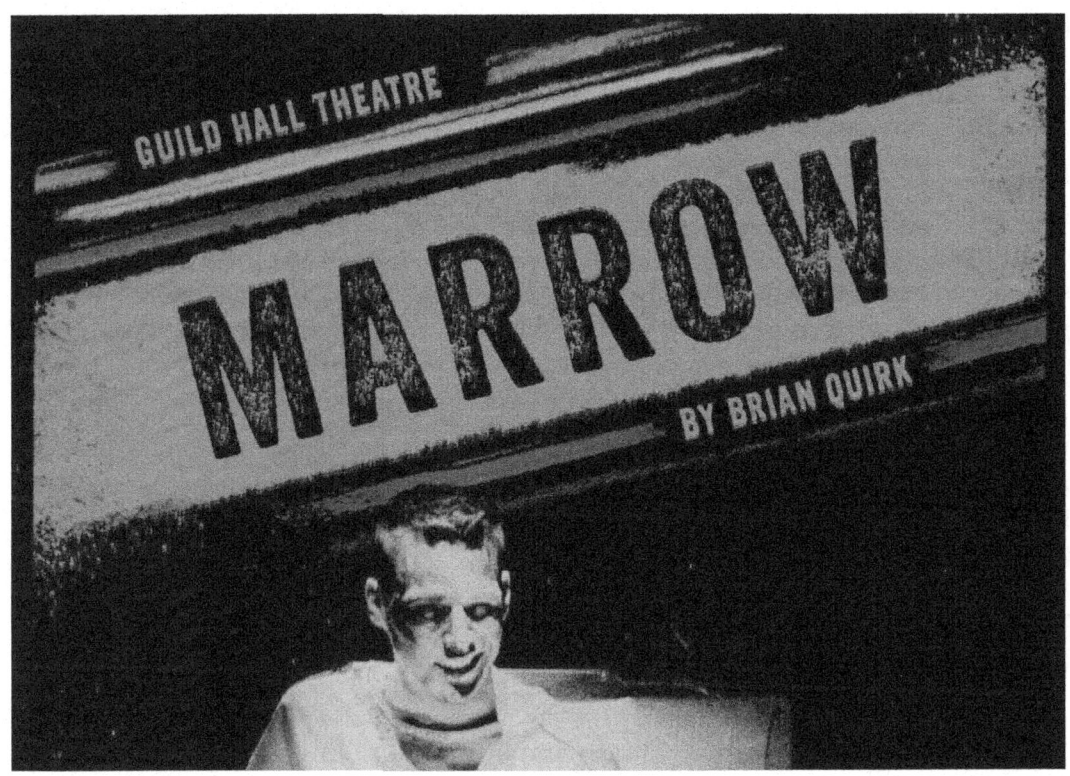

Marrow

Reviewed for HI! DRAMA by William J. Cataldi

- Produced by **Resolve Productions** in residence at the **Episcopal Actors' Guild**
- Written by Brian Quirk
- Performed by Craig MacArthur
- Directed by Melissa Firlit
- Stage Manager: Gabriela Gowdie
- Sound Design: Matt Bitner
- Lighting Design: Matthew D. McCarren
- Dialect Coach: Diego Daniel Pardel

THE PLAY

Unless I could see Brian Quirk's *Marrow* on paper, I cannot have much to say about the play itself. This particular work seems to be all about the performance. I can't remember ever seeing or reading a more difficult-to-perform piece, and young Craig MacArthur could not have picked a bigger challenge to his acting acumen. He does an outstanding job. The solo performance focuses on a twenty-seven-year-old gay man who is beaten in a hate crime and left for dead on a city street. The play is a series of impressionistic memories, conversations, explanations and ruminations during his time in the hospital, where he starts out in a coma (they don't know how much brain damage has been done) and proceeds through regaining consciousness to rehab. Mr. MacArthur's characterizations are generally persuasive. His ability to memorize and perform a 55-minute, word-dense monologue, requiring radical momentary shifts in time and space, and ranging from the principal character who has suffered serious brain damage to an assortment of other folks who have populated his world, astonished me. If he plays his cards right, Mr. MacArthur may become a significant actor.

Part of the proceeds from these performances goes to the Episcopal Actors' Guild, which offers member actors support of all kinds, from free space to emergency rent money. A trip to see *Marrow* will not disappoint, and helps support a great cause. If you're interested in experimental theater, or just theater at the Off-Off-Broadway level, don't miss a chance to see Mr. MacArthur's fascinating performance.

THE PERFORMANCE

Director Melissa Firlit has decided to encourage Mr. MacArthur to perform with great haste. Usually, haste is a fault in theater, because it doesn't give the audience a chance to process the words, meanings, implications or dimensions of what's being said. Haste in this performance did indeed undercut my ability to grow to love the principal character and to emote over his plight. Sometimes, my mind wandered. On the other hand, Mr. MacArthur (in Ms. Firlit's hands) never jammed characterizations together, always enunciated appropriately, and gave sufficient psychological nuance with voice, facial expression, and body to his characters, despite the haste. That was quite something.

One of my favorite writing techniques employs list making. I love lists. Mr. Quirk obviously loves lists as much as I do, because he seems to be a master of the technique. A list is a meaningful, coherent set of discrete elements. When I compose a list, I want my reader to contemplate each discrete element. How does it fit into the list? How does it's inclusion change the nature of the list as a whole? What is the meaning of the list, based on an assessment of its elements?

In his haste, Mr. MacArthur ventured often into recitation of the many lists in this play. Frequently, I was only able to glean the overall meaning of the list (he's attracted to this man), but the poetry of the list (he's turned on by the man's pout, his shifty stance, his tattooed muscles) got lost. That, in turn, meant that a great deal of the poetry and multi-dimensionality of the writing got lost.

Why 55 minutes? If Mr. MacArthur had paused, even just halves of a second, over his many list items, these lists may have come alive for me. This might have ballooned the performance to 90 minutes, but I wouldn't have noticed even if I'd had to go to the bathroom. I would have been too busy crying. The impressionism of the play would persist, even in a slower performance. Earlier, I wrote that I wouldn't have much to say about Mr. Quirk's writing. I suspect it was brilliant. But I'd have to have time to contemplate it more, before the action moved on. Or I'd have to read it.

This was Mr. MacArthur's night. His stunning performance lit up the room. He needs to be able to give better characterizations of straight people. His work with a wide range of gay men was a miracle of nuance. But he requires more psychological depth to be a great actor. This doesn't mean much. He's in his twenties. It's simply an impossibility for him to have much in the way of "psychological depth" yet. He's got to keep acting, keep honing those awesome skills — and, above all, keep living. Like I wrote earlier: all he's got to do is play his cards right and he'll have a great future. Bravi to one and all. **HAPPY FACE MINUS**

PERFORMANCE INFORMATION

- Thursday – Saturday, February 20th – 29nd @ 7pm, 2020
- Episcopal Actors' Guild
- One East 29th Street, NYC
- New York City 10016
- Tickets: https://www.artful.ly/store/events/19498

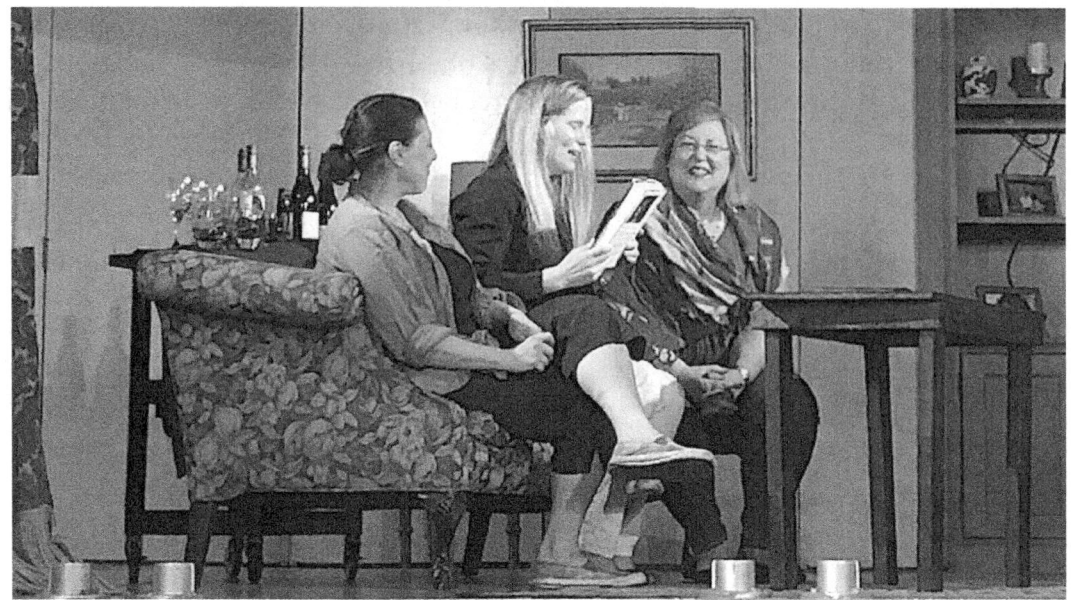
Claudia Terry, Kristin Hardwick & Leslie DiLeo

Forgotten Falls

- Presented by the **Black Orchid Theatre Group**
  @ the **Church of the Resurrection**
- Play by Ryan Kaminski
- Director: Craig Hutchison
- Stage Manager: Jackie Price
- Property Mistress: Inez Lambert
- Photo: Sara Howell

THE CAST (in order of appearance)

- Mallory Barnes: Leslie DiLeo
- Grace Barnes: Claudia Terry
- Sheriff Fred Watson: Michael Cramer
- Audrey Lawrence: Rebecca Collier
- Lena Lawrence: Kristin Hardwick
- Stephen Lawrence: Abrian Rivera

THE PLAY

When her mother dies, Mallory Burnes returns home after a long absence. At first, it seems everything is fine. Her sisters, Grace and Audrey, welcome her back. She's a successful writer, so she has always been considered the family high flyer, and after their devastating loss they are more than happy to have her help. But, things are not what they seem. Audrey's husband, Stephen, and his family, seem reluctant to let Audrey interact with her sisters. Why this is happening, and how it affects them, is the basis for Forgotten Falls, Ryan Kaminski's new play.

I wish I could be more positive about this work. Billed as a "mystery," Forgotten Falls details family conflict and murder, but there's nothing particularly mysterious about it. From the beginning, the conflict is obvious, and there's never any question as to who is guilty of the crime. The only mysterious element is why the crime was committed, and that isn't all that mystifying, either.

Mr. Kaminski seems to have a talent for drama. But, if he wants to write mystery plays, he needs to learn how to create a puzzle, develop clues, and build towards an appropriately dramatic denouement. Needless to say, Agatha Christie's books and plays offer perfect examples. Mr. Kaminski is a young man. It's possible he doesn't know who Agatha Christie is. But, if he truly seeks a career in the theater, reading her work would be a good beginning.

THE PERFORMANCE

The acting was pedestrian, at best. Perhaps that had to do with the play's problems. I've seen several of the Black Orchid actors in other productions and they've done a fine job. This time, however, there didn't seem to be any focus. The dialogue was simply recited, with frequent fumbling for lines. The direction was acceptable, but the fight choreography was clumsy and badly done. The single set was serviceable, as were the costumes, but the lights were not properly focused. The floor in front of the stage was brighter than the stage itself.

CONCLUSION

I thought about this performance for several days before writing this. I don't like to be negative. But, this time, I had no choice. Mr. Kaminski shows promise, but he needs practice and concentrated study. He's young. He has time for that, and I wish him luck. On the other hand, the Black Orchid Theatre Group is quite capable of professional work. Why it was missing this time, I can't say. For whatever reason, this performance was not up to their previous standard. The best thing about this production was that it gave a novice playwright a chance to showcase his work. For that, I'm giving *Forgotten Falls* a **MIXED FACE MINUS**.

PERFORMANCE INFORMATION
- February 21st, 22nd & 23rd, 2020
- Church of the Resurrection
- 117 East 74th Stree t, NYC
- (212) 879-4320

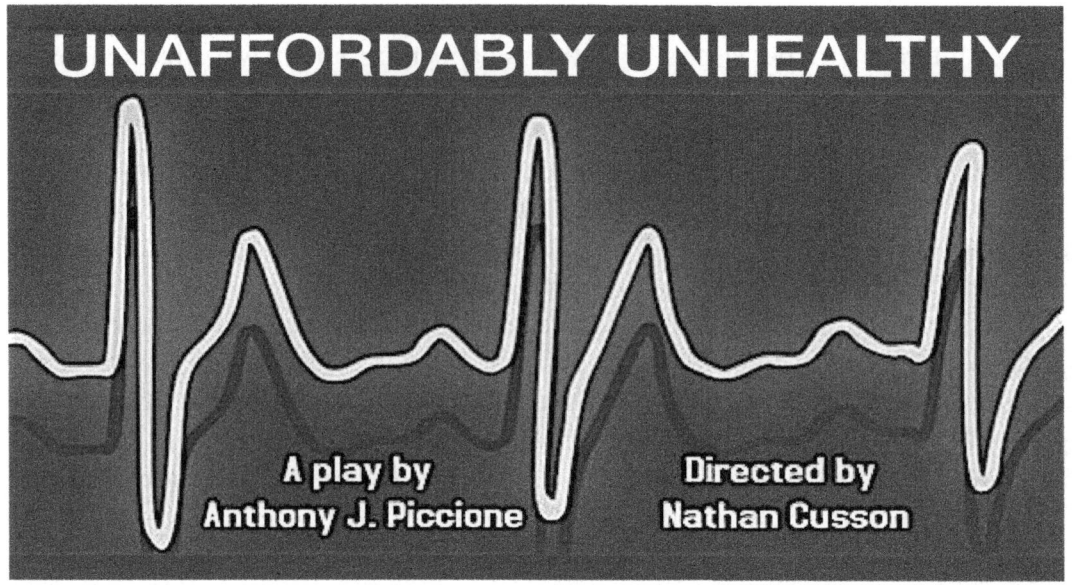

Unaffordably Unhealthy

- Presented by Anthony J. Piccione in association with **The Tank**
- Play by Anthony J. Piccione
- Director: Nathan Cusson
- Stage Manager: Cody Motivans
- Lighting Designer: Davida Tkach
- Press: Jay Michaels Arts & Entertainment

THE CAST

Ishani Basu, Emily Brady, Cathy Cavender, Chelsea Clark, Scotty Corn, Carson Frost, Sarah Elizabeth Haga, Louise Heller, Mason Mickley, Susan O'Doherty, Holly Painter & Jordan Schreiber

BACKGROUND

It's obvious to everyone these days that our health care system is in crisis, mainly because of the obscene amounts of money everything seems to cost. On the one hand, the almost miraculous advances in medical science we've seen since the computer revolution changed our lives, have made it possible to deal with conditions that, until recently, were inevitably fatal. Diabetes and AIDS immediately come to mind.

On the other hand, what difference does that make if the treatment is denied to the people who need it. The reasons for that are diverse and complex. As someone who has been observing the gradual but inexorable rise of the oligarchy for many years, I believe we lost control when our august business schools began insisting that lawyers and accountants were better at running businesses than the people who founded and loved them. Too many of our health providers are now run by business majors, not by charities or religious orders or even medical professionals; people who consider health care a vocation, not just an investment. I have no complaint about the need to make a profit. But, in some cases — when lives are at stake being one of them — that should not be the primary consideration.

THE PLAY

Anthony J. Piccione's *Unaffordably Unhealthy* takes a fascinating look at the harm unbridled capitalism has brought to our health care system. In a short, sixty minutes, we hear twelve heart-rending anecdotes detailing how our fellow citizens — from the upper middle-class down — have died, or been financially ruined, by insurance companies or hospitals that have either refused them treatment because of their inability to pay, or treated them and then demanded payments that have driven them into poverty and life-long debt.

THE PERFORMANCE

Why this has happened is beyond the scope of this review. *That* it has happened is what's relevant, and Mr. Piccione has done a splendid job combining these true stories into a riveting, dramatic narrative. The set is simple, the lighting as good as it can be in the space available, and Nathan Cusson's direction clean and focused. Everyone in the cast was sympathetic and engaging, intimately interacting with one another while drawing the audience into each story with skill and conviction.

I have one tiny caveat. Toward the end of the performance, the lights went out and the audience burst into applause. But, it wasn't the end of the play. The lights came back on for another three or four minutes before it actually ended. The first "ending" was so dramatically appropriate, however, that I would suggest the play be ended there. Nothing would be lost, and it happened at a dramatic high point that fully justified the early applause. Just a thought, and not a reason to withhold the **HAPPY FACE** the performance deserves.

PERFORMANCE INFORMATION

- February 25th, 26th, 29th, 2020
- March 3rd, 4th, 7th, 2020
- The Tank
- 312 West 36th Street, NYC
- Information: http://bit.ly/at-azER5
- Tickets: www.thetanknyc.org

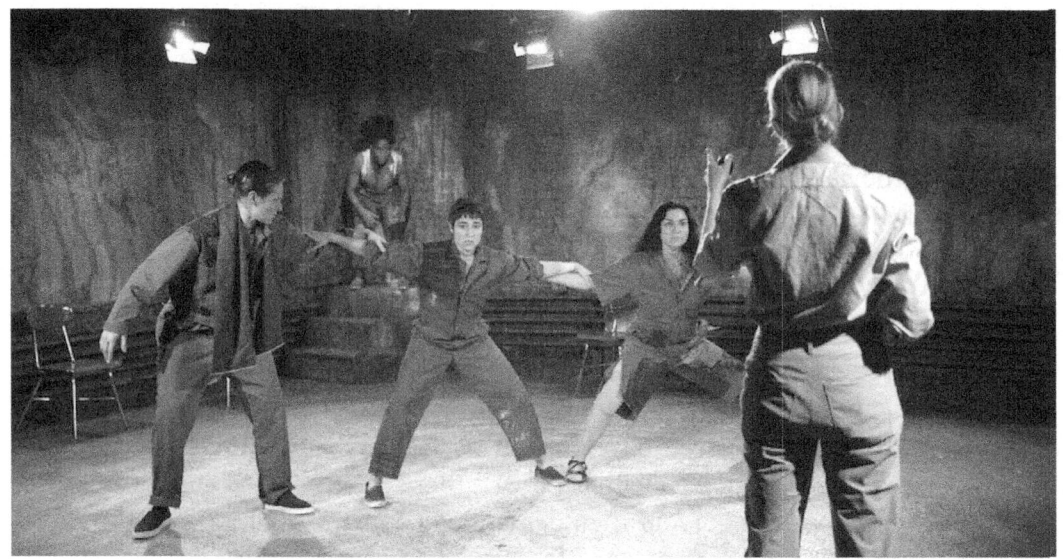

(L–R) Fleece, Hope Ward, Melissa Navia, Lucille Duncan & Laura Jordan

Bundle of Sticks
Reviewed for HI! DRAMA by William J. Cataldi

- Presented by **INTAR Theater** and **The Radio Drama Network**
- Playwright: J. Julian Christopher
- Director: Lou Mereno
- Production Design: Meghan E. Healey
- Lighting Design: Harbour Edney
- Sound Design: Jesse Mandapat
- Stage Manager: Fran Acuña-Almiron
- Assistant Production Manager: Alejandra Maldonado-Morales
- Production Assistant: Celina Revollar
- Intimacy Coach: Chelsea Pace
- Casting: Paul Davis, Caleeri Casting
- Press: David Gersten & Associates
- Photos: Carol Rosegg

THE CAST (Members of Actor's Equity Association)
- Francisco: Melissa Navia
- Abram: Fleece
- Gregos: Lucille Duncan
- Gemi: Zo Tipp
- Otto: Laura Jordan
- Tyree: Hope Ward

THE PLAY

J. Julian Christopher's *Bundle of Sticks* introduces us to five enrollees at the Global Conversion Therapy Center, appropriately underground in Coober Pedy, Australia. In between sessions with the sadistic instructor, Otto, the play explores some of the stories of this international assortment of gay men who are seeking to become straight. What brought them to conversion therapy? What internal resistance do they face in converting? Interwoven throughout the play is a mythology of a rainbow serpent, who consistently thwarts Otto's efforts. It should be noted that none of the six characters are played by men, and the play contains what I can only describe as much explicit sexuality. (If you are uncomfortable with verbal and graphic depictions of sex of any kind, this play will not be for you.)

The play's great strength is its fascinating handling of honesty versus dishonesty, with one's world or with oneself; and how persistent dishonesty can lead to perversion of the soul. Also, when moral confusion pervades the whole world, the world can seem upside-down like a madhouse. Mr. Christopher writes with humor, facility, intelligence and great clarity. This last is not always a given, but Mr. Christopher wants to be understood. His language is often poetic, but never jejeune.

The play's great drawback is its occasional trite forays into current LGBTQ propaganda. For example, homosexuality must not be a choice, because obviously no one in their right mind would ever choose something so awful. There are times when the play conflates sex and love, implying that sex outside of a monogamous, romantic relationship really would make homosexuality deserving of conversion therapy. Some of the story lines are cliché: for example the gay man married to a woman because of social duty, which damages both man and woman. However, to be fair, I am a 52 year old homosexual man, who has lived with both LGBTQ propaganda and cliché for my entire adult life. I also see a lot of LGBTQ theater and film. What is propaganda or cliché to me, may mean liberation or novelty to many other audience members. There is room in this world for all kinds of art.

Why were the six characters (who were all men) played by women or non-binary individuals? Currently, many theatrical productions at this level (off- and off-off-Broadway in New York) engage in gender swapping of this sort. Sometimes, the effort flops because the production team has no good reason for it, which leaves many audience members scratching their heads. In this case, the decision paid off. The non-male actors gave the play a whole other quality. It allowed for an exploration not just of homosexuality, but the lack of masculine gender specificity in many gay men. Gender fluidity is a major preoccupation of queer theory and therefore of New York theater of the moment. This has kicked masculine men off the top of the food pyramid, which aids in promoting diversity and inclusion, especially when it doesn't specifically threaten masculine spaces. Mr. Christopher doesn't suggest that masculinity itself is a problem that needs to be corrected. On the contrary, he's keenly aware of the intense attractiveness of masculine imagery, especially penises. By writing a play that requires women or non-binary actors, however, he offers the world alternatives to cisgender stereotypes, and allows his characters to struggle with gender alongside homosexuality. This approach enriches the play tremendously.

THE PERFORMANCE

The actors were uniformly outstanding. Otto, played by Laura Jordan, was the star of this production. She was thoroughly convincing as the patriarchal white man, hell-bent on making men out of the queers. She captured the nuances of Mr. Christopher's writing beautifully. Gemi, played by non-binary actor Zo Tipp, consistently resisted Otto. They were the child of billionaire Indonesian parents who sent them to Otto's boot-camp to make a man out of them. Their performance was charming and powerful. Francisco, played by Melissa Navia, vacillated between self-loathing brought on by his latin background, and a powerful, undeniable love of dick. Ms. Navia's transformation from Otto's lap dog to independence lit up the stage. Abram, played by Fleece, exuded humor as the slavic, butch, Balkan stereotype, who couldn't resist getting pounded by Gregos, played by Lucille Duncan, a masculine, Greek Top, with a penchant for drag. The pair gave rich performances full of heart. Finally, Tyree, played by Hope Ward, an American, black dude in love with Gemi, rounds out the six with her fine portrayal.

Lou Moreno directed *Bundle of Sticks* wonderfully with only a small, awkward space, and limited assets for set, lighting and sound. His attention focused on the actors, sharpening their performances into precise and powerful instruments. The props and costumes (the program lists Seamstress Aislinn Smith, but no costume designer) brilliantly exceeded what was required of them. You'll see what I mean when you go see this play. So, too, intimacy director Chelsea Pace did a miraculous job of making women look like actual gay men having sex. How she did that will remain a mystery to me forever. The sex scenes were undeniably arousing. Imagine my confused brain.

There was only one bad thing about this night, March 1st, 2020. The theater had no heat. We all shivered in the cold. I pray the staff can fix the problem by opening night, tomorrow, March 2nd. Just in case, bring a warm coat or at least a sweater. *Bundle of Sticks* was good enough, though, so that I didn't really notice the cold that much except at intermission. I definitely recommend a trip to **INTAR Theater** to see this excellent production. **HAPPY FACE MINUS**

PERFORMANCE INFORMATION

- February 22nd – March 22nd, 2020
- The INTAR Theatre
- 500 West 52nd Street, 4th floor, NYC
- (212) 695-6134
- https://www.intartheatre.org/home

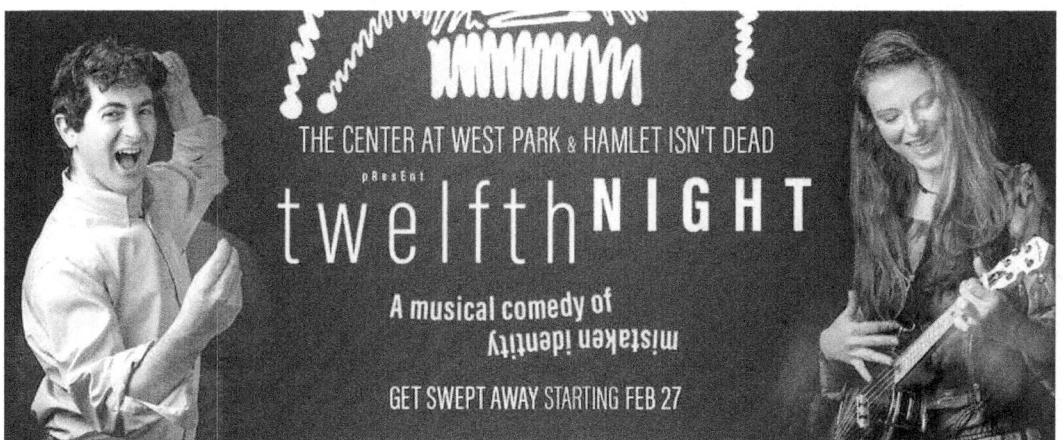

Michael Luca & Maureen Fenninger

Twelfth Night A Musical Comedy of Mistaken Identity

- Play by William Shakespeare
- Presented by **Hamlet Isn't Dead**
- Director: James Rightmyer, Jr
- Musical Director: James Powers°*
- Lighting Designer: Alan Waters
- Set Designer: Rachel Langley
- Costume Designer: Amelia Dudley
- Resident Stage Manager: Nicole Amaral
- Assistant Director/Fight Director: Michael Fleischer
- Composers: David Anthony Hentz° & James Powers°
- Technical Director: David Andrew Laws
- Assistant Stage Managers: Megan Necovski & Deanna Amaker
- House Manager: Elizabeth Ruelas*
- Marketing Coordinator: Gracie McBride
- Graphic Designer: Joshua Stauffer
- Production Photographer: Valerie Terranova*

THE CAST (°Hamlet Isn't Dead company member)

- Curio/Captain/Priest: Justin Bennett*
- Feste: Maureen Fenninger°*
- Viola: Taylor Harvey*
- Valentine : David Anthony Hentz°
- Malvolio: Travis Klemm°
- Sebastian: Michael Luca°
- Olivia: Stephanie LaVardera°*

- Sir Toby Belch: Mike Marcou°
- Duke Orsino: Joey Mulvey
- Drummer/Attendant: Duke Norsworthy
- Sir Andrew Aguecheek: Rahoul Roy
- Maria: Cameron Silliman
- Antonio: Jordon Waters

THE PRODUCTION

Where can you go and laugh yourself silly while reveling in some of the most ravishing dialogue ever written? At the moment, the answer is simple. **Hamlet Isn't Dead**'s hysterical production of William Shakespeare's brilliant comedy, *Twelfth Night,* now playing at **The Center at West Park Sanctuary Theater**, is the place to be.

When we think of Shakespeare, too many of us remember being forced to plod through pages of tiny print, confused by the vocabulary, lost in the cultural references, turned off by the listless rendering of the Bard's deathless prose or poetry by some bored teacher's assistant. This is truly a chance to remedy that misconception. With well chosen Rock 'n Roll, original music, and some of the most consistently well-spoken Elizabethan diction in New York City, this fine company has created an entertainment for the ages.

THE PLAY

Identical twins Viola and Sebastian are shipwrecked, then separated before being washed ashore in the Dukedom of Illyria. Believing Sebastian to be dead, Viola disguises herself as a boy and enters the service of Duke Orsino. Almost immediately, she falls in love with the Duke who is already in love with Countess Olivia. Believing Viola to be a boy, Orsino sends her to woo Olivia for him. But, Olivia falls in love with Viola, which leads to all sorts of confusion when Sebastian turns up and is mistaken for his sister. Whatever, all's well that ends well, and almost everyone gets what they want in the end. I say "almost" everyone. To find out who doesn't, see this play. It's romantic and funny from beginning to end, a perfect way to impress your date.

THE PERFORMANCE

The performance opens with a rousing round of Rock 'n Roll presented by Justin Bennett, David Anthony Hentz, Duke Norsworthy, and the remarkably versatile Maureen Fenninger. All are fine musicians, as we have come to expect here in New York City. But, they are also excellent actors, the three men stepping in and out of the action as needed. Ms. Fenninger as Feste, the play's "fool," was exceptionally funny, a joy to watch whenever she appeared. Her vocalization of *Mistress Mine,* a lovely musical setting of Shakespeare's lyrics by David Hentz and James Powers, was a stunner.

Taylor Harvey played Viola with dignity and reserve, bravely trying to make Duke Orsino's case with Olivia even after falling in love with him herself. As the

Duke, Joey Mulvey gave us something of a scatter-brain, overwhelmed by his passion for Olivia until common sense finally returns. As Olivia, Stephanie LaVardera was aloof and aristocratic. At least, she was that until she fell in love with Viola. After that, she was as silly as anyone in love seems to be. Michael Luca, as Sebastian, was an absolute stitch, a bad boy with a smile that lit up the stage. He didn't hesitate to take full advantage of Olivia's misconception when she mistook him for his identical sister.

As Malvolio, Olivia's infatuated manservant, Travis Klemm offered a superb picture of an idiot in love. Willing to demean himself in every possible way to impress his mistress, he was taken in and manipulated effortlessly by Sir Toby Belch and Sir Andrew Aguecheek, two of the funniest characters in theatrical literature. As Sir Toby, Mike Marcou played a classic enabler, wicked and more than willing to turn anyone into a fool for his own amusement. Rahoul Roy's Sir Andrew was simply delicious. He milked every line for its humor (something I've seen him do in other plays) and he did it with extraordinary skill. Cameron Silliman played Maria with great humor and she appeared to enjoy every moment. In concert with the other slapstick characters, Feste, Sir Toby, Sir Andrew, Sebastian, and the actor/musicians, she was remarkably engaging.

Leaving Jordon Waters as Antonio. Not to suggest that he was inadequate in any way; his Antonio was replete with understanding and gravitas. But, for whatever reason, the part of Antonio seemed almost superfluous, probably because the play was cut to some degree and part of his subplot removed. I can't be sure of that without comparing this version with the original script. Be that as it may, Mr. Waters did a fine job with what he was given to do.

CONCLUSION

Director James Rightmyer, Jr. and his company are simply remarkable. They sound as if they speak Elizabethan English every day, which I think they must do. Their dialogue is beautifully spoken, with joy and panache, every subtlety made perfectly clear. Nor, is it sullied or confused by attempts to sound like Lawrence Olivier. Just saying the lines as they normally speak and understanding what they're saying makes Shakespeare's immortal work real and accessible to everyone. Add to that their continuing effort to attract young audiences and Shakespearean "newbees" with clever new concepts and intelligent productions and it's clear why **Hamlet Isn't Dead** is one of my favorite companies. **HAPPY FACE PLUS**

PERFORMANCE INFORMATION

- February 27th – March 14th, 2020
- The Center at West Park (Sanctuary Theatre)
- 165 West 86th Street, NYC
- www.hamletisntdead.com/twelfthnight

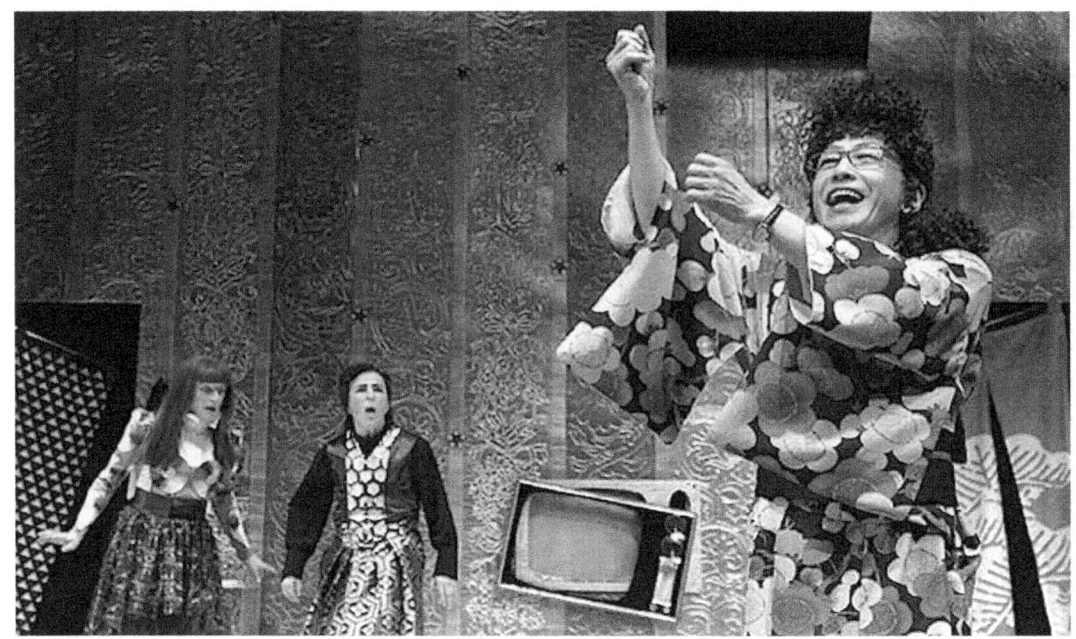

Glyn Pritchard, Lilo Baur & Hideki Noda

One Green Bottle

- Presented by **La MaMa** in association with **Tokyo Metropolitan Theatre** and **NODA-MAP**
- Written and Directed by Hideki Noda
- English translation by Will Sharpe
- Set Design: Yukio Horio
- Lighting Design: Christoph Wagner
- Costume Design: Kodue Hibino
- Composer: Denzaemon Tanaka XIII
- Sound Design: Marihiko Hara
- Sound: Junko Fujimoto
- Traditional Dance Advisor: Kikunojo Onoe
- Noh Movement Advisor: Reijiro Tsumura
- Video: Shutaro Oku
- Hair & Makeup: Eri Akamatsu
- Back translation: Keiko Tsuneda & Peter Marsh
- Assistant Director: Ragga Dahl Johansen
- Production Manager: Ayumu Poe Saegusa
- Stage Manager: Toshiko Takihara
- Press: Michelle Tabnick PR
- Photos: Helen Maybanks

THE CAST

- Boo (Mother): Hideki Noda
- Bo (Father): Lilo Baur
- Pickle (Daughter): Glyn Pritchard
- Musician: Genichiro Tanaka

BACKGROUND

Hideki Noda's *One Green Bottle* is an hysterically funny tragedy, a Japanese import detailing one night in the life of a family that's destroying itself. Bo, Boo and Pickle all have plans for the evening, but one of them must stay home to care for Princess, their pregnant dog. As they argue over who's going to do that, trivial arguments awake long-standing resentments, painting a remarkably apt picture of the sort of short-sighted stupidity that's presently destroying our world.

THE PLAY

Recently, I've had the great pleasure of experiencing some remarkably witty Japanese theater. Last December it was an hilarious evening of Rakugo, a 400 year-old Japanese storytelling tradition presented at New World Stages by well known Canadian expatriate Katsura Sunshine (a naturalized Japanese citizen). Now, at the storied **La MaMa Experimental Theatre Club**, direct from the **Tokyo Metropolitan Theatre**, we have a gender-bending farce, skillfully translated into English by Will Sharpe, that reminds us not only how much we have in common, but also what we are all facing if we keep on going as we are.

THE PERFORMANCE

Boo, Bo and Pickle haven't actually communicated for years. Boo just wants to get out of the house. Her husband, Bo, a Kabuki Theater star, is impressed by his own fame, assuming that it gives him the right to prevail in every argument. Pickle, their daughter, lives in another world entirely, obsessed with selfies, memes, texts, and tweets, she is unable to communicate without the help of a technological device.

As Boo, author Hideki Noda is the very picture of a scatter-brained wife. Extraordinarily funny, she manipulates Bo at every turn. She's determined to go to a Noisy Boys concert, something Bo does not understand. Bo, played by Lilo Baur as a self-centered celebrity, insists that Boo should just give in. He refuses to understand why she won't. Nor, does he have any understanding of modern technology, as becomes clear when he demands that Pickle send emails to various inanimate objects later in the play. Pickle, deliciously played by Glyn Pritchard, is droll and remote. She considers her parents to be non-woke idiots, utterly incapable of understanding anything. As the evening progresses, these characteristics become more and more pronounced. No one will give an inch, resulting in a cataclysmic stand-off that one must see to appreciate.

CONCLUSION

Yukio Horio's set is open and colorful, with clever projections and well designed sound effects and lighting throughout. The music, composed by Denzaemon Tanaka XIII and performed by Genichiro Tanaka, is based on Japanese Noh and Kabuki traditions. Subtle and frequently powerful, it serves as an appropriate backdrop for this highly entertaining portrayal of societal alienation. **HAPPY FACE**

PERFORMANCE INFORMATION

- February 29 – March 8, 2020
- The Ellen Stewart Theatre
- La MaMa Experimental Theatre Club
- 66 East 4th Street, NYC
- www.lamama.org

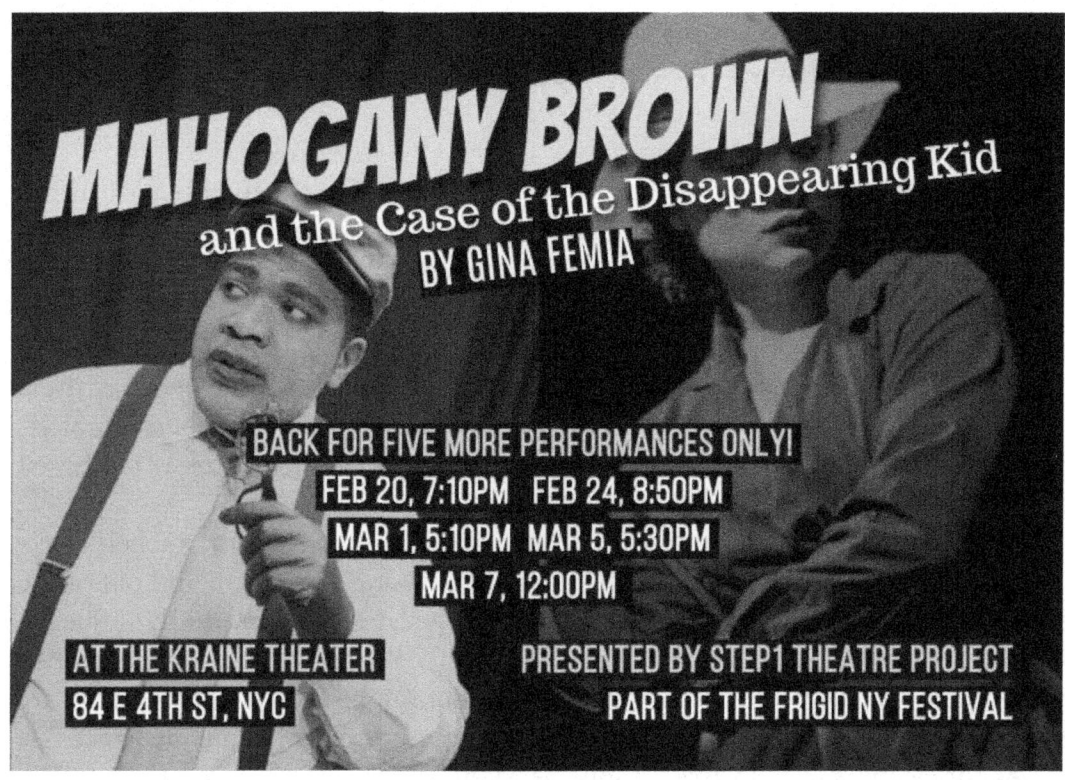

Mahogany Brown

Reviewed for HI! DRAMA by Jan Ewing & Eva Heinemann

- Presented as part of the **Frigid Festival** in association with the **Step 1 Theatre Project**
- Written by Gina Femia
- Directed by Janelle Zapata Castellano
- Set & Light Design: Jak Prince
- Original Sound and Music: Jacob Subotnick
- Movement: Rachel Weekley
- Make Up: Charisse Simone
- Production Manager: Kate Lagana
- Stage Manager: Cordelia Senie
- Press: Jay Michaels Arts & Entertainment
- Photos: Step 1 Theatre Project

THE CAST

- Mahogany Brown: Charisse Simone
- Jimmy Jones: Xavier Rodney

- Sunshine: Lara Fox
- The Nameless: Rachel Weekley, Alexis Plaza, Ashley Rodgers

JAN EWING

Gina Femia's *Mahogany Brown,* currently running at **The Kraine** as part of the Frigid Festival, is the story of a kidnapping, a father's attempts to find his missing son, and the intercession of a mysterious private eye named Mahogany Brown (Charisse Simone). Conceived in the film noir style, it begins with a great deal of style and cinematic flare. As the action proceeds, however, it loses focus and slowly turns into a melodramatic soap opera. I'm not sure why this happens, as there doesn't seem to be any justification for it other than the somewhat supernatural aspects of the production. Which brings up an important question. Are we supposed to believe there are paranormal forces at work?

There are three, very effective white-face "Nameless" characters (Rachel Weekley, Alexis Plaza, Ashley Rodgers) changing the sets and moving in and out of the action. They are quite ghost like, which does suggest an other-worldly influence might be at play. Those, combined with the noir-like narrative from Xavier Rodney as Jimmy Jones, the bereaved father, suggests that might be the case, but they are not developed beyond just being there, so that assumption might be incorrect.

At the beginning, Charisse Simone as Mahogany Brown is remarkably sultry and intriguing, a fascinating 1940s femme fatale. As the narrative moves forward, however, her projection of that quality becomes inconsistent, moving from erotic to strident.

Basically, the end of the play seems to have little to do with the beginning. That, and the inadequate lighting at The Kraine (most peculiar because they do have adequate spotlighting which was not used at all), is why I have to give this play a **MIXED FACE PLUS.**

EVA HEINEMANN

I have to disagree with Jan Ewing on this one. There are very subtle clues given throughout this short 50 minute play that reveals where it may be headed. But that made the mystery even more mysterious.

Sunshine (Lara Fox) was a rather confusing character until the mystery was revealed but I enjoyed her cartoony interruptions to the plot.

I liked the white face with black clothes and white gloves which gave it a ghostly quality and I picked up on all the dead puns so I knew something wasn't quite on the up and up as it took a downward spiral into the truth of what was going on.

I was incredibly moved by this haunting story of love and loss and how to cope with tragedy.

I found the props and cut out puppet quite effective.

Janelle Zapata Castellano's direction had to maneuver a fine line between the surreal and the reality of the situation.

I thought the cast did a remarkable job of maintaining the heightened beginning with the Surprising ending which left me going from appreciative laughter to uncontrollable weeping.

Anyone who has ever lost a child even temporarily like I did at a Daffy's and subway will connect to the raw emotions in this. **HAPPY FACE**

PERFORMANCE INFORMATION

- February 20th – March 7th, 2020 (click below for dates & times)
- The Kraine Theater
- 85 East 4th Street, NYC
- https://www.frigid.nyc/events/mahoganybrown

Rules of Desire

- Produced by Eric Krebs
- Play by William Mastrosimone
- Directed by William Roudebush
- Production Stage
  Manager: Michael J. Tosto
- Sub Stage Manager: Esti Bernstein
- Set: Robert F. Wolin
- Lighting: Joan Racho-Jansen
- Costumes: Joseph Shrope
- Sound: Andy Evan Cohen
- Props & Special Effects: Cosimo Mariano
- Casting: Stephanie Klapper
- House Manager: Vironika Puricelli
- Press: Richard Hillman, PR
- General Manager: Prayatmi Shakya

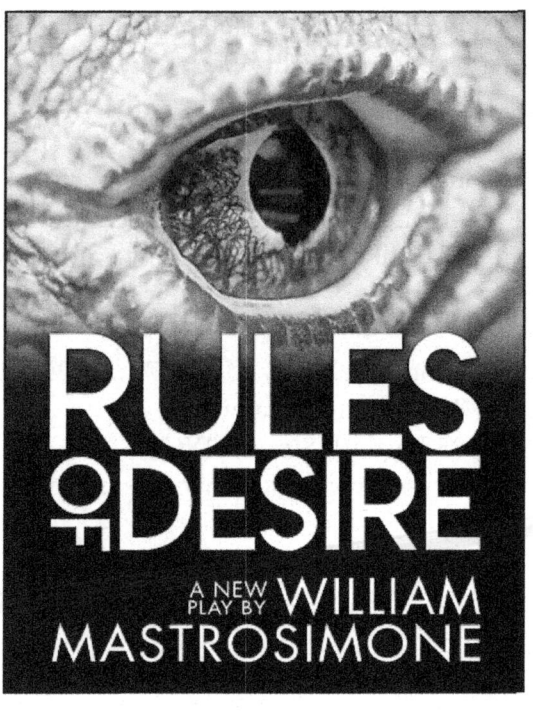

THE CAST

- Matt: Tristan Biber
- Felicia: Mckenna Harrington
- Alex: Christopher Sutton

THE PLAY

William Mastrosimone's gripping *Rules of Desire* is a tale of toxic masculinity, this time told from a man's point of view. Matt, a 20-something sailor, falls in love with Felicia, a young woman with an uncertain past. When his aircraft carrier is ordered back to sea, the two of them cook up an improbable, but not impossible scheme. Matt smuggles Felicia aboard and stows her away in a tiny space below decks. An aircraft carrier is basically a floating city, as long as three football fields with over 5,000 inhabitants. The chances of being caught are slim, and, of course, it's done in the name of love. But, like so many bad decisions made in moments of unreasonable passion, it's totally illegal — a court marshall offense — and neither Matt nor Felicia have given any thought to the possible consequences.

Enter Chief Alex, an uptight petty officer, widely disliked by his subordinates because of his unbending disciplinary demands. He catches them in the act and threatens exposure unless Matt shares Felicia with him whenever he's on duty. Reluctantly, since they have no choice, they agree. Thus, for twelve hours every day, Alex is "free" to do whatever he wishes to Felicia. It's sexual slavery, pure and simple.

THE PERFORMANCE

As a former Navy officer, I was extremely impressed by Mr. Mastrosimone's command of the military vernacular. It was remarkably similar to the language one hears every hour of every day on a ship, not to mention that the level of anger expressed by Chief Alex, powerfully played by Christopher Sutton, is more common than it should be. Mr. Sutton is an intense actor, to say the least. His portrayal was right-on in so many aspects — up to and including the emotional suppression needed to support Alex's facade, blocking the extravagant humanity trying to break through — that I was extremely moved. It's not easy being a man in 2020. Mr. Sutton's vivid performance does a fine job suggesting why.

McKenna Harrington gives us a Felicia seemingly oblivious to whatever Alex is trying to achieve. She is so tightly locked into herself that she can't appreciate what he's talking about, which saves her in the end. Matt, sympathetically played by Tristan Biber, is appropriately helpless. He's an ordinary seaman, after all. He belongs to the Chief. In a very subtle way, he is also a slave.

CONCLUSION

This was an entirely engrossing performance of a viewpoint we don't see often in this day of #MeToo. It was refreshing to see an honest picture of the things contributing to "toxic" masculinity. There are multiple sides to every story. We need to understand the other guy's viewpoint or risk becoming what we accuse him of being.

I want to apologize for not getting this review up before the play closed on March 7th. I saw it late, and several performances were cancelled. It should not have closed early. It was too good for that. Christopher Sutton fell apart with heart-rending skill. For that, and all those appropriately dirty words, *Rules of Desire* gets a real **HAPPY FACE**.

PERFORMANCE INFORMATION

- February 11th – March 7th, 2020
- The Playroom Theater
- 151 West 46th Street, 8th Floor, NYC
- (212) 967-8278
- info@rulesofdesiretheplay.com

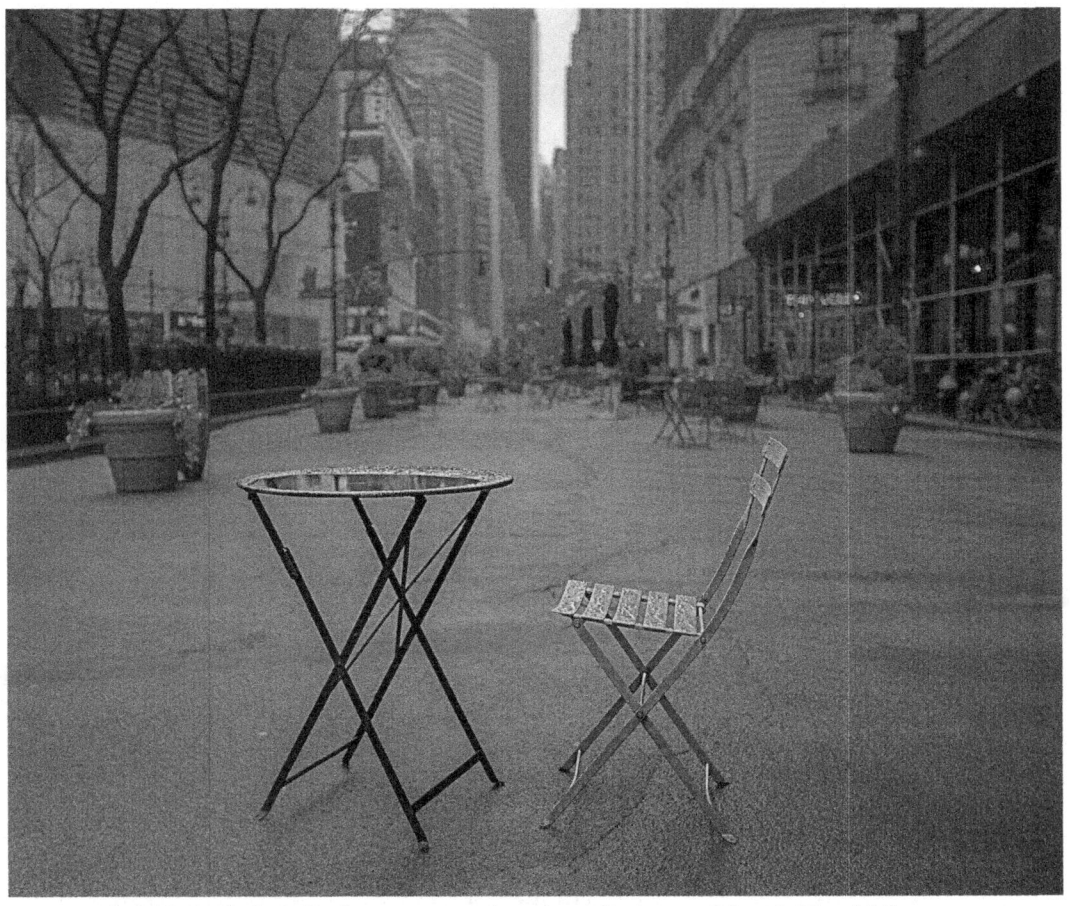

A table and chair in the empty pedestrian plaza near Macy's Herald Square

Bright Lights, Covid City Broadway in the Dark
A photo essay by Dan Lane Williams with Kristen Noel

Broadway in the Dark is an ode to the artists, theatres, industry and the city I call home — the one that has been put on hold during these unprecedented dark days. And, this feels personal because I am an actor, a photographer, a New Yorker. This place houses my heart and my hopes. It sits dark, quiet and uncertain. Yet, it still remains stoic and majestic — and that is what I choose to hold onto and see.

Just as this city never sleeps, this isn't about the demise of a craft. It is a peek towards the future, fueled by the belief that we will be able to go back to entertaining, and attending, and creating and communing. The lights and the curtains will go back up. But for now, I celebrate my city differently, in her solitude.

The idea for this collection came about while taking a long afternoon walk up Broadway in the rain in late April. Early spring always feels like a time of transition, caught within limbo of seasons. And this April it had already been dictated that we operate in as much isolation as possible — a city surrounded by people, yet isolated by "social distance."

That particular day I walked all the way from Union Square to 50th and Broadway — just me, my camera and my city — and the first image of this body of work was born with the table and chair in the photograph at the head of this essay; Macy's Herald Square, devoid of humanity, energy, traffic, sounds, vibrancy — all seemingly muffled. These first image was the seed from which this collection blossomed.

After arriving home, the reality of what was transpiring hit me harder and the inspiration for this work evolved even further. It first started with the streets upon which the theatres lived. The quiet desolation at curtain time with few, if any people or cars was eerie and jarring. What had always notoriously been one of the busiest times in the theatre district — packed with enthusiastic theatre-goers bustling about in and out of pre-show dinners, meeting up with friends, was now still. Not even a whisper of its normal self. Though still, there was also a notable sense of hope.

I exhaled when I saw that the theatre lights were still aglow, both inside and out, as if to say … *We will be back as soon as we can* … as if that solitary light in the middle of the stage was proudly standing there, eagerly yet patiently waiting for the next show to raise its curtain. Yes, we will be back.

During the first session, I was drawn to the famous Barrymore Theatre. After I shared the initial images I captured with a good friend and fellow photographer, he suggested that I continue to explore this and document more of the dormant theatres in the district — to tell their collective story. The project extended from there to multiple excursions into the area to create the rest of the images that became a part of this collection. Broadway and Times Square demonstrate the effect of these times, this collective timeout, probably more than any other.

The nature of Broadway and of New York City is rooted in resilience — and it is poised to rebound, to rise and to reemerge out of our quarantine. Capturing this moment in time feels important, almost sacred. I believe we will resume our passions as artists, creators and lovers of the arts. We will sing and perform. We will play beautiful music and we will dance in the streets. We will attend productions and meet up with friends. The lights will go back up on Broadway — and I will sit with a *Playbill* in hand. Until we meet again… my dear theatre.

ADDITIONAL INFORMATION

- Dan Lane Williams: dlwphotography.com
- Kristen Noel: www.bestselfmedia.com
- To purchase prints: http://bit.ly/DLWBroadwayPrints

PLATE 1: 42nd Street looking east & west

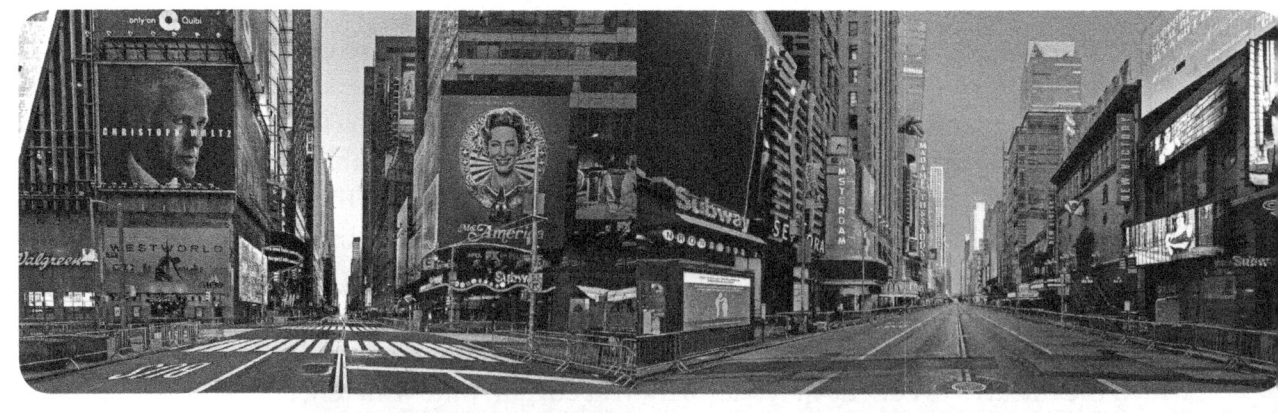

PLATE 2: 42nd Street looking west

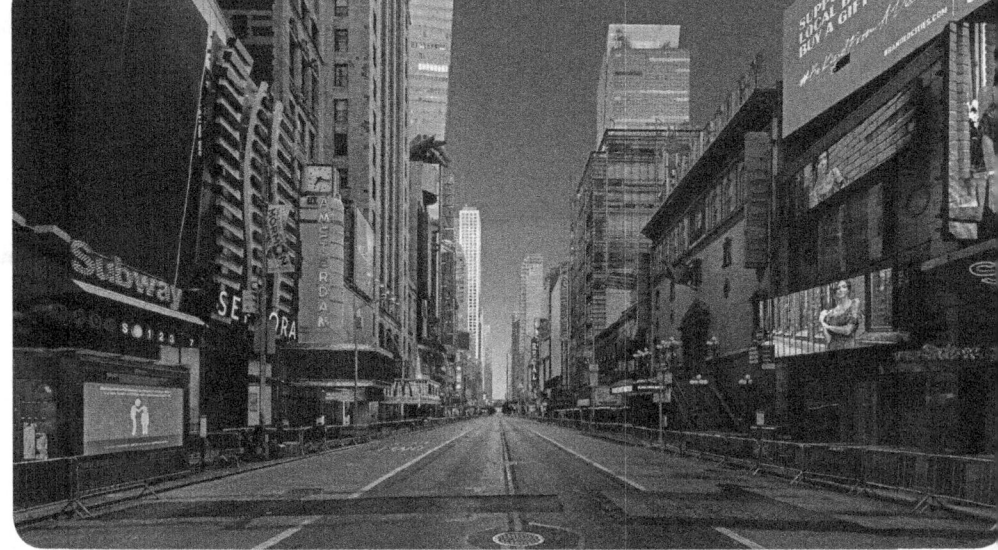

PLATE 3: 42nd Street looking east

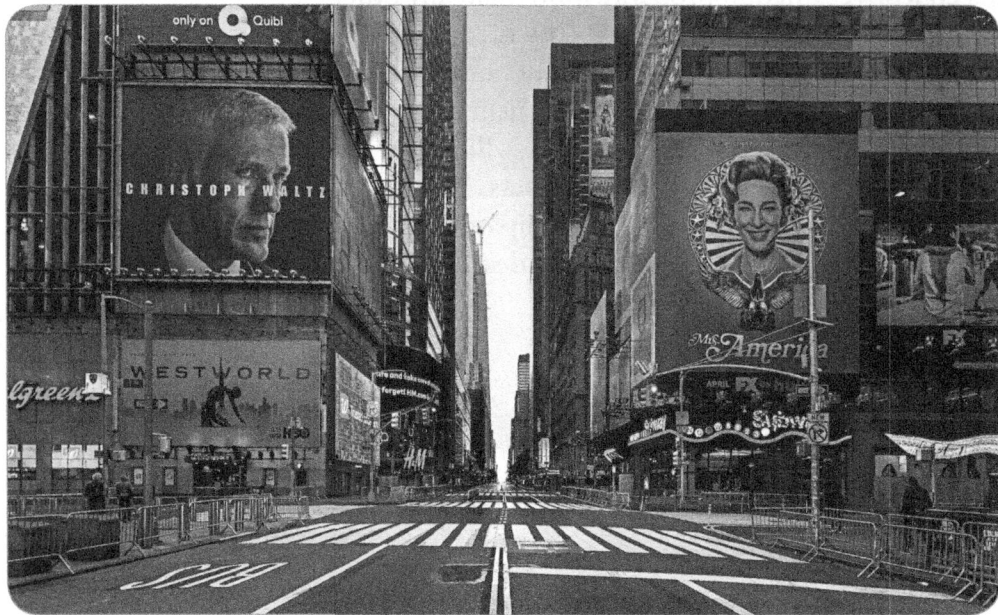

Plates 1–3

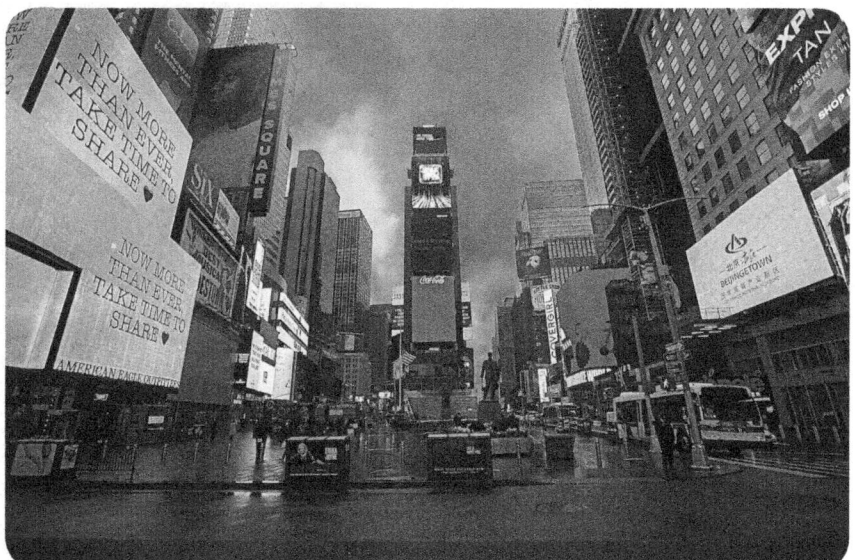

PLATE 4: Times Square looking north

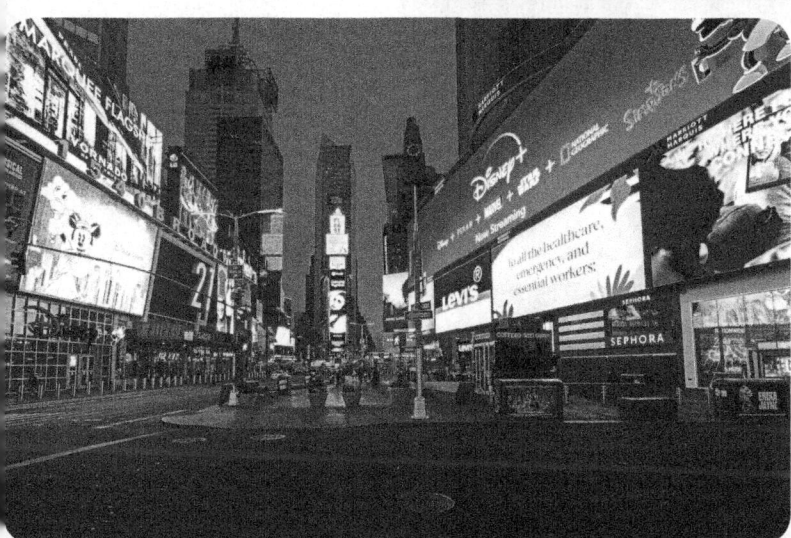

PLATE 5: Times Square looking south

PLATE 6: Duffy Square

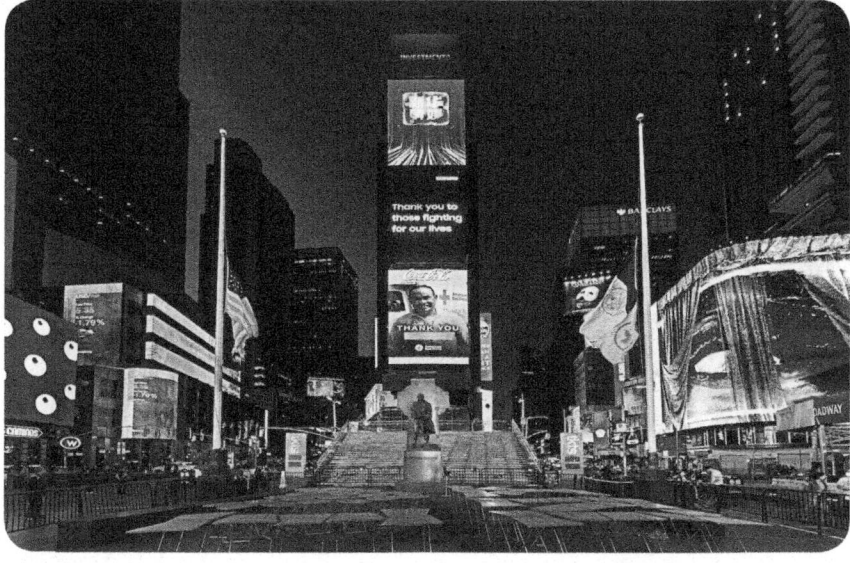

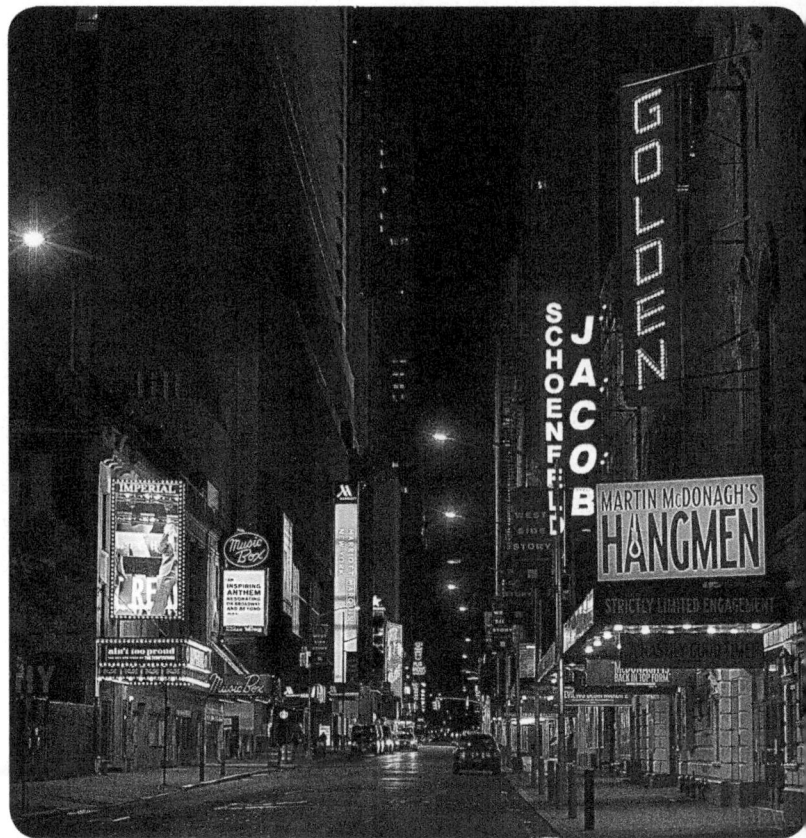

PLATE 7: 45th Street looking east

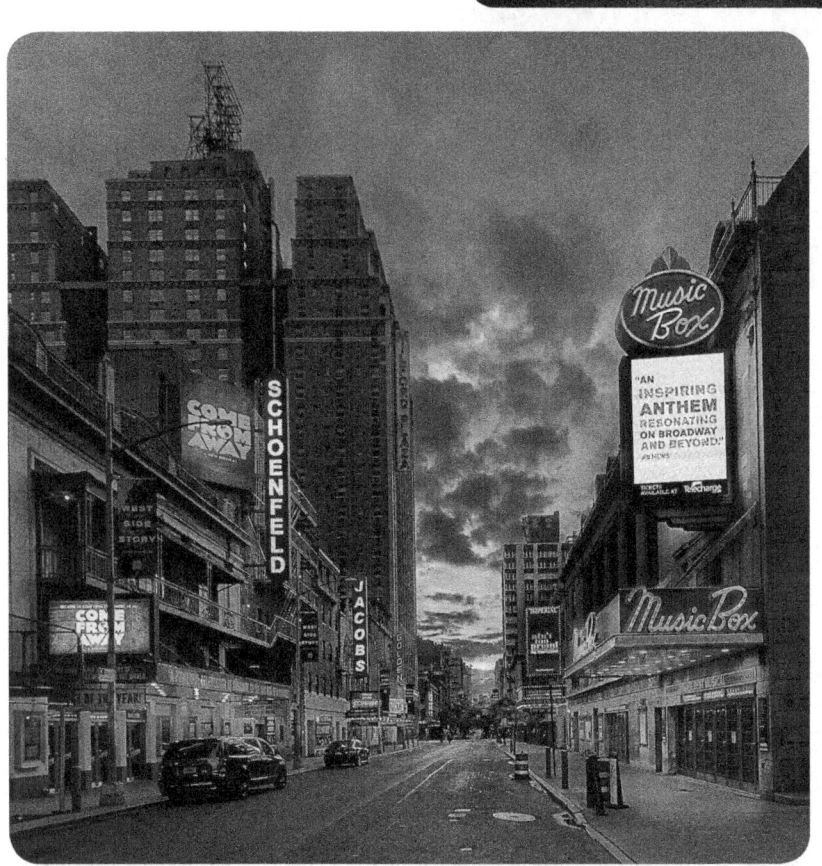

PLATE 8: 45th Street looking west

Plates 7–8

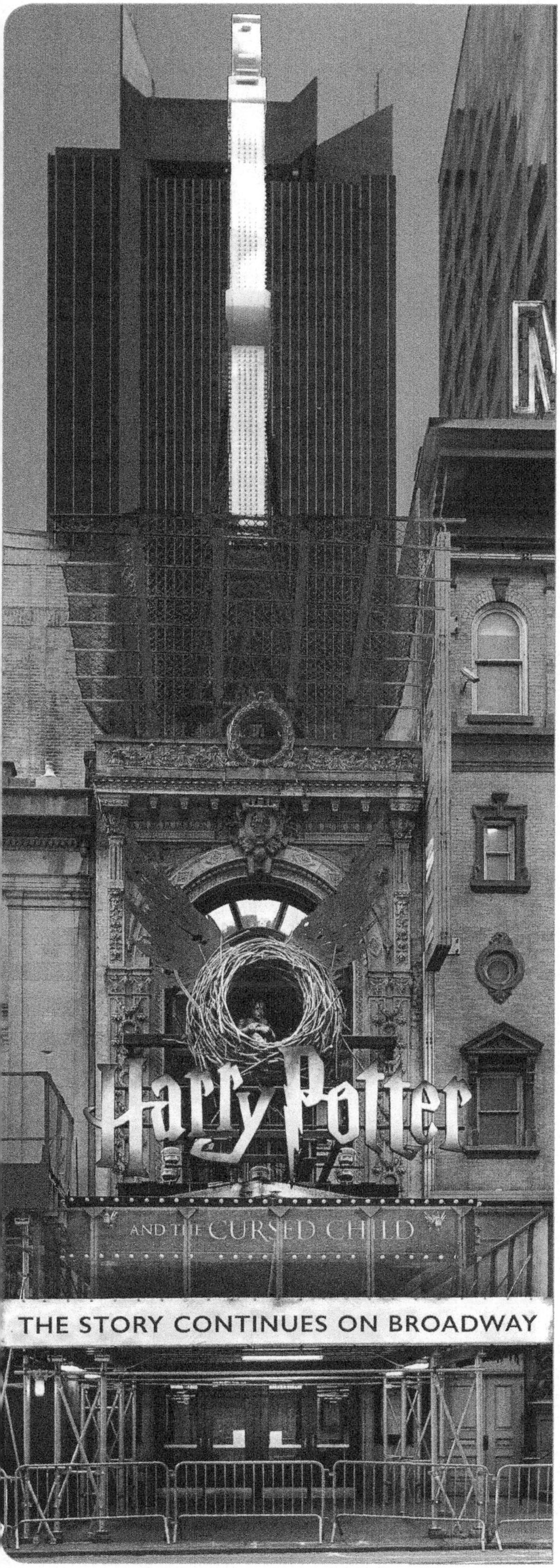

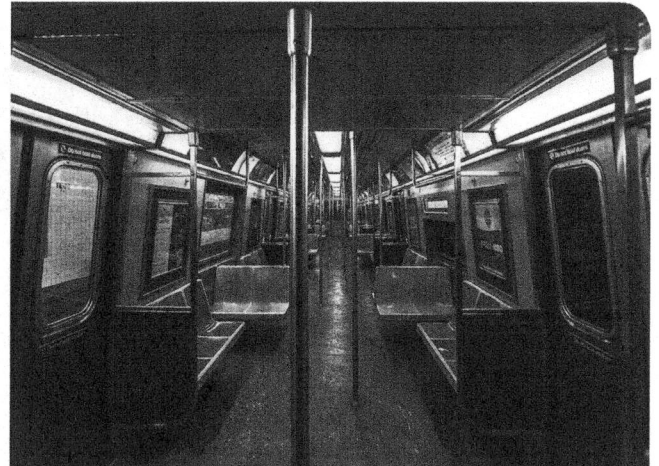

PLATE 9: Pandemic subway

PLATE 10: The Lyric 42nd Street

PLATE 11: 50th Street at rush hour

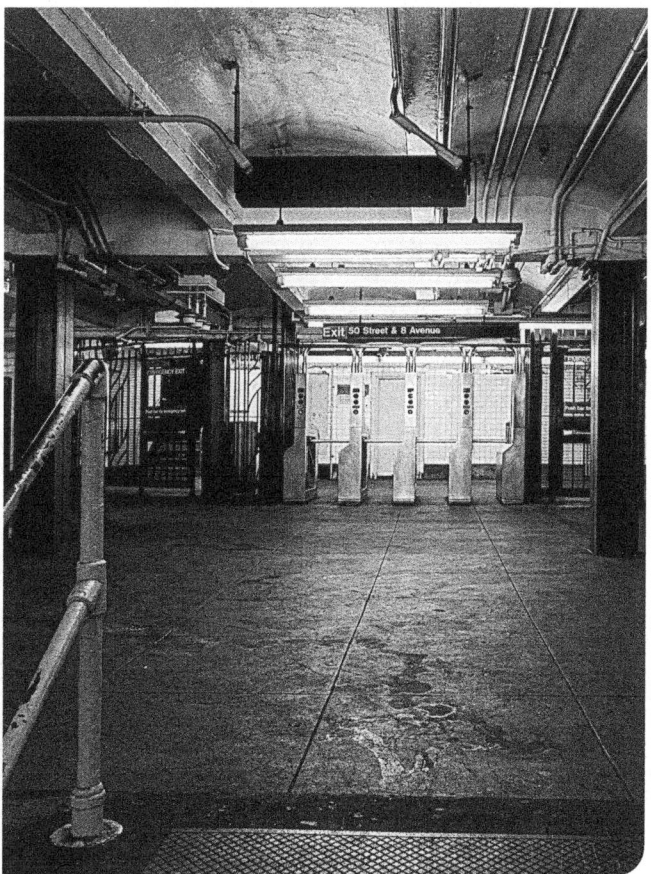

PLATE 12: Harry Potter at the Lyric on 43rd Street

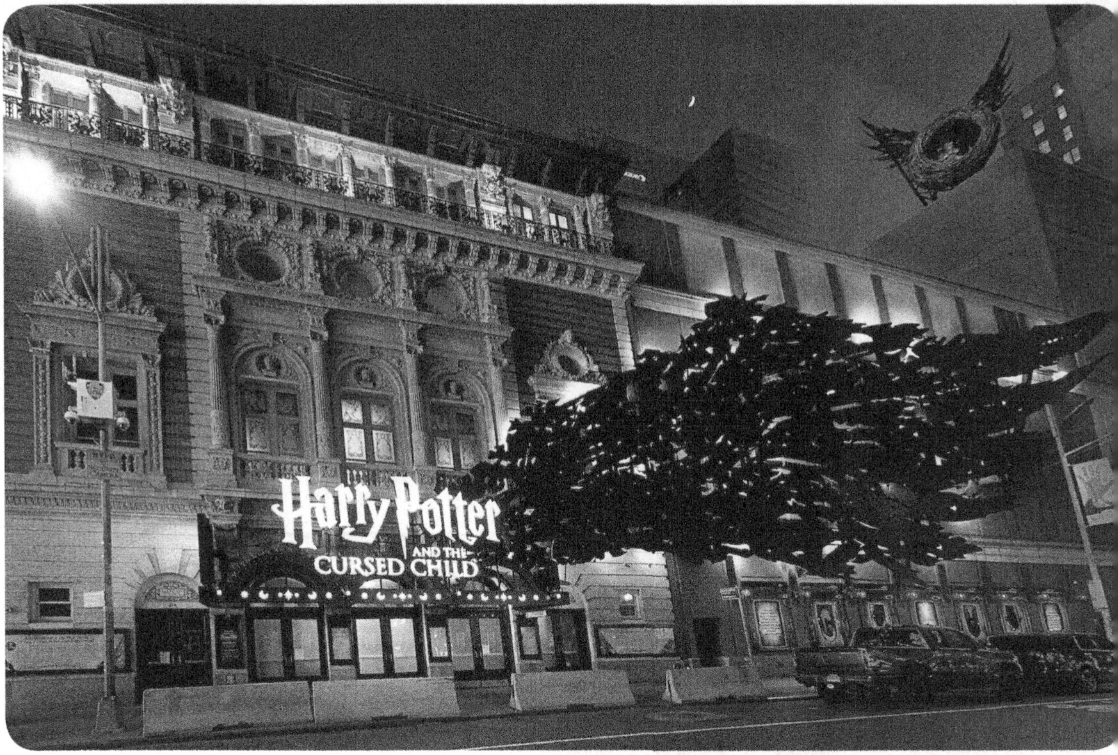

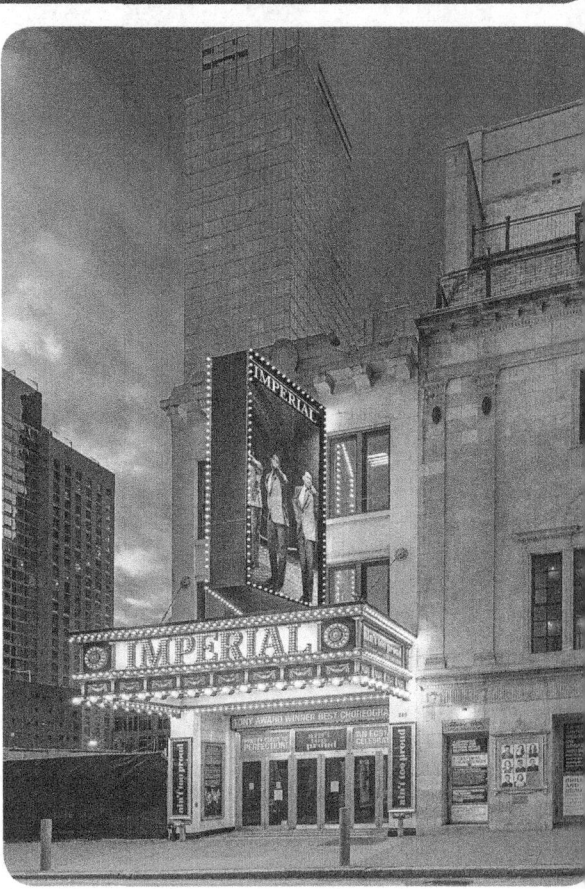

PLATE 13: The Imperial Theater

PLATE 14: The Booth Theater

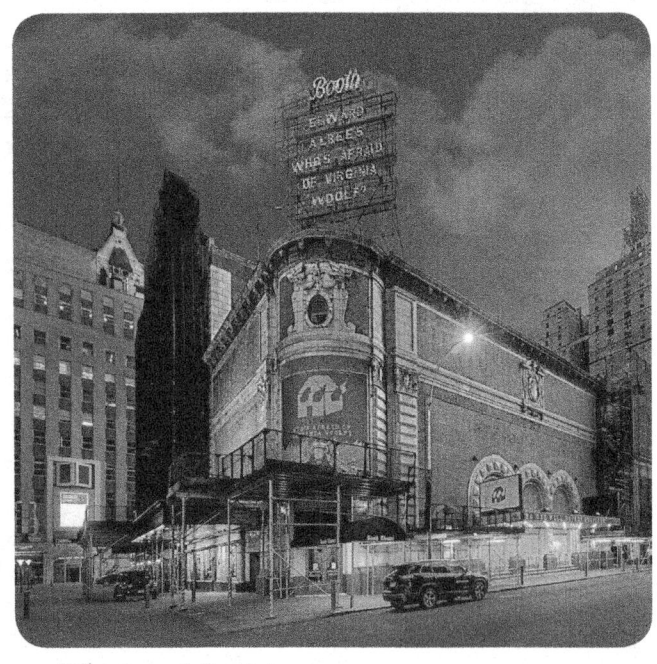

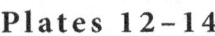

Plates 12–14

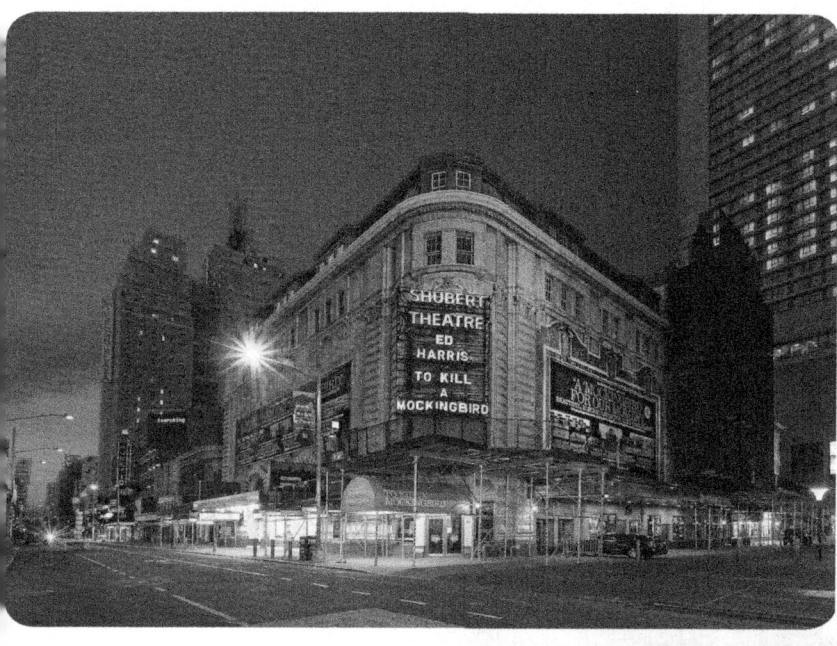

PLATE 15: The Shubert Theatre

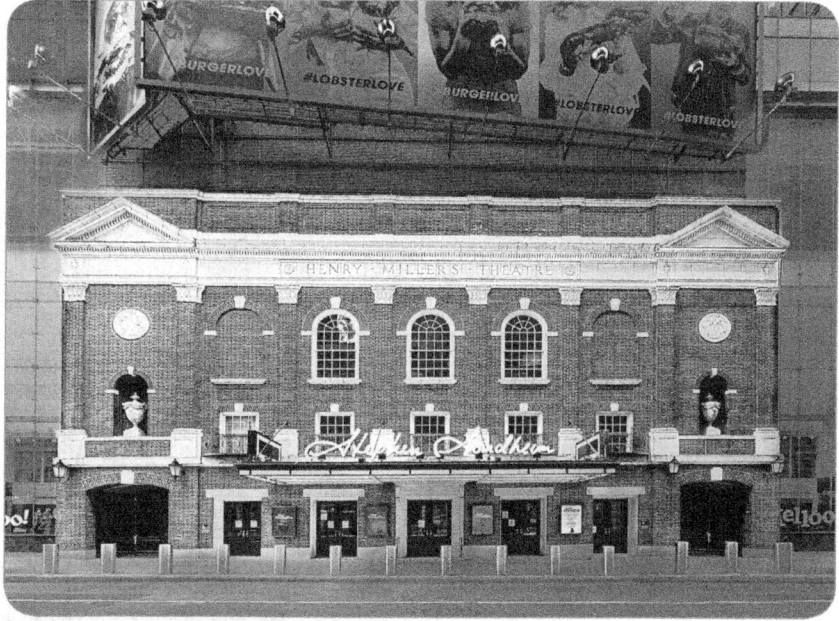

PLATE 16: The Stephen Sondheim

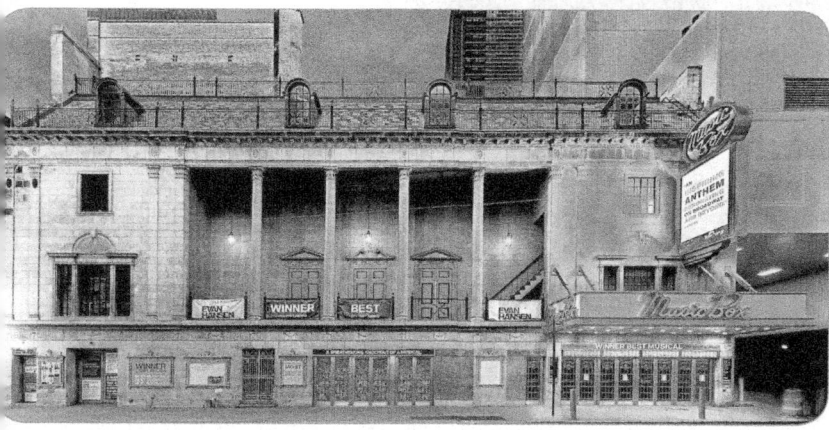

PLATE 17: The Music Box Theater

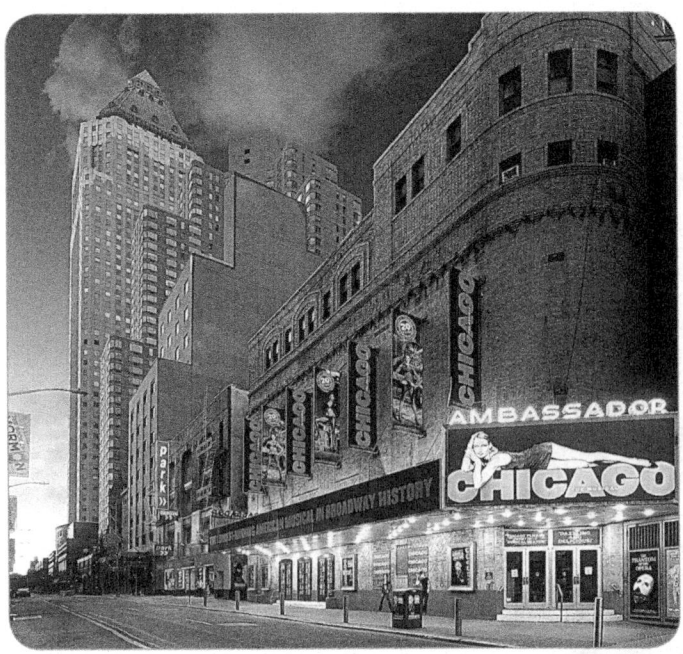

PLATE 18: The Ambassador Theatre at 49th Street

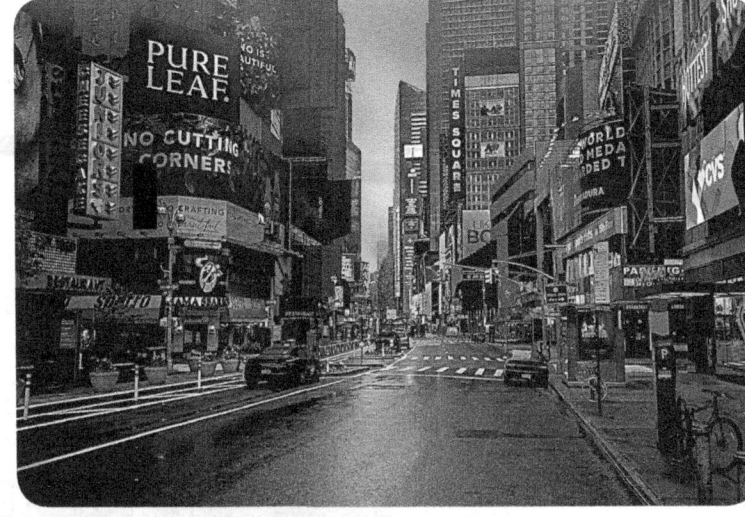

PLATE 19: Broadway looking south from 50th Street

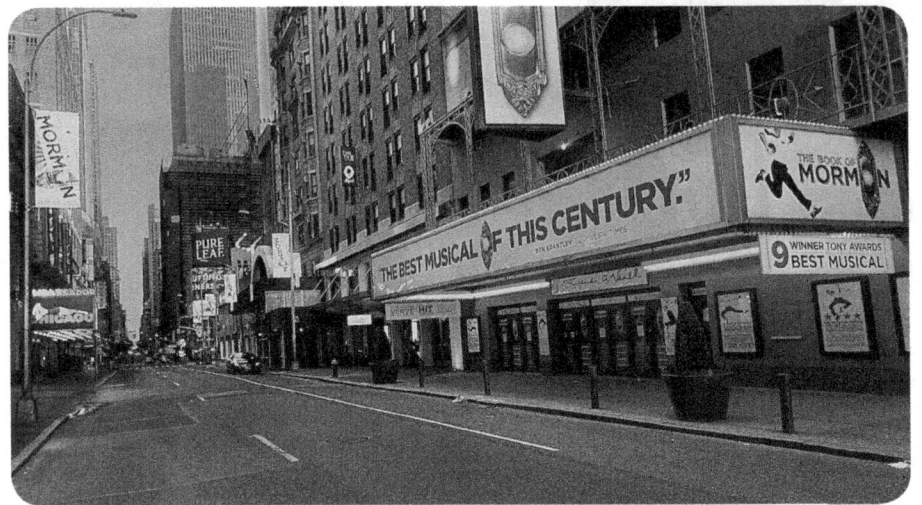

PLATE 20: The Eugene O'Neill at 49th Street

Plates 18–20

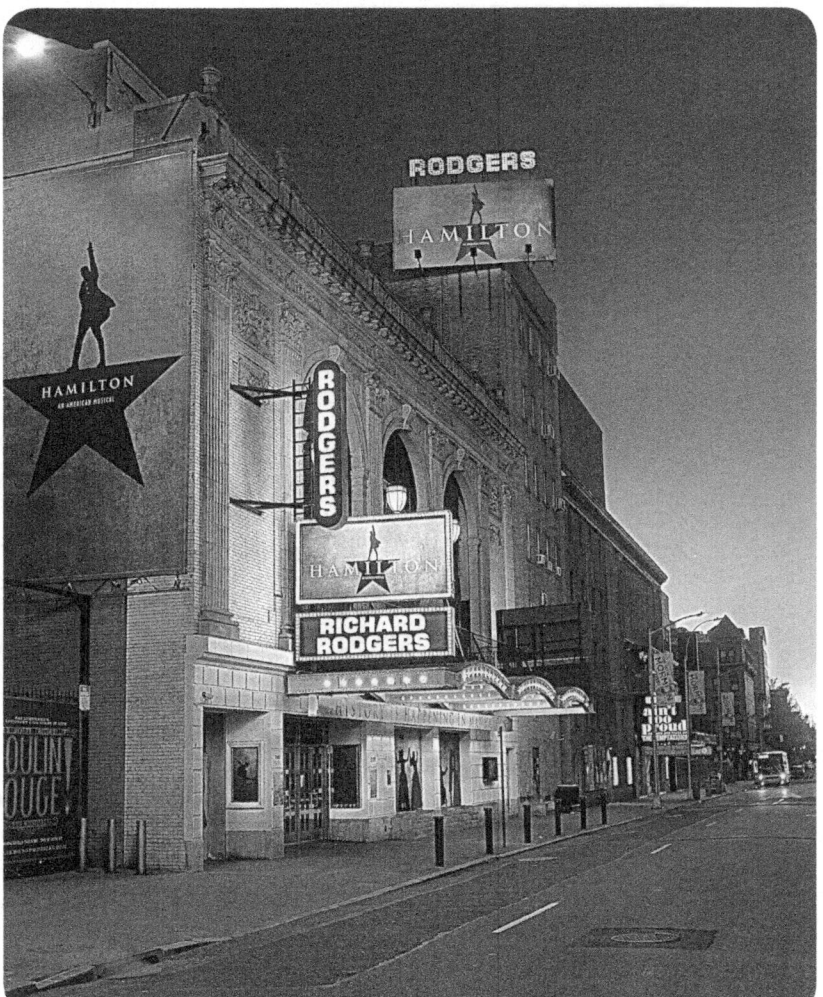

PLATE 21: The Richard Rogers Theater at 46th Street

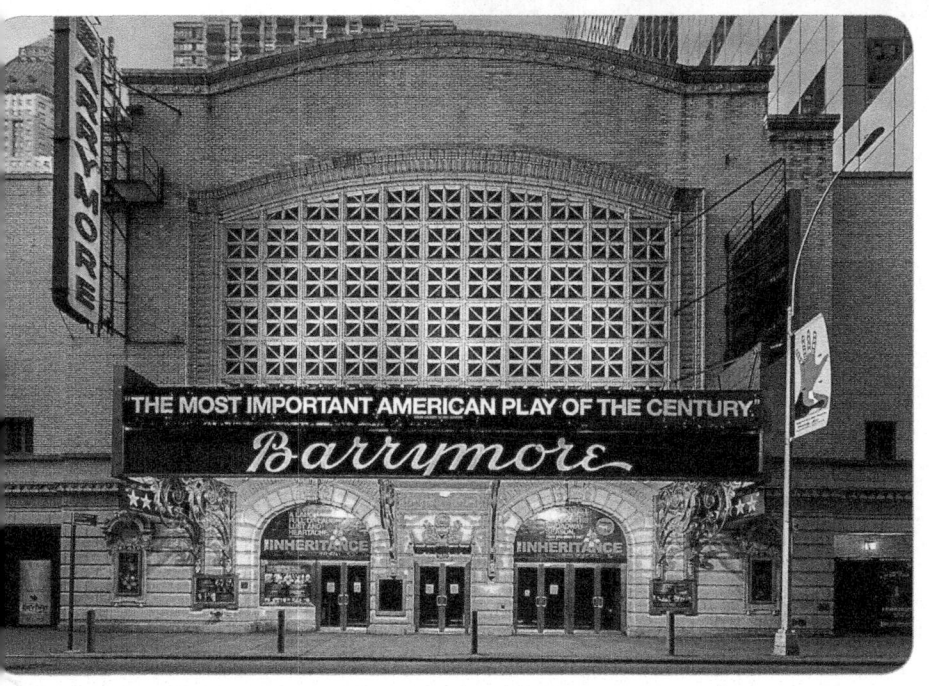

PLATE 22: The Barrymore Theater

PLATE 23: The
Gershwin at 51st Street

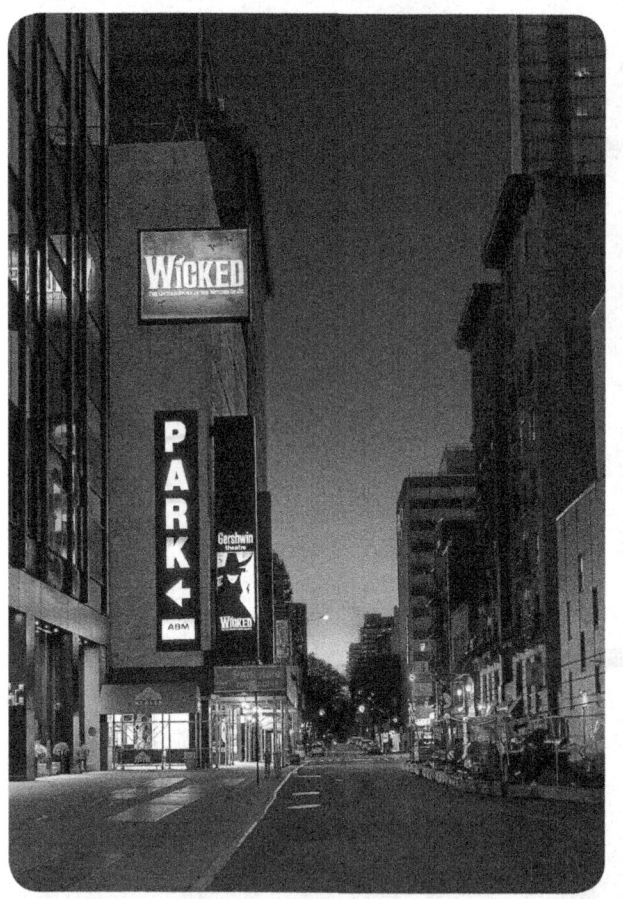

PLATE 23: The
Gershwin at 51st Street

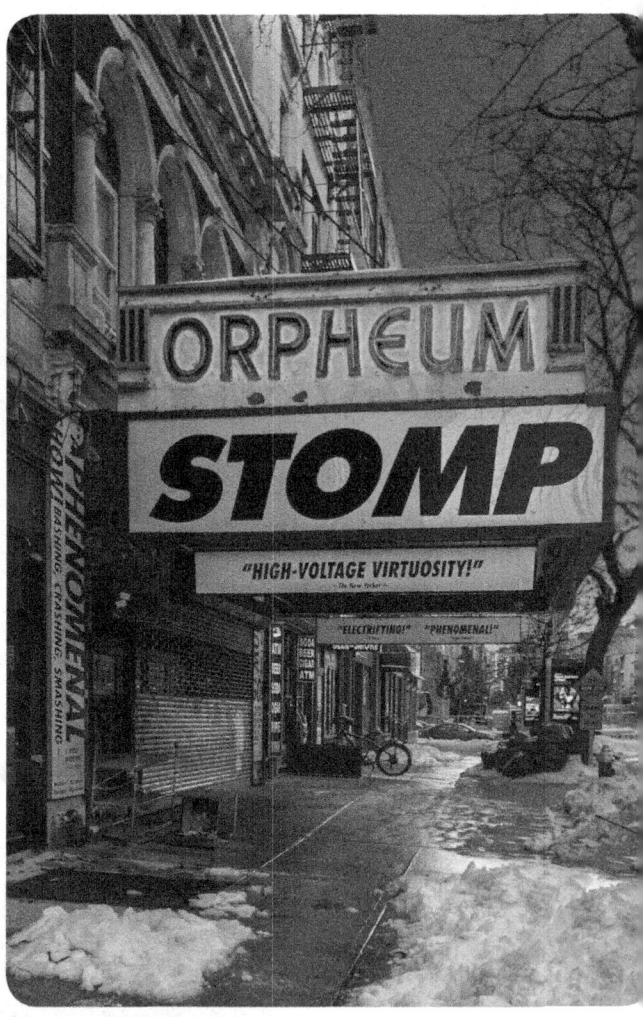

PLATE 24: The
Orpheum (Off-Off
Broadway)

PLATE 25: The
Walter Kerr Theater

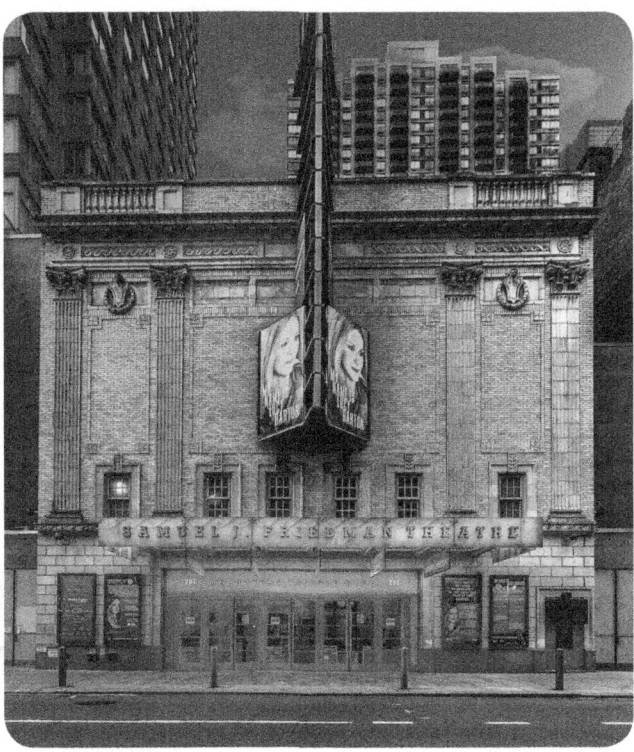

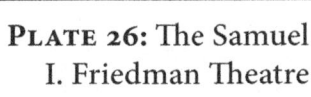
PLATE 26: The Samuel I. Friedman Theatre

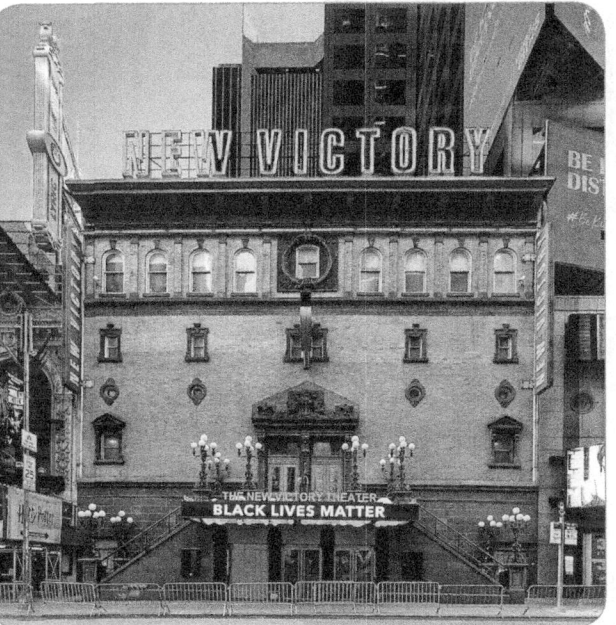

PLATE 27: The New Victory Theater

PLATE 28: The Bernard B. Jacobs Theatre

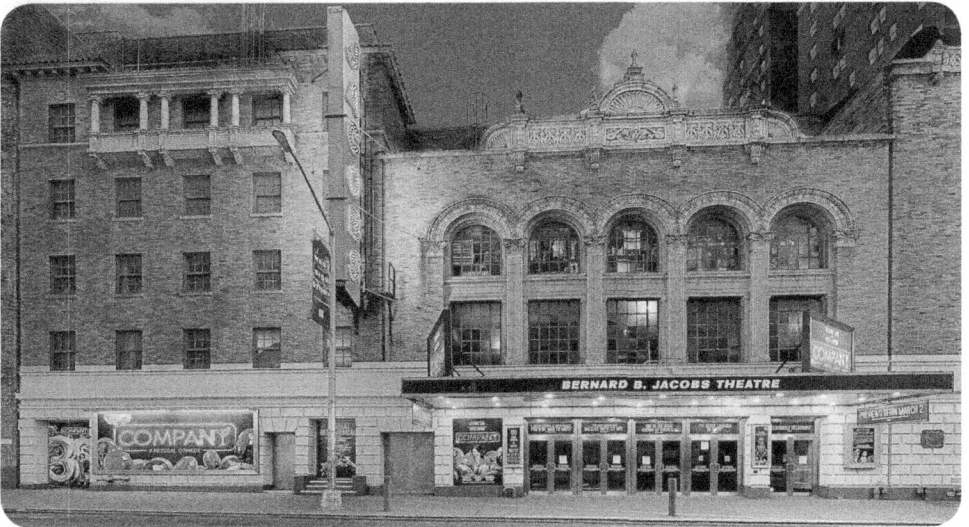

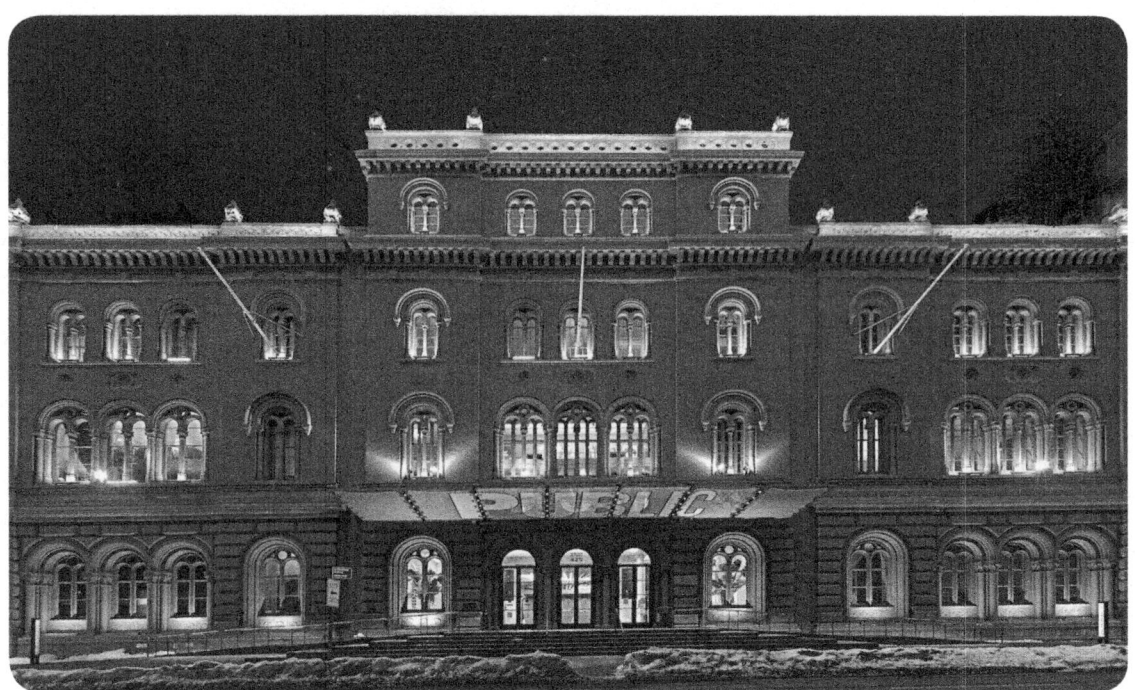

PLATE 29: The Public Theatre (Off Broadway)

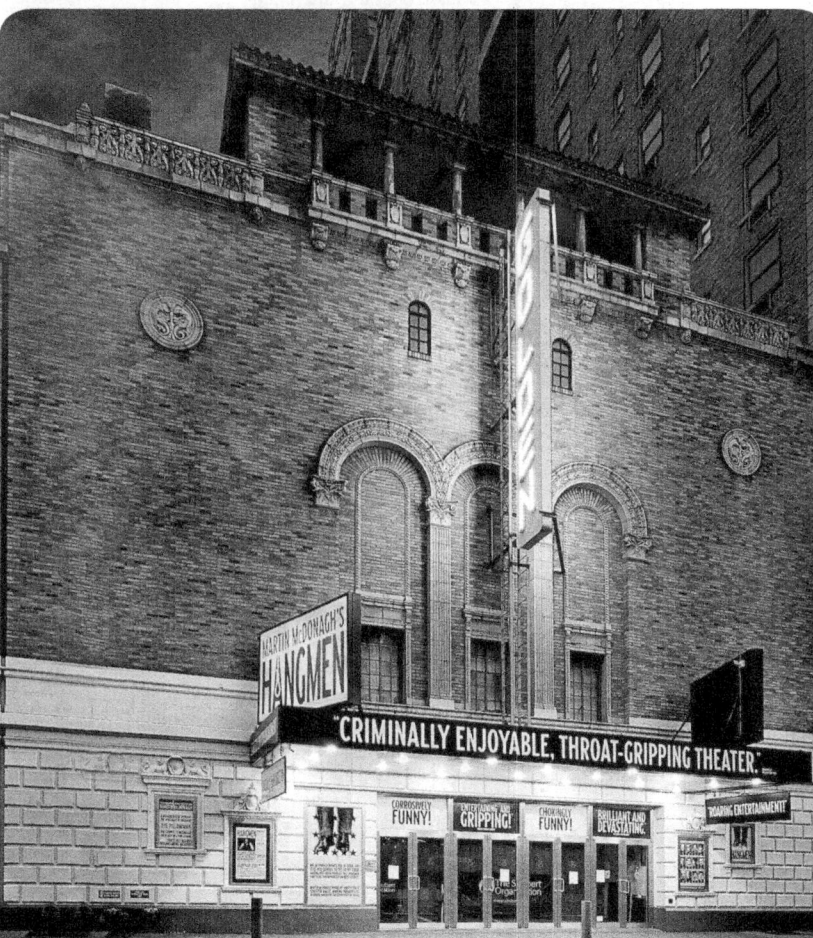

PLATE 30: The Golden

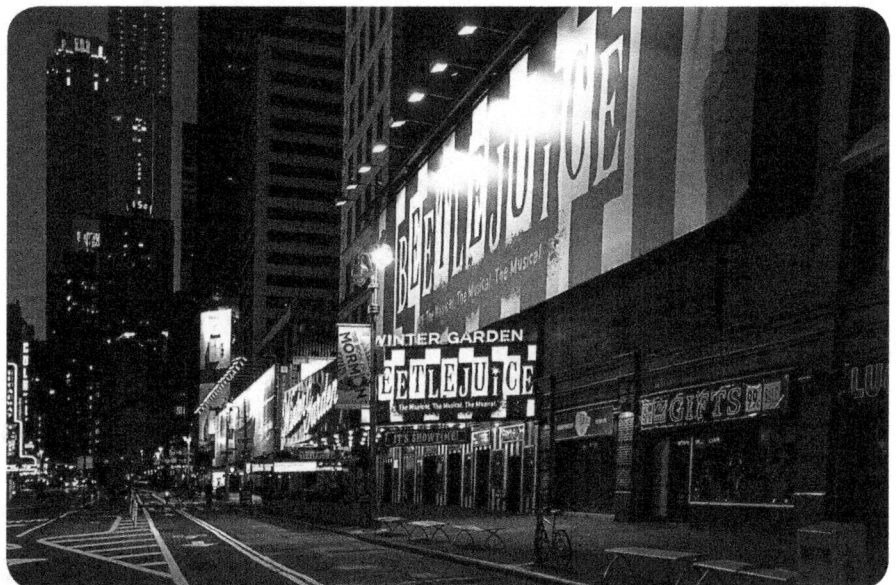

PLATE 31: The Winter Garden

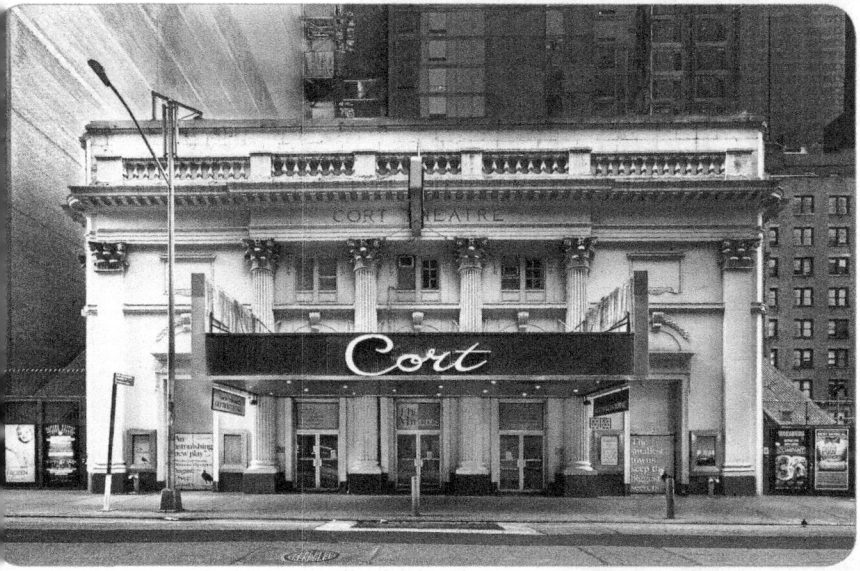

PLATE 32: The Cort Theatre

PLATE 33: The 13th Street Repertory Theatre (Off-Off Broadway)

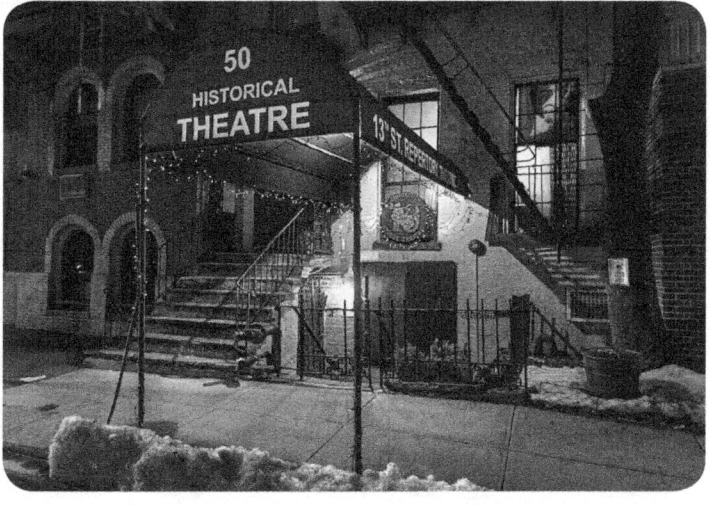

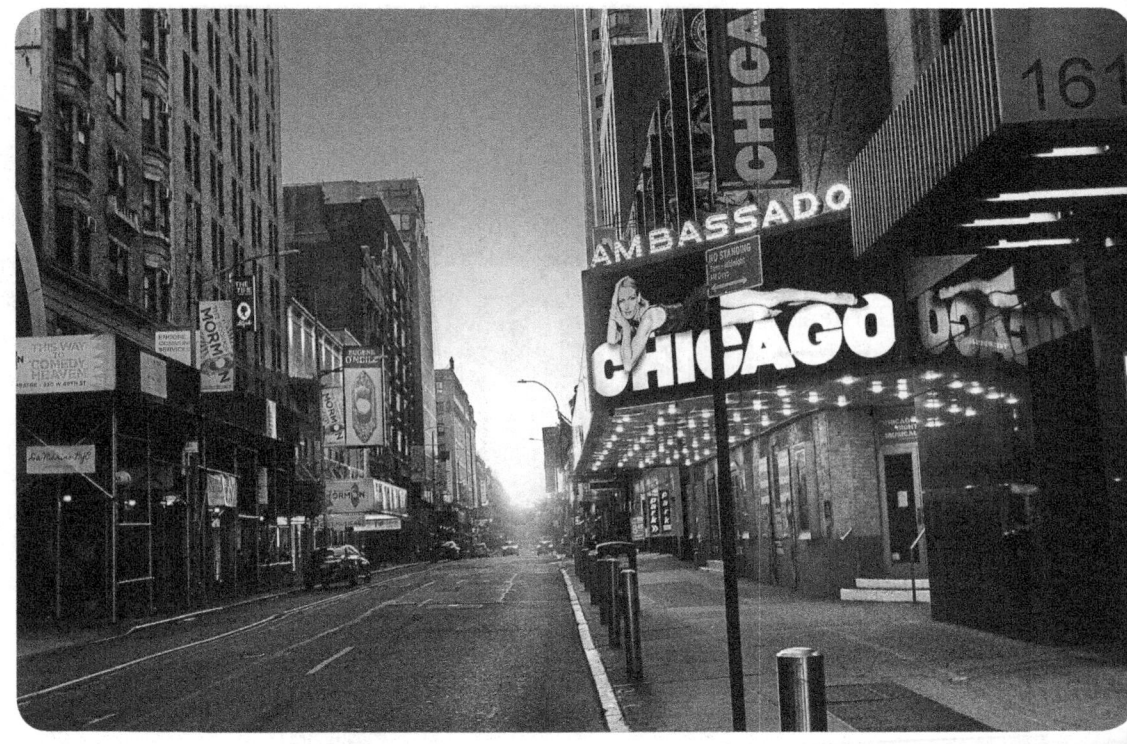

PLATE 34: 49th Street looking west

PLATE 35: Theatre 80 St. Marks (Off-Off Broadway)

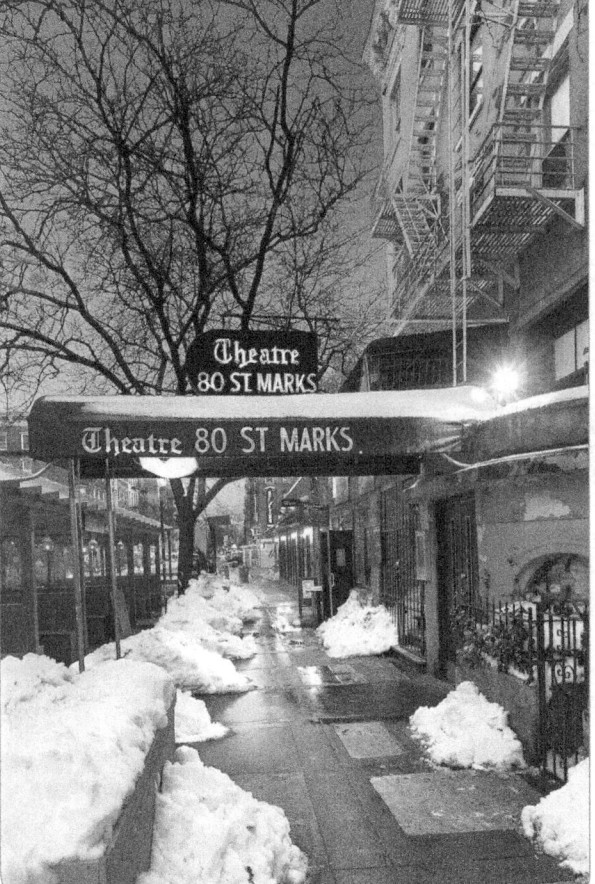

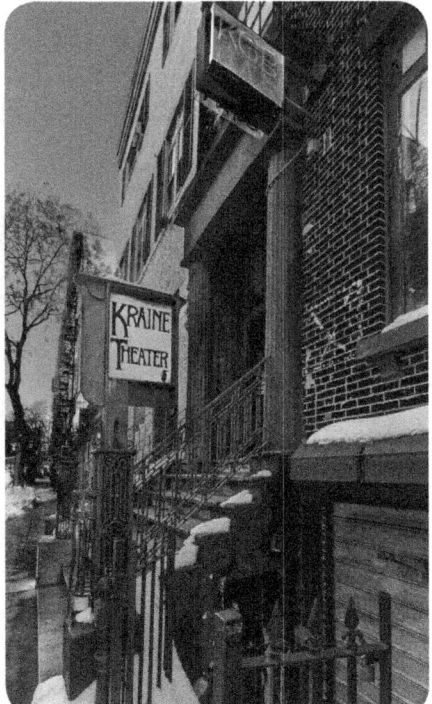

PLATE 36: The Kraine (Off-Off Broadway)

Plates 34–36

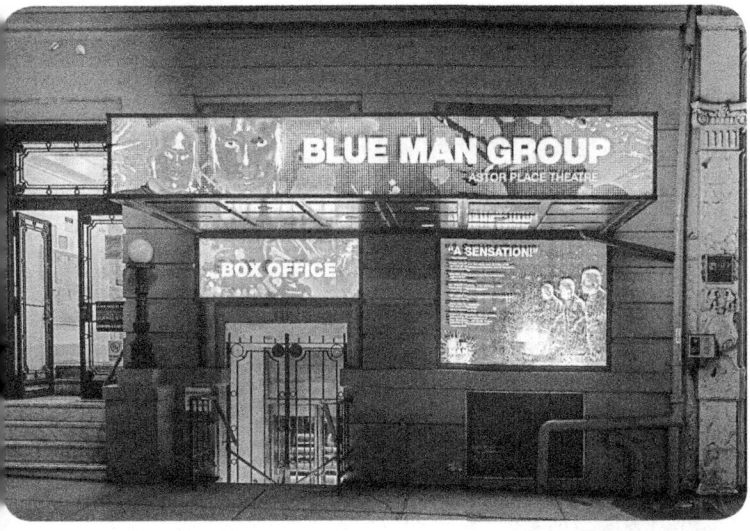

PLATE 37: Astor Place Theatre (Off-Off Broadway)

PLATE 38: New York Theater Workshop (Off-Off Broadway)

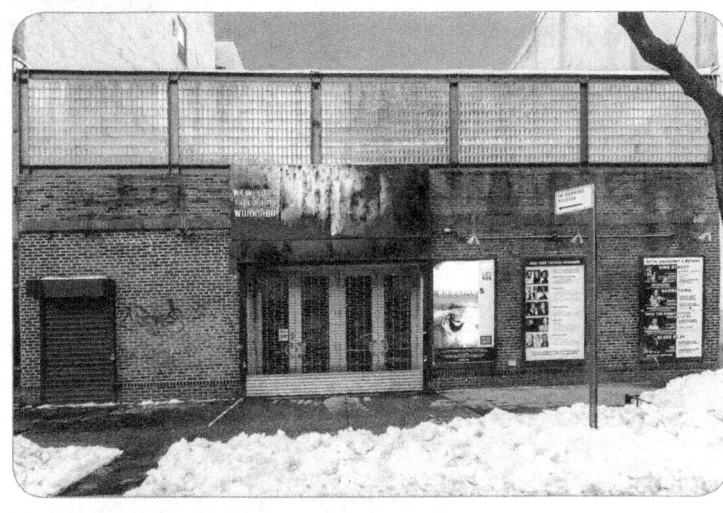

PLATE 39: The Longacre

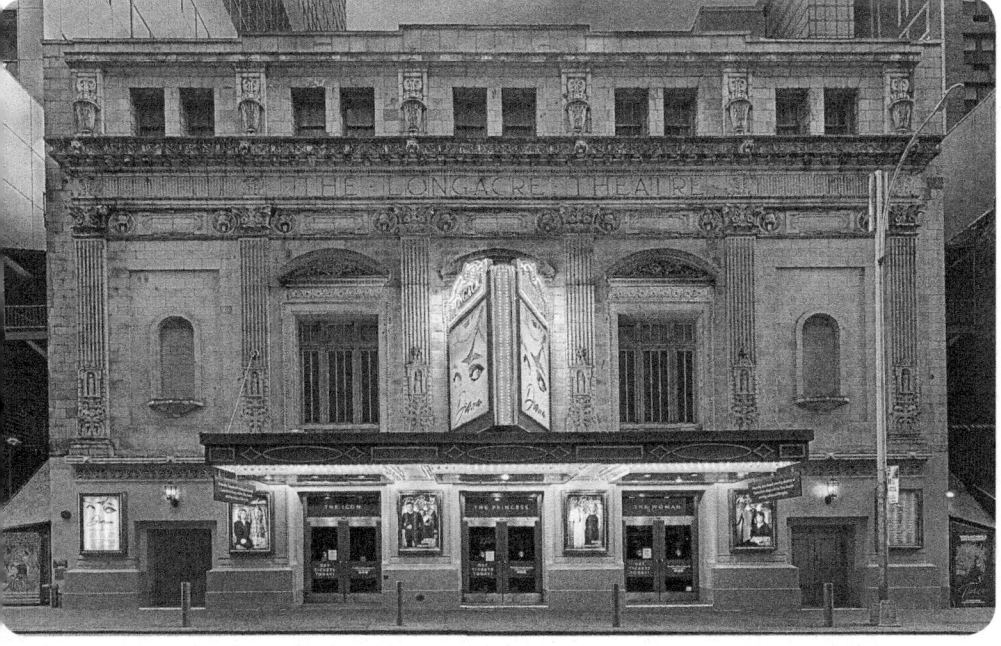

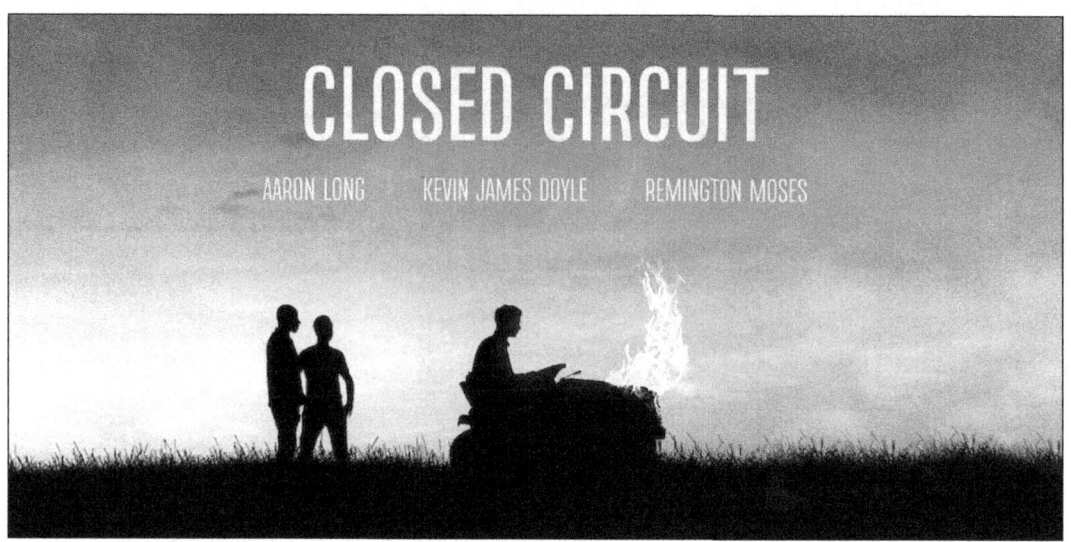

Closed Circuit

Reviewed online during the pandemic shutdown

- Presented as part of the **Frigid Festival**
- Play by Remington Moses, Kevin James Doyle & Aaron Q. Long
- Directed by Mary Chieffo

THE CAST

- Shannon: Remington Moses
- Charles: Kevin James Doyle
- Pat: Aaron Q. Long

BACKGROUND

In a very real sense, this review marks the beginning of a new age. I was scheduled to see *Closed Circuit* on March 7th at the **Kraine Theater**, where it was being presented as part of the recently concluded **FRIGID New York Theater Festival**. A health issue intervened (nothing fatal) and I had to cancel. When I contacted the company, they were most kind, and mentioned they'd made a video of that last performance. We discussed it, and the result is this piece, an online review of a *live* play, watched online for publication on a website. The fact that this occurred on March 16th, 2020, the day the Old World stopped, somehow makes it significant.

THE PLAY

I confess, video is not as engaging as a live performance, not for a New Yorker, anyway. But, it'll serve in a pinch, and I'm happy to say that *Closed Circuit* survives the transition quite well. Remington Moses, Kevin James Doyle, and Aaron Q. Long, the talented writer/actors who play Shannon, Charles, and Pat, are all experienced stand-up comedians, with a flare for comic delivery and polished timing. The plot is revealed in a set of "interlocking monologues, (as) three individuals recount the mysterious death of a family member."

As might be assumed, the actors wrote their own material, which is both the blessing and the drawback of this play. It's witty, intelligent, and the monologues are perfectly suited to each actor's style, but the interaction of the plotline needs more thought. Having watched it once, in an effort to replicate the sort of experience one might have in a theater, I had trouble keeping the "narrated" characters straight, mainly because their stories were being *told* and they were not quite real. There was also a great deal of laughter, which was as it should be for such an entertaining show. But, the performance seemed more a "stand-up" than a play, and the laughter itself was dramatically disorienting. It's a dark, "Chinese whisper" of a plot that needs more coherent interaction if it's to make a lasting impression.

THE PERFORMANCE

That said, *Closed Circuit* was very entertaining, certainly worth a look, and I hope we'll see it move on as we slowly climb out of this strange viral stasis we're all in. I also want to mention that the lighting at the final performance was some of the best I've seen at the **Kraine Theater**. Well defined areas; discrete, well-timed, and bright enough to see what's going on. Good stagecraft, there. Not always the case with festival plays.

As I understand it, Director Mary Chieffo has been quite instrumental in the development of this play, working particularly on some of the narrative interactions I mentioned above. I'm sure it's been an interesting project for her, its intellectual complexity depending upon which came first, the routines, or the plot. Whichever, I believe it's a worthwhile endeavor and my comments are made with the best of wishes. This innovative play deserves a **HAPPY FACE** as it moves on down the road.

PERFORMANCE INFORMATION

- February 22nd – March 7th, 2020 (various dates & times)
- The Kraine Theater
- 85 East 4th Street, NYC
- https://www.frigid.nyc/events/closedcircuit

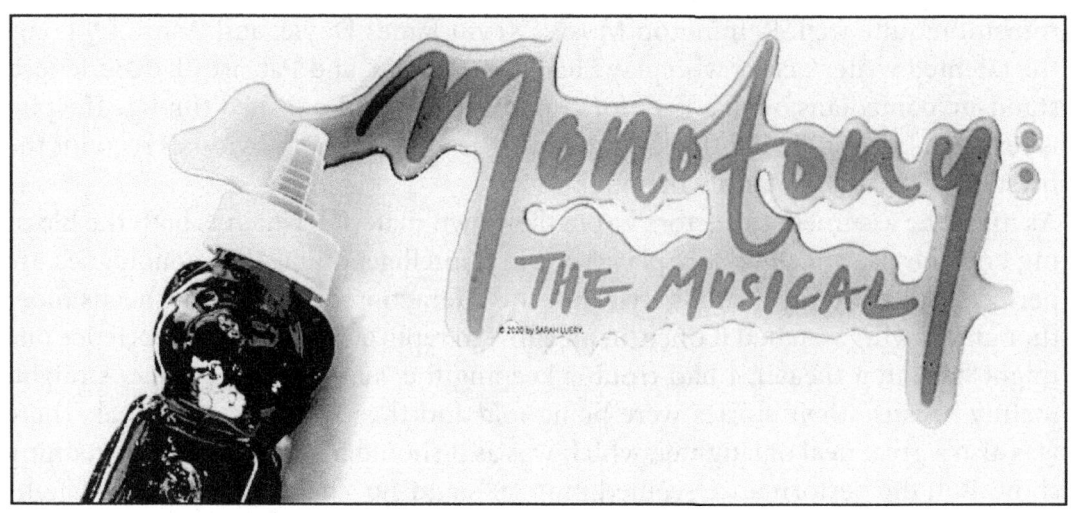

Monotony

Reviewed online during the pandemic shutdown

- Book & Lyrics: Sarah Luery
- Music: Jared Chance Taylor
- Dramaturg: Kathleen Coombs
- Graphic Design: Karen Sori
- Press: Dan DeMello PR

THE CAST (Working under a SAG-AFTRA collective bargaining agreement)

- Herbert Handler III: Alden Bettencourt
- Theodore McGiver: Jon Gibson
- Marnee McDougal: Kelsey Ann Sutton
- Mr. McGiver/The Bear: Tod Macofsky
- Ms. McDougal/Kyle: Alixandree Antoine
- Herbert Handler, Sr./Bode: Ahamed Weinberg
- Frank Collins/Trey: David Castillo
- Deacon: Pat Regan
- Thomas: Evan Allgood
- Lucinda: Karen Trachtenberg

BACKGROUND

I had the great fortune to grow up with radio. I mean RADIO. Not the repetitious, propaganda that passes for it today. I mean *real* radio; with comedies, dramas, soap operas, documentaries, remarkably diverse music, and Edgar R. Morrow signing in from London.

I have to confess, I was reminded of that with the first notes of *Monotony*. Author Sarah Luery and composer Jared Chance Taylor have created a charming, tuneful romp into the daily life of a millennial Everyman. They've given us a funny, romantic script, well-defined characters, with immediately recognizable vocal characteristics (vital in radio acting), and well thought-out performances of some beautifully written and exquisitely realized original music.

THE PLAY

Herbert Handler is bored. Being too young to have yet experienced any particular passion of his own, he has mindlessly given in to his father and taken a job as an accountant with the somewhat monstrous J. M. McGiver & Co., thus making one of the greatest mistakes a twenty-something can make. Barely old enough to shave, he has locked himself for life into what he already views as a monotonous dead end, and the fact that "life" means every week-day for sixty-plus years is just becoming clear.

Enter Theo, the boss's son, the prince of the palace. He's everything Herbert is not; intelligent, talented, and beautiful enough to defy his father and follow his own path. When they first meet, Herbert is overwhelmed. But, his office buddy Marnee, sensing that "interaction" with Theo might cheer Herbert up, initiates a campaign to get the two of them together.

Thus, lives go by. Day after repetitious day passes as these little games are played, father's disapproving as son's resist. To find out what happens, pour a drink, sit down, close your eyes and click below. The script is clever and funny, the musical score polished and positively stunning at times. It's an audio experience — like radio used to be — that engages the senses and creates pictures in the mind.

THE PRODUCTION

Sarah Luery's detailing of office tedium is spot-on. Not to suggest there's anything tedious about the play. The dialogue is tightly constructed and consistently funny, with witty lyrics skillfully set by Mr. Taylor. Through composed in the jazz-influenced classical style introduced by Leonard Bernstein in the 1950s, his music is clever and fresh on its own. The vocals are beautifully arranged, the orchestrations positively rhapsodic. Mr. Taylor has marshaled his considerable abilities and crafted what might be described as an authentic original cast album, which, given the cost of hiring a full orchestra, leads me to guess that a great deal of this fine performance was realized electronically. Whatever, it all sounded remarkably authentic.

THE PERFORMANCE

As Herbert, the reluctant accountant, Alden Bettencourt is engaging and funny. He has a fine singing voice. His diction is superb, and his infatuation with Theo a delight. Jon Gibson plays Theo like the star child he's supposed to be, charming, entitled, and oblivious of his effect on those around him (until the end). As Marnee, Kelsey Ann Sutton gives us an office match-maker that many of us will recognize, while Tod Macofsky plays Mr. McGiver (the Boss and Theo's father) as an overbearing martinet, frequently reminiscent of the great character actor Gale Gordon, famous on both radio and television as the nemesis of Eve Arden ("Our Miss Brooks") and Lucille Ball (the "Lucy" TV shows).

Musically, everyone in the cast was first rate. The ensembles were frequently stunning, enabled, as one might guess by Mr. Taylor's remarkable arrangements. They also made a grand attempt at radio-acting, although only someone as old as I am might look at it that way. I doubt the producers set out to create a radio show. That's just MY take on it. Everything about *Monotony* suggests that it was intended for the stage.

CONCLUSION

It was a pleasure to sit back, relax, and let my mind roam into *Monotony*'s millennial world. It's a well known fact that listening is a much more intense experience than viewing. It engages more of the brain and can set the imagination on fire. The only caveat I have with this piece are some of the technical aspects of the podcast. At times, the underscoring was too heavy and it overwhelmed the dialogue. But, that's a small thing. This excellent offering is beautifully put together and great fun to hear. I look forward to one day seeing it on the stage. **HAPPY FACE**

PERFORMANCE INFORMATION

- Premiered as a podcast on April 15, 2020
- Podcast – https://s.disco.ac/ozauuhzmzewt
- https://www.monotonythemusical.com/
- https://www.instagram.com/monotonythemusical/

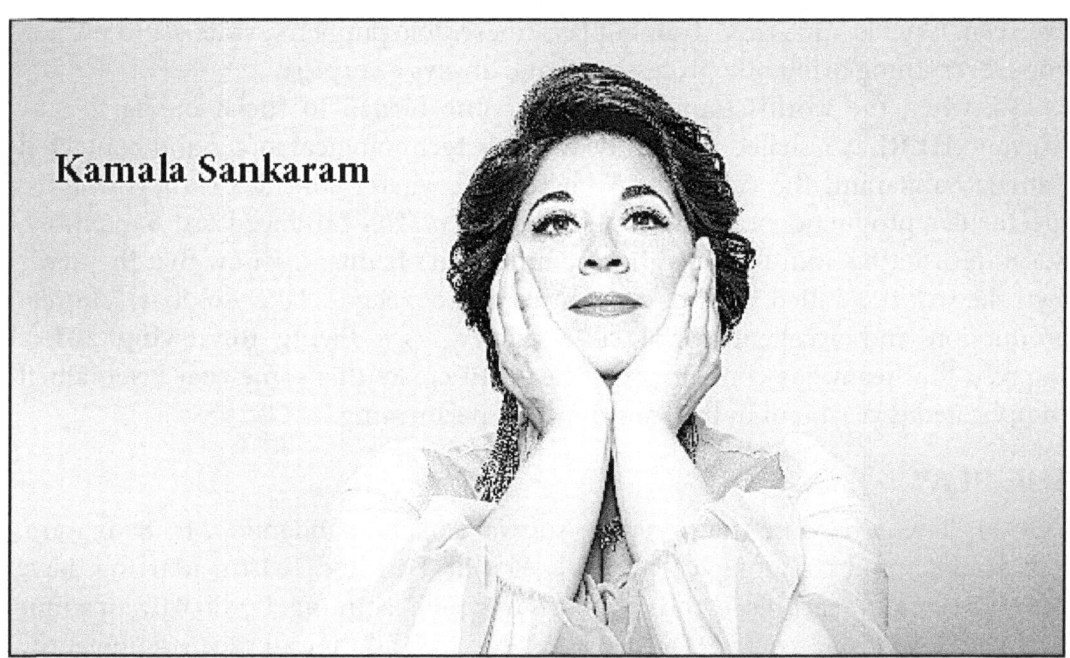

Kamala Sankaram

The Zoom Opera
Reported during the pandemic shutdown

- Produced by the **HERE Arts Center**
- Book & Lyrics: Rob Handel
- Music: Kamala Sankaram
- Director: Kristin Marting
- Press: Everyman Agency

THE CAST

- Paul An
- Hai-Ting Chinn
- Zachary James
- Joan LaBarbara
- Adrian Rosas
- Kamala Sankaram
- Joel Marsh Garland

BACKGROUND

I've been reviewing for a number of years, now, and I've seen hundreds of Off-Broadway plays all over New York City (until last March, anyway). As I've said many times, the technical work at the **HERE Arts Center** is consistently the best

I've seen. Operas, musicals, straight plays, incredible puppetry, videos and projections, everything brilliantly professional and always a surprise.

So, when the world stopped, and everyone turned to social media to stay relevant, **HERE** marshaled its readily available technological forces and contacted Kamala Sankaram, the composer who created what I consider to be the most spectacular production I saw in 2019. *Looking at You* produced last September, was a devastating, multi-media glimpse into what's happening now that the nerds own the world. I called it a work of genius, my colleague, Jake Goldbas, "A great production and excellent social commentary" (*see* **Ewing Reviewing 2019**). Happily, that team has come together again to create this somewhat brief, albeit complicated experiment in live, multi-screen performing.

THE PLAY

ZOOM, having become the signature software of the pandemic, Ms. Sankaram, Rob Handel, and technologically astute Artistic Director, Kristin Marting, have used it to create an art piece, the very basis of which is timing. Ordinarily, in a musical work, everyone knows exactly where they are and they all start singing at the same time. When two of the singers are in Philadelphia, one in the Bronx, two in Brooklyn, others in Manhattan, and the "orchestra" is coming from an undisclosed (in this case) location in New York City (if there even *is* an actual orchestra), and all of it is being controlled from yet another venue, the **HERE Arts Center** on 6th Avenue, the timing difficulties are staggering.

Every element in this performance is subject to the technological restraints we are all learning about every day. Some network data-pipes are slower than others. Computers run at different speeds. Nothing happens instantly, as many people believe. Thus, closely coordinated ensembles or character exchanges are almost impossible. Mr. Handle has met this challenge by creating a seven-character matrix he calls *All Decisions Will Be Made by Consensus*. The performers are presumably opining about the same subject, but they are doing it "in and around" one another rather than directly "to" one another.

Ms. Sankaram explains how she solved this "delay" problem in the question/answer session at the end. She used sophisticated musical notation, similar to that developed in the 1950s by composers John Cage and Karlheinz Stockhausen — another example of her knowledge and skill. That solved the problem this time. In the near future, however, I don't doubt that some clever programmer should be able to compensate for this electronic delay and fix the problem in the software. It's all like magic already. Who knows what will be available next year?

THE PERFORMANCE

I must admit, after a single viewing, I'm not entirely sure *what* they were singing about, other than that there is only ONE subject in the world at the moment, and everything anyone is doing is about that. In this instance, I don't think it matters. The result was a glorious cacophony of sound, reminiscent of *Moses & Aaron* by Arnold Schoenberg. I can't praise Ms. Sankaram more than that.

All of the performers, including Ms. Sankaram, are fine singers and extraordinary musicians, and their performances were first rate. Paul An gave a powerful reading, easily living up to his memorable performance in *Looking at you,* while Joan LaBarbara was incredibly moving, singing "I will come back" directly into the camera with a maternal warmth that went straight to the viewer's heart. The composer gave us a fine, strong soprano, which she admitted she had to hold back because it sometimes overwhelmed the equipment. Indeed, everyone in the cast was clearly a trained musician. This isn't a time for amateurs, is it?

CONCLUSION

I'm writing a report instead of a review because this small opera is just the beginning. Primarily, it explores the morphing of a mature art form into a totally new medium. As a fascinating experiment, a step toward revolution, it's stunning. Esthetically, because of the tech limitations, it isn't yet ready for prime time. When it is, I'm sure this fine team will be ready to present it in the highest resolution, and I, for one, can't wait.

PERFORMANCE INFORMATION

- Performed online April 24 – 26, 2020
- www.here.org

The Confession of Lily Dare

Reviewed online live 05/13/2020

- Presented online by **Stars in the House**
- Introduced by Julie Halston
- Play by Charles Busch
- Directed by Carl Andress
- Photo: Live online

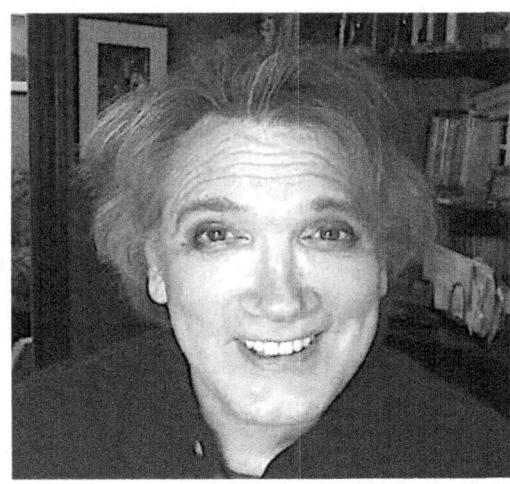

Charles Busch

THE CAST

- Lily: Charles Busch
- Mickey: Kendal Sparks
- Blackie: Christopher Borg
- Emmy Lou: Nancy Anderson
- Aunt Rosalee/Baroness/Mrs. Carlton/Louise: Jennifer Van Dyck
- Louis/The Baron/Dr. Carlton/Maestro Guardi: Howard McGillin
- Narrator: Carl Andress

THE PLAY (from the company website)

Charles Busch's *Confession of Lily Dare* tells the story of one woman's tumultuous passage from convent girl to glittering cabaret chanteuse, to infamous madame of a string of brothels — all while hiding her undying devotion to the child she was forced to abandon.

THE PRODUCTION

Mr. Busch is really a remarkable playwright. His script is not only funny, it's tight, witty, and intelligent — chock full of historical and cultural references — and it works remarkably well without the usual tools for which he is famous — no props, no gorgeous costumes, no artifice of any kind. The result is warm, tender, and quite moving. It gives us a new picture, I think, of the wide range of the author's talents.

Indeed, all the actors were extremely engaging, skillfully guided by director Carl Andress, who did a superb job moving this complicated stage piece into a format where acting is scrutinized in an extraordinarily intimate way. Everyone played directly to the camera. There was not a single moment when any one of them lost concentration or dropped character.

THE PERFORMANCE

As Mickey, Lily's lifelong friend and musical accompanist, Kendal Sparks was energetic and charming. Together with Emmy Lou, Lily's disciple and sometime employee, engagingly played by Nancy Anderson, he always tried to be there when Lily went through a bad patch, which happened constantly. Christopher Borg played Blackie, the bad guy, as slick and devious, an underworld character who consistently used Lily as a tool to make money.

Jennifer Van Dyck and Howard McGillin were particularly challenged as both played multiple roles (see above). Mr. McGillin, who was an absolute hoot, had to change his makeup and recomb his hair at least four times, which is not always easy to do in a live performance. Ms. Van Dyke played parts ranging from Lily's wicked Aunt Rosalee to her innocent daughter, Louise, with skill and panache. She was great fun to watch.

Mr. Busch is a treasure, a well-known New York theater personality with a considerable following. He is a true female impersonator, an actor who plays female parts. That should be obvious, but these days, many young people do not seem to know the difference between a female impersonator and a drag queen. There is no Betty Davis here, although in *Lily Dare* Mr. Busch does sound remarkably like Barbara Stanwick in the 1937 movie, *Stella Dallas*.

I also want to mention the resemblance of his speaking voice to that of Anne Elstner Matthews, who played Stella Dallas in the radio soap opera of that name from 1935 until radio suddenly died in 1955. Based on a famous novel by once well-known author Olive Higgins Prouty, *Stella Dallas* also concerns a blue-collar mother unable to be part of her daughter's life. The similarity *does* end there, however, as Lily Dare and Stella Dallas certainly did not follow the same paths in life. I mention this because I was so reminded of classic radio as the play progressed. Concentrating on the character and narrative flow, the high quality of Mr. Busch's ability and intelligence were clearly in evidence. In every way, this version of *The Confession of Lily Dare* deserves a warm **HAPPY FACE**.

PERFORMANCE INFORMATION

- Performed online live May 13th, 2020
- Performed onstage January 11th – March 5th, 2020
- The Cherry Lane Theatre
- 38 Commerce Street, NYC
- (866) 811-4111

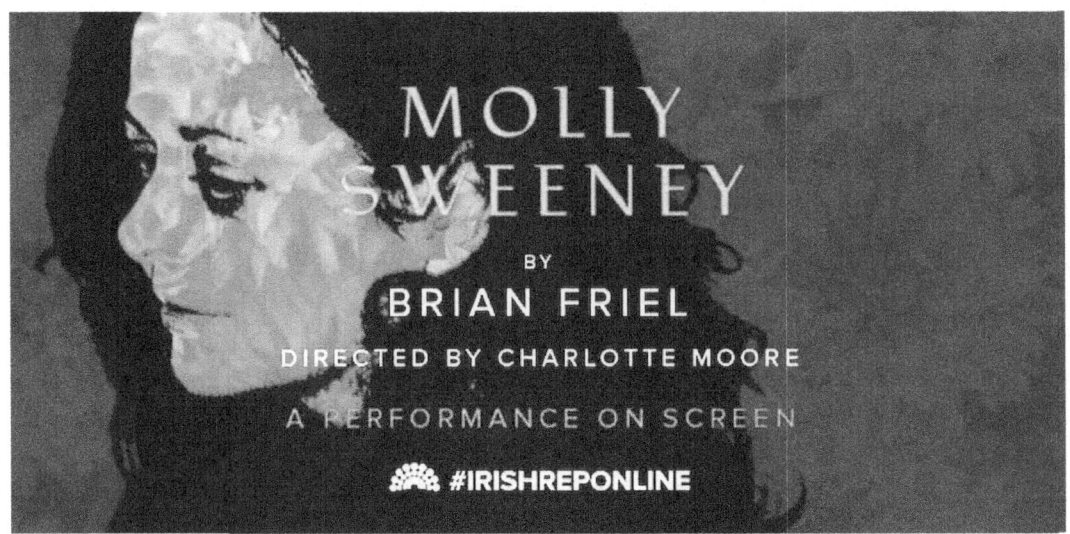

Molly Sweeney
Reviewed online live May 16, 2020

- Produced by the **Irish Repertory Theatre** [#IrishRepOnLine]
- Play by Brian Friel
- Directed by Charlotte Moore

THE CAST

- Molly Sweeney: Geraldine Hughes
- Dr. Rice: Paul O'Brien
- Frank Sweeney: Ciarán O'Reilly

THE PLAY

Brian Friel, one of Ireland's most famous playwrights, wrote *Molly Sweeney* as three riveting monologues, skillfully interwoven to create a single narrative, making it a perfect choice for an online presentation. It concerns a forty-two year old woman, blind almost from birth, who undergoes an operation to restore her sight. It is a remarkable consideration of what happens when a person's world is suddenly upended — the dangers of being torn away from the familiar, however odd that "familiar" condition might appear to others.

People who are deaf or blind, for instance, are under constant pressure. They're treated by everyone around them as if something's wrong. To a sighted person, it's almost incomprehensible that a blind person might not want to be *fixed*. I've never had a personal conversation about this with a blind individual, but I have discussed it with a number of deaf friends, and those who have grown up with the condition are often passionate as to why they don't want to change. They have learned to cope with their world in their own way, and to suddenly change that world means learning everything over again; essentially starting over. Few adults want to do that. And, I'm delighted to say that Mr. Friel's play presents the arguments on both sides with intelligence and clarity. I came away with a much greater understanding as to why it isn't necessarily a good thing to encourage such a profound change, and I sincerely believe that no one other than the patient involved is qualified to make that decision.

Geraldine Hughes was remarkable as Molly. Her speech about the party she was given the night before her surgery, detailing what she was going to lose, was heartbreaking.

As Dr. Rice, Molly's surgeon, the man who had the most to gain by restoring her sight, Paul O'Brien gave us a stunning portrayal of a genius in decline and desperate to restore his reputation, while Mr. O'Reilly played Molly's husband as an Everyman, unable to comprehend why restoring Molly's sight destroyed her, something so many of us can't understand when we encounter a disabled person who does not *want* to change.

Molly Sweeney is a very moving play, beautifully performed. This is another **HAPPY FACE** all the way.

PERFORMANCE INFORMATION

- Performed onlive live May 12th & 14th @ 7pm, 13th –16th @ 3pm, 15th & 16th @ 8pm
- https://irishrep.org/show/2019-2020/molly-sweeney-2/

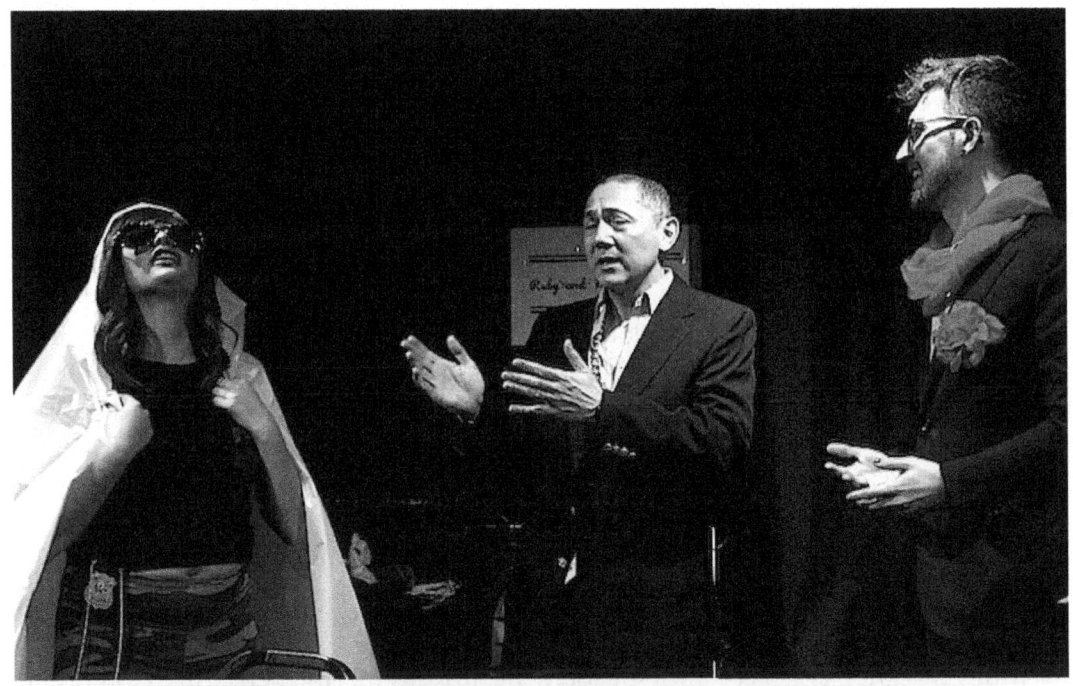
Natalie Hunter, Robert Baumgardner & Lars Montanaro

Diner on the Edge
Video reviewed online March 14th, 2020

- Produced by the **Improvisational Repertory Theatre Ensemble (IRTE)**
- Artistic Director: Nannette Deasy
- Executive Director: Robert Baumgardner
- Concept and Direction: Bill Berg
- Original Music: Tym Moss
- Press: Jay Michaels Arts & Entertainment
- Photo: Roberto Tobar

THE CAST (in no particular order)
- Leonard D'Coy: Robert Baumgardner
- Ruby Lavin Spivak: Nannette Deasy
- Bubba Mothershead: Curt Dixon
- Terri "Corkscrew" McGruff: Natalie Hunter
- Styx Mahoney: Sam Katz
- Patsy Love: Esther Lu
- Janusz Pouha: Jamie Maloney
- Chauncey Curio: Lars Montanaro
- The Haunted Jukebox (VO): Tym Moss

BACKGROUND

I've been following the **IRTE** for a while now, having reviewed their spirited productions of *Tammy's Bachelorette Party* and *Go To Sleep, Stupid Kids* last year at the **Producer's Club**. They've performed in more festivals than I can count, played to packed houses all over the country, and received many honors for their creative approach, which seeks to bring together "traditional theatrical elements with the immediacy and spontaneity of comedy improvisation." As far as I'm concerned, they deserved every honor they got.

Writing a review for an improvised play is not the same as reviewing a work with a fixed narrative. An improvisation can go anywhere. One can't look for intriguing plot twists or clever double entendres. Philosophical musings are out of the question, as are detailed character analyses and intellectual expositions on writing styles and language. It's the performance itself that matters, and, in this case, I'm delighted to be able to say that this play provides a lot of very funny material to consider.

THE PLAY (paraphrased from the program)

"You're a weary traveler in need of a cup of coffee, a hot meal, and a friendly smile. This place looks fine and there's nothing else around for miles. Ask about the blue plate special, but beware: you've stumbled into **IRTE's** *Diner on the Edge!* Join our diner denizens and the unlucky stiffs who serve them as they teeter on the edge of a catastrophe determined by you, the audience, in this improvised story of workaday life and adventures into oblivion."

THE PRODUCTION

With *Diner on the Edge,* which ran onstage at the **Producer's Club** just before everything stopped, founders Nannette Deasy and Robert Baumgardner and their talented troupe have taken a slightly different approach. Most often, an improvision is based upon a slight concept; no more complicated than an adolescent sleepover or a wedding shower. It's kept simple and succinct, thus allowing the actors to wander in any direction they wish. This time, however, director Bill Berg's concept seems a bit more detailed. It concerns a decrepit diner on its last legs, how it serves as a social venue for the locals, and how they react when an unexpected catastrophe (freshly suggested by a member of the audience at each performance) destroys them all.

It also seems as if the characters might be more fully detailed than usual. Ruby, skillfully played by Nannette Deasy, is a lonely, middle-age woman pining for her long absent husband. Robert Baumgardner plays Leonard as a sleek con man, who passes himself off as a financial advisor, managing to get banking information and social security numbers off anyone in the cast who might have money. Sam Katz and Lars Montanaro played Styx and Chauncey as a sort of vague odd couple. Sam Katz has been a hoot in everything I've seen **IRTE** do, with snarky remarks and off-the-wall connections that sometimes move the narrative into an uncomfortable place. Mr. Montanaro made a good contrast, somewhat withdrawn, maybe gay, or maybe just sneaky. In this case, it wasn't clear if Styx was a mobster or a hand puppet. Whichever, he was oddly dependent on a strangely influential Chauncey for his opinions.

Company stalwart Jamie Maloney played Janusz the dishwasher as a grumbling outlier. His characterizations are always great fun to watch, particularly when he plays somebody's mom, as he did in *Go To Sleep, Stupid Kids*. Generally speaking, he is a nuanced actor, but he needs to speak a little louder. At times, it was hard to understand what he was saying. Kurt Dixon played Bubba as a horny truck driver, ready to take on practically anybody or anything, while Natilie Hunter gave us "Corkscrew" McGruff, ex-cop, happy to kill anyone and unwilling to stand back in ANY situation. Which leaves Esther Lu to provide adolescent charm and uncertainty as she keeps trying to find out what's going on.

Then there's that catastrophe. On the evening in question, it was an enormous tidal wave advancing toward the diner. I'm not sure where that suggestion came from, possibly from an earlier performance. Chauncey saw it first, and warned everyone in the diner, but several of them couldn't swim, and some of them didn't believe him. Whatever the case, the tidal wave was terrific, with the cast members waving huge swatches of blue and white cloth, and Chauncey tripping across the stage with a dolphin puppet in each hand, bobbing up and down and in and out of the waves. It was a real pièce de résistance. The entire cast died with great aplomb.

CONCLUSION

Diner on the Edge played very well on the small screen. The video I saw was not originally intended to be more than a record of the performance; one camera from a single angle. But, I really think that's the best way to watch a performance intended to be seen live. There's no cinematic artistry to divert one's attention from the play itself. I had been scheduled to see it live before it closed because of the pandemic, and I was disappointed when that happened. But, this video (see below for the link) was still funny and entertaining, an excellent example of this creative company's commitment to the improvisational art. A **HAPPY FACE** all around.

PERFORMANCE INFORMATION

- Performance video streamed online March 14th, 2020
- March 13th – 28th, 2020
- The Producer's Club
- 358 West 44th Street, NYC
- (212) 315-4743
- www.irteinfo.com
- Online: https://youtu.be/zbjoAatyFOw

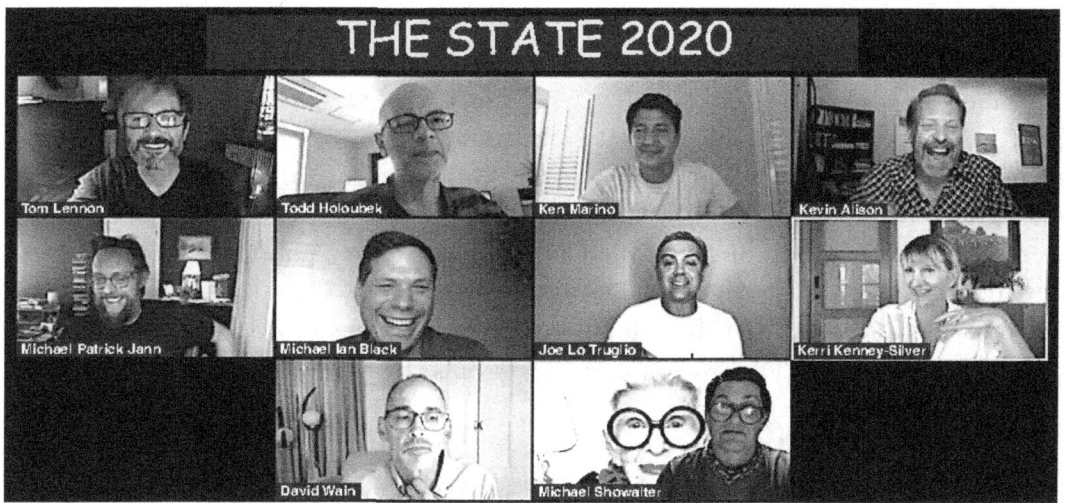

Zoom with the State

Reviewed onlive live June 10, 2020

- Produced by David Wain

FEATURING

- Kevin Allison, Michael Ian Black, Todd Holoubek, Michael Patrick Jann, Kerri Kenney-Silver, Thomas Lennon, Joe Lo Truglio, Ken Marino, Michael Showalter, David Wain

BACKGROUND

The State was a well known sketch comedy troupe that appeared on **MTV** from 1993 until 1995. Based loosely on *Saturday Night Live* and *Monty Python* (maybe a bit less sophisticated) the eleven members of the cast, who had been working together since high-school, wrote and performed material designed specifically for **MTV**'s adolescent audience. Since then, they have gone on to play an important role in many memorable projects, both as solo performers and in collaboration.

THE PRODUCTION

ZOOM with The State was an interactive online reunion featuring ten of group's original members (excluding Ben Garant who was unable to appear). It was conceived as a way to commemorate the troupe while encouraging their many fans to make contributions to both the **NAACP**, which received the money raised by an auction of memorabilia from the show, and **The California Immigrant Resilience Fund**, which received the proceeds raised by ticket sales (see the links below). As Michael Patrick Jann said so succinctly, "We all just felt we needed to DO something, and, as a comedy group of advancing age, a Zoom event is very bursitis friendly!" Really funny if you get it, and it worked VERY well.

Before this event, I wasn't familiar with *The State*. I was out of the country quite a bit in the early 1990s and not watching much television. But, obviously, many people were, and the number of people who tuned in for this event was quite remarkable. The "chat" function was active during the broadcast, and legions of fans were constantly responding and sharing their current reactions and memories. During the program, itself, it was announced that over $25,000 had been raised, and I now understand that the total after the auction was more than $85,000. Kudos, guys. What a glorious way to celebrate your celebrity.

THE PERFORMANCE

The show opened with a rousing rendition of *The Jew, The Italian, and The Red-Headed Gay 2020* performed by David Wain, Ken Marino, and Kevin Alison, who were joined by the entire cast as they cavorted about in separate windows and settled into their respective Zoom frames (see the link below to hear the opening number). The mood was relaxed and informal, with personal memories and anecdotes interspersed with film clips from the past (i.e., *The Manzelles*) and sketches recreated for this event (i.e., *The Sideways House*), which were all recognized and commented upon by the viewers. Add to that the new pieces, chosen by fans based on their titles, and at least one old sketch that had never been seen before, and you have an engaging pastiche of their past and present work.

CONCLUSION

It was a tonic to see this troupe, a group of old friends, working together so well after twenty-five years. So many musical and theatrical ensembles fall apart as its members pursue their own careers, but *The State* cast seems to have maintained their friendships, and the warmth they feel toward one another was evident. *ZOOM with The State* was entertaining and remarkably engaging. The auction was a hoot, with one patron donating $6,000 for Tom Lennon's "Booger Booger & Fartybutt" plaque (go figure). My understanding is that this performance, which was scheduled as a "one time only" affair, will soon be offered for sale online, with the proceeds again going to worthy charities. As to whether *The State* will follow up with a second Zoom show is still an open question. But, stay tuned. The charm of the cast and the excellent results they achieved make that very likely. So, see it if you have a chance. It's being done for a very good cause. **HAPPY FACE**

PERFORMANCE LINKS

- Information: https://davidwain.com/thestate
- Charities: https://www.immigrantfundca.org/ ; https://www.naacp.org/
- Sample from this performance: https://youtu.be/4bSO_GEprYI

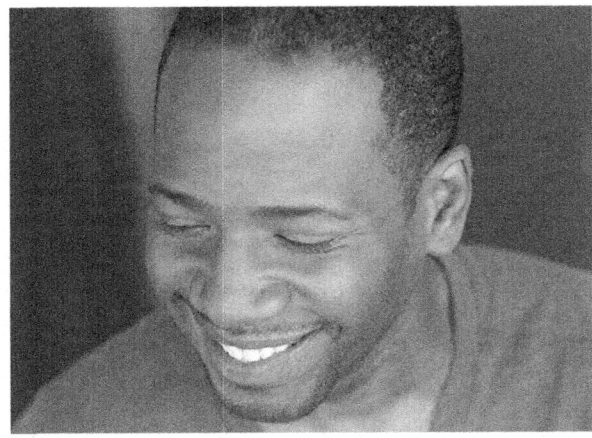

Gregory Marlow

PartiTime

Reviewed online live by William J. Cataldi June 14th, 2020

- Produced by the **Fresh Fruit Festival**
- Artistic Director: Dennis Corsi
- Playwright & Director: Gregory Marlow
- Press: Jay Michaels Arts & Entertainment

THE CAST

- Lenzo: Cooper Howell
- Bouncer: David Hughes*
- Orlando: Corey Wright*
- Butler: Sean Parris
- Brandon: Rejinal Simon
- Doug: Kwame Remy*
- Marcus: Christian Bradford*
- Leo: Nathan Streifel
- Lawrence: Terrence Clowe*
- Jeremy J: Cameron Barnett*
- Serge: Joshua Bennett
- Stage Direction Reader: Larry Whitfield

THE PLAY

Gregory Marlow's *PartiTime* thoughtfully and sincerely depicts a weekly Saturday night sex party for black men in midtown Manhattan in the current day. The party's owner, Doug, must close down and move it to New Jersey (a symbolically charged move) because he has lost his lease. Doug carefully chooses amongst the would-be attendees as they arrive hopefully at the front door. The men arrive, peel off to have sex, talk, take a lot of drugs and drink, and seem to have an almost universally bad time. The party ends in the early morning, as the men file out onto the street, squinting from the Sunday morning sun, sinking into mighty hangovers.

Readings deprive us of a lot of visual help useful in experiencing a play. That was the case here. The speaking characters, and other non-speakers, seem to have a lot of great sex, which could have been enacted on stage in suggestive, non-explicit ways. That would have given us a glimpse, at least, of why these men went to the sex party in the first place. Without this visual asset, relying only on the dialogue, one wonders why anyone would ever have sex at all. Some characters are couples (or one side of a couple), who have laid down the rules and come out for a good time, only to let jealousy, insecurity, fear and their need to possess the other, eat them alive.

Some characters are single guys, who spend the whole time longing for a stable, monogamous pair-bond (and a house in the country, with kids in the yard), and wondering why they don't have one. A few of the characters, the lone white attendee, young Leo; Lenzo, a muslim dude who comes to New York, because he'll get the death penalty for having sex in his home country; and Orlando, a single, hot, black guy, who seeks out anonymous sex because he has been "hurt," seem to have a good time, but are either punished, or probably will be punished for it in the end.

The play fleetingly explores issues of heteronormativity, ageism, and race. It correctly portrays the self-loathing of many, maybe most, gay men, especially men of color. And it effectively makes the conservative case for bourgeois, romance-based pair-bonds as the antidote for that self-loathing and unhappiness.

The zoom reading was technically proficient with character boxes flashing on and off the screen depending on who was relevant in a particular scene. Occasional pauses, when actors lost their place in the script, were not too distracting. The actors were not fully rehearsed, sometimes flubbing their lines, but this was not a performance, it was a reading, so no harm done. Oftentimes, the actors did an outstanding job with the script, conveying complexity of emotion, and naturalistic banter.

However, the play left me feeling irritated. Men have testosterone flowing through their veins that inclines them toward lust. They get horny. Mr. Marlow strongly urges us to see this as a moral flaw. I do not. The self-loathing of gay men comes from their assumption that they should be ashamed of the drive to explore their lust. Exploring one's lust means spreading one's seed far and wide. Bourgeois, heteronormative commandments to form monogamous pair-bonds won't always satisfy this natural urge to have sex with a lot of different men. The suggestion that men who need sex parties, clubs and hook-ups in their lives are bad men is homophobic and reeking of self-hatred.

This is coming from a man in a twenty-five year partnership which has never, ever been monogamous. My partner and I have had sex with hundreds of other men during those twenty-five years. We don't have any jealousy, any mutually-agreed upon rules, any desire to "own" one another, or any shame. When we went to sex parties in the past (we are older now and don't have as much sex anymore), we had a great time always. We love each other profoundly. We have always approached our partnership as mature men, and we have eschewed the ethics of sixteen year old girls in forming our life together.

But that's just my two cents. The play is poetic and beautiful at times, quite an accomplishment for Gregory Marlow. I would love to see it performed on stage, if we ever return to live performances again. Kudos to the author. **HAPPY FACE MINUS**

PERFORMANCE LINKS

- www.FreshFruitFestival.Com
- http://www.freshfruitfestival.com/developmental-reading-series-2020/PartiTime/

Hamlet

Reviewed online live June 14th, 2020

- Play by William Shakespeare
- Produced by **Shakespeare Sports** in association with **Jay Michaels**
- Directed by Michael Hagins
- Artistic Director: Carrie Isaacman
- Press: Jay Michaels Arts & Entertainment

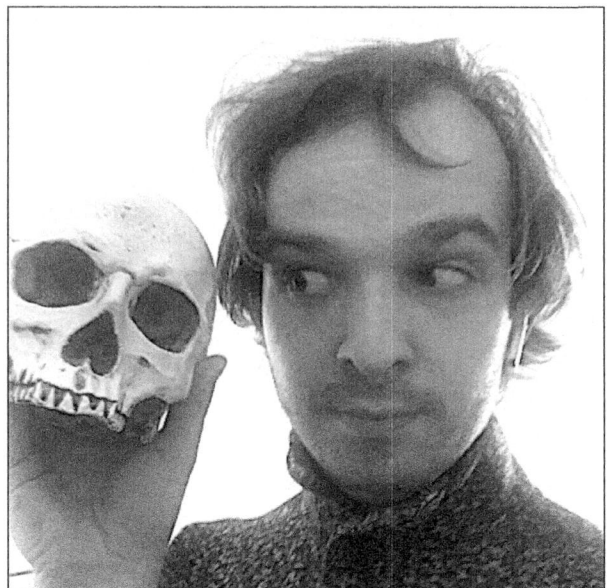

Matt Tiemstra

THE CAST

- Hamlet: Matt Tiemstra
- Horatio: Charlie Aleman
- Gertrude: Mary Sheridan*
- Ophelia: Jordyn Morgan
- Laertes/Player King: Tucker Dally Johnston
- Rosenkrantz/Marcellus: Gigi Principe
- Guildenstern/Osric: Aaron Kapner
- Gravedigger/Player Queen: Carrie Isaacman*
- Polonius: Stevie Roetzel
- Claudius: Bradley J. Sumner*

BACKGROUND

Hamlet, first performed in 1609, is probably the best known play in the English language. It's replete with quotes that have entered our thoughts and influence our everyday lives; "Neither a borrower nor a lender be." "What a piece of work is a man …," "To be or not to be …," "Good night sweet prince, may flights of angels sing thee to thy rest," among many others. Stunning language, noble thoughts, thrilling concepts that never fail to lift our spirits and make us think.

THE PLAY

For anyone who might have been living in a cave for the past 400 years, Hamlet, Prince of Denmark, is seeking revenge on his stepfather and mother for the murder of his father. Basically, he is an unbalanced child who manages to destroy his entire world; a typical spoiled brat, refusing to cooperate, pulling rank on his subordinates, making lethal decisions until everything and everyone is gone. Whether or not my opinion is shared by others, I don't know. But, it's evident to me, and this online production makes it even more so.

THE PRODUCTION

Shakespeare Sports has made a brave attempt to present this well known classic under very difficult circumstances. Director Michael Hagins and his cast have given us a somewhat truncated staged reading of the play — supporting a worthy cause (see below) — which I believe they intend to present onstage at the Clemente Center when theaters reopen later this year (if they do).

The reading was well done but not thrilling. There were technical glitches (not unexpected as we all learn to dance around the new software) which caused the tightly written dialogue to occasionally disconnect. Matt Tiemstra, the play's Hamlet, apparently learned his lines, while almost everyone else read from a script. That, combined with mostly modern dress and hair styles, particularly noticeable in the otherwise decent reading of Stevie Roetzel as Polonius, served to undermine the suspension of disbelief we all need to lose ourselves in a 15th century Shakespearean tragedy.

THE PERFORMANCE

As Hamlet, Matt Tiemstra needs a stage. His energy and enthusiasm was evident, and his descent into madness particularly effective. Also, the fact that he knew his lines allowed him to act, not just read. It made a lot of difference in his performance. As Claudius, Hamlet's stepfather, Bradley J. Sumner was proficient but lacked gravitas, possibly because of the unfamiliar acting style into which we've all been plunged (see below). Mary Sheridan convincingly played Gertrude, Hamlet's mother, with love and an uneasy concern as she watched her son self-destruct.

As Ophelia, one of the most tragic heroines in theatrical literature, Jordyn Morgan was more than sympathetic. Aristocratic and fragile, she seemed totally lost as her innocence crashed around her. Tucker Dally Johnston played Laertes with great anger, befitting a son whose father was murdered by a thoughtless prince, while Aaron Kapner as Guildenstern and Osric was a stitch every time he appeared. Also seeming to have memorized his lines, Mr. Kapner gave a strong performance, with great charm and subtle humor.

Leaving Charlie Aleman, Gigi Principe, and Carrie Isaacman to carry on as Horatio, Rosenkrantz, Marcellus, the Gravedigger and the Player Queen, frequently unappreciated roles to which they all brought charm and energy. Kudos, guys. Good jobs.

CONCLUSION

I intend to see this production when (if) it opens as intended, at the Los Kabaytos Theatre at the Clemente Center next year. In general, I think online readings of such a famous play might be a mistake, that the medium is better suited to new and infrequently performed works. We all look for certain things in famous dramas that are difficult to reproduce in the new "in-the-face" acting style forced upon is by the pandemic. And, make no mistake, our actors have to learn how to do it. Performing for an opinionated viewer who is (virtually) one or two feet away staring directly into your face is *not* easy. It's an acquired skill that takes a lot of practice, and I do believe that's why I was less than excited by this Hamlet. Mr. Hagins is a good director. His cast is definitely capable of a more engaging performance. In this case, I believe, a new, demanding acting style, combined with a relatively unfamiliar technology, threw them all a curve. Because of that, and in honor of their support of the fine Citizen Schools charity (see below), **Shakespeare Sports** gets a **HAPPY FACE MINUS.**

FURTHER INFORMATION

This online production of *Hamlet* is a fundraiser for **Citizen Schools**, an American nonprofit that partners with middle schools across the United States to expand the learning day for children in low-income communities. Its stated mission is "Educating Children and Strengthening Communities."

PERFORMANCE LINKS

- Performed onlive live June 14th, 2020
- Charitable donations: https://citizenschools.rallybound.org/Donate

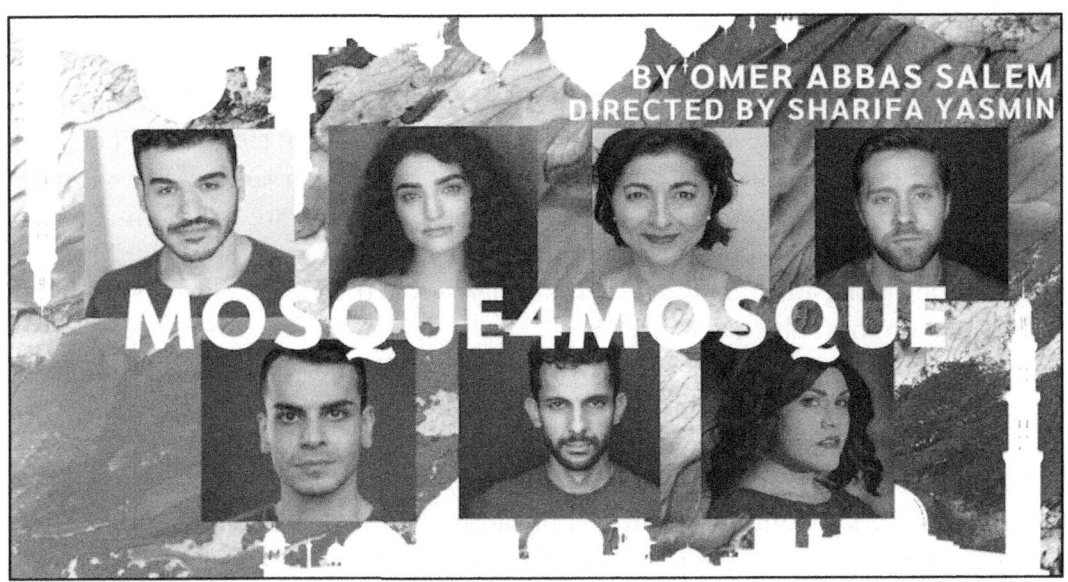

Mosque4Mosque

Reviewed online live by William J. Cataldi June 19th, 2020

- Produced by **National Queer Theater** as part of the **Criminal Queerness Festival**
- Artistic Director: Adam Odsess-Rubin
- Playwright: Omer Abbas Salem
- Director: Sharifa Yasmin
- Press: Everyman Agency

CAST

- Ibrahim: Noor Hamdi*
- Sara: Rula Gardenier
- Lena: Bahar Beihaghi
- James: Connor Bryant*
- Karim Philip Algiers/Ensemble: Martin Zebari*

THE PLAY

ZOOM productions just keep getting better and better. At first we struggled with the software and alienating format. The actors were all in their own box, reading lines. Now production teams have relaxed, and we can imagine sets, imagine actors interacting, touching one another. Think radio plays from the 1940s. Plays can come alive in this unfortunate format. Omer Abbas Salem's *Mosque4Mosque* did just that as the first theatrical entry of **National Queer Theater**'s annual **2020**

Criminal Queerness Festival.

Ibrahim, a muslim gay man around thirty, has made it a habit to visit the confessional at the Church affiliated with the university where he works. His confessions give us an interesting gaze at his inner life. He struggles with an eternal conflict: play the field and have a lot of great sex with relative strangers, or settle down into the warm embrace of his new, white boyfriend, James. At home are his mom, Sara — overbearing, subtly manipulative, and sister Lena — in love with her older brother, long suffering alongside him under their mother's love. The play is a detailed analysis of the situation these characters live in.

As has been universally the case with **Queer Criminal Festival** play choices, the playwright clearly loves his home culture. The care and craftsmanship with which Mr. Salem offers up the many details of life in this muslim home, right down to smells and descriptions of menu items, belies his undying affection for a culture Ibrahim and Lena struggle with in complications of the heart. Islamic homophobia is backpedalled, since the only homophobic character is Ibrahim's father, who is long dead, and makes his case through Ibrahim's remembrances in the confessional. These are hip muslims. Nonetheless, Ibrahim sits and stews over his eternal conflict. I wanted to know once and for all what Ibrahim would do. I listened for clues. We are asked to root for the joys of a monogamous pair-bond with James. But by the end, we have no definite choice. This play has no resolution.

Some might consider this a major flaw. Narratives have to have an exposition, crisis and denouement. Art knows no rules, however, except for the ones being broken. Elaborate descriptions of people and events — all exposition — can offer a lot of food for thought, and make excellent art. John Cheever, the great American short story writer, wrote a brilliant story entitled "The Worm in the Apple." He describes a family in the preppy suburbs of Connecticut in much detail. He teases the reader with details that make us wonder, "Is this the worm in the apple?" We keep expecting the crisis. Did the father embezzle funds? Did the mother have an affair? But in the end the family just lives on happily ever after. The surprise is, there's no surprise.

In *Mosque4Mosque,* the characters do face a significant, last-minute issue that comes up, unrelated to the ongoing, psychological drama amongst these characters, but the psychological drama remains unresolved. Ibrahim is still Ibrahim. Some will find that a flaw. In this case, I'm so happy with the beautifully crafted exposition, that I'm content with the ambiguous ending.

THE PERFORMANCE

Noor Hamdi did a great job in last year's *Drowning in Cairo*. I'm happy to say his acting skills are coming along nicely. I have conversed with him, and I can attest that his Ibrahim was not really a version of himself. I'm glad to see this fine actor progressing. Rula Gardenier as Sara was the other star of this production.

Her portrayal was delightful and funny, an every-(muslim)-mom, who makes us love her while rolling our eyes at her antics. Both Ibrahim and Sara needed actors with a great deal of psychological dimension and Mr. Hamdi and Ms. Gardenier were more than up to the task. Lena and James were played by Bahar Beihaghi and Connor Bryant respectively. Both made excellent supporting performances in roles that required them to have appealing personalities that filled out the script, but didn't shift attention too much away from Ibrahim and Sara. Martin Zebari had the thankless task of playing extra parts that were needed to further the story, which he did with much warmth and professionalism. The cast was stellar one and all.

THE PRODUCTION

That brings us to the ZOOM production itself. With one small exception, when Mr. Hamdi's link froze, causing a long break in the scene; the use of ZOOM was outstanding. Frozen links are unfortunately a problem with the medium. No problem at all. The rest of the time, I was able to imagine the family kitchen down to details, which were filled in by the dialogue; costumes; and interactions between cast members; all described by the narrator. I was able to imagine them so well, that I felt afterward as if I had seen this play on video. The actors were all acting, not reading a script they were unfamiliar with, and their acting was thoroughly persuasive. My experience resembled that of hearing an excellent radio play, as I mentioned. Mr. Salem's play lived and breathed on my desktop.

Ibrahim had a very tough life so far, and I'm not sure why everyone couldn't just leave him alone for a few years and let him have his fun with casual sex. That's just my take on Ibrahim's plight. We are given a chance to explore this family's complex dynamic, however, combined with the demands of current American culture, along with current LGBTQ culture. I still think Ibrahim should have told everyone to go to hell. This is a funny, exciting play by Omer Abbas Salem that deserves a full production in a theater. When, oh when, can we go back to full productions? **HAPPY FACE**

PERFORMANCE LINK

- http://dixonplace.org/category/criminal-queerness-festival/

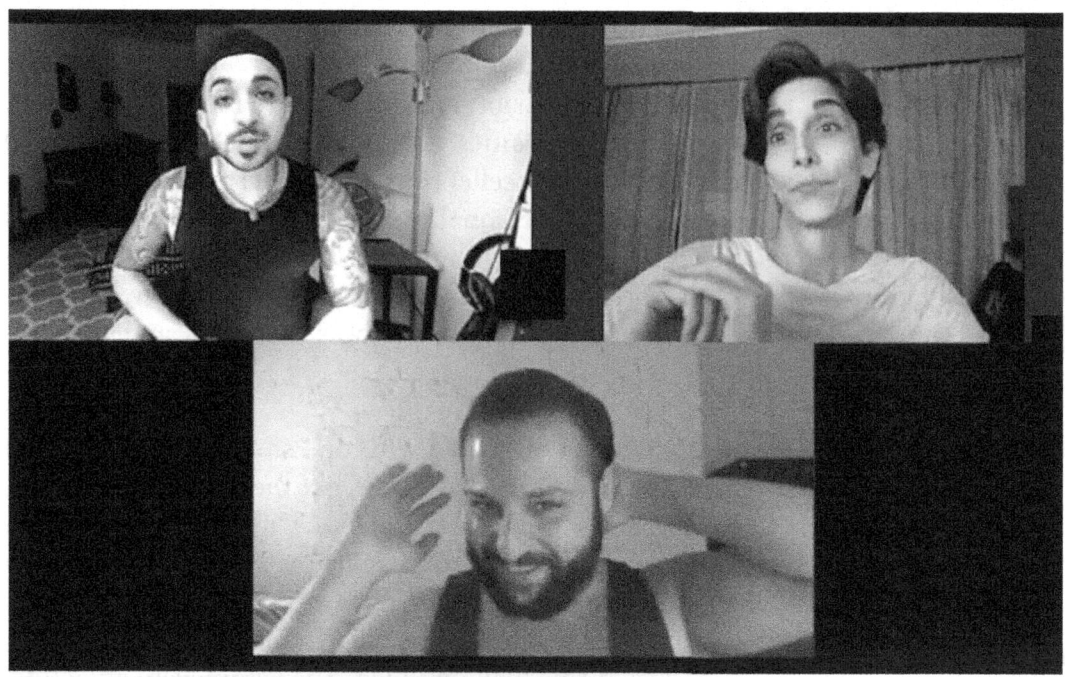

(L–R) Samy Nour Younes, Louis Sallan, Pooya Mohseni

She He Me

Reviewed online live by William J. Cataldi June 19th, 2020

- Produced by **National Queer Theater** as part of the **Criminal Queerness Festival**
- Artistic Director: Adam Odsess-Rubin
- Playwright: Amahl Khouri
- Director: Sivan Battat
- Press: Everyman Agency

THE CAST (*Courtesy of Actors' Equity Association)

- Randa: Pooya Mohseni*
- Rok: Samy Nour Younes*
- Omar: Louis Sallan

THE PLAY

Let's face it. Gay and lesbian people have pretty much achieved their political and social goals for full equality. They have become the mainstream. Pete Buttigieg is the poster child for gay and lesbian political activism in the United States, a friendly guy anyone can relate to, who doesn't think we can afford Medicare for All. It's become the fashion for gay and lesbian voices to promote conservative values: service in the military; marriage and kids in a suburban context. America has learned to like gays and lesbians.

I'm bored with "equality." That's why, in 2015, I became a homosexual and abandoned my gay past. I'm an ex-gay. I went looking for something real, something that could address the anger and hurt in my heart; and what did I find? I found my predominantly black and brown workmates justifiably worried about encounters with cops. I found poor folks beaten for jumping the turnstiles in the subway. And I found gender activism. I found people with female brains in male bodies. I found people with male brains in female bodies. I found people who couldn't (didn't want to) self-identify with male gender norms or female gender norms, who were looking for something else — a third way.

Amahl Khouri's *She He Me* thoroughly explores gender issues in the context of the tense, war-torn Middle East and North Africa, where non-conformity of any kind finds no quarter. Randa, a transgender woman who originates in Algeria, endures being forced to abandon her child, extreme poverty, beatings, expatriation, imprisonment, multiple rapes, and eventual alienation from the entire muslim world, as she finds asylum in Sweden. Her story is the worst one of three, a story of survival. Rok, a young, transgender man in Lebanon, fares better. I imagine his problems more closely resemble those of any western transgender man, except for the fact that Lebanon lives under the eternal threat of Israeli bombardment. As someone says (I paraphrase), "People in the Middle East live life to the fullest, because any moment the building you're standing next to might collapse from a bomb." His is a story of defiance and resilience. Omar, a "social dysphoric" homosexual, doesn't feel comfortable with masculinity — a double whammy in a world where a male's lack of masculinity "will bring disgrace upon the entire family" and almost all men constantly try to out-man each other. He eventually finds no solace in a gay community obsessed with gender conformity in its own way. His story is about fabulousness in the face of adversity.

Each character takes turns telling his or her story, with the other two playing roles that come up with the current narrator — parent, sibling, policeman, guard, government agent, whatever is needed. This way the narrations interlock in a tight-fitting, gorgeous, self-reflective, balanced, and beautifully structured play. Khouri is a master of the art. I'm an emotional and empathetic man. I started crying fifteen minutes into *She He Me,* and barely stopped until the end. There is *no* trace of manipulation here. None of these characters want sympathy. I think what they want is the proper respect due any human being we may encounter. And they earn way more than mere respect.

I had to wonder. Could I have endured the abuse these characters suffered and come out the other end okay? I mean, "abuse" is putting it very mildly. Would I have had the stamina, could I have found a will to live sufficient to survive the kind of universal condemnation and battery that Randa survived? I don't know. I think of myself as a strong, masculine guy, but Randa found the inner resources of a goddess, a Persephone banished to a recurring hell. Randa's womanhood, Rok's manhood, and Omar's humanity were of a magnitude many orders greater than anything I have ever even considered. But then I don't live in a world where bombs fall from the sky or the police abduct and rape me.

THE PRODUCTION

The ZOOM production values were excellent. There were no glitches. This particular play is well-suited to a ZOOM production. In fact, I'd venture to say it may be better in this format than it would have been on stage, but I'm not sure. Pooya Mohseni as Randa broke my heart. She did such an outstanding job with Randa that it's easy to see why she has had success as an actor. She was sweet perfection. Samy Nour Younes was sexy and cool as Rok. He played his role casual with a touch of ambivalence. Rok was sure he was a trans man; there was no equivocation. His performance wasn't as powerful as Mohseni's, but Rok had a much easier time than Randa. There was a lot of humor and youth in his portrayal of Rok. Louis Sallan was not so convincing as Omar. He seemed to be an American-born and -bred gay man. This is purely an issue of his current acting acumen. There was too much of himself in his portrayal. I had to imagine the role instead of experiencing it directly. Some more lessons might clear this up. That said, all three actors did a fine job with a harrowing script.

Amahl Khouri's *She He Me* is the best of the seven National Queer Theater productions I have seen. It is one of the best plays I have ever encountered. It has the one quality that always makes great art — cruelty. Amahl Khouri doesn't care how much it hurts. He wants to tell his story. His cruelty shows in the details, and the careful structure, and the craftsmanship. He holds nothing back. Greatness is his. HAPPY FACE PLUS

PERFORMANCE INFORMATION
- http://dixonplace.org/category/criminal-queerness-festival/
- Livestreamed on Facebook Live and Youtube Live. Available until June 26

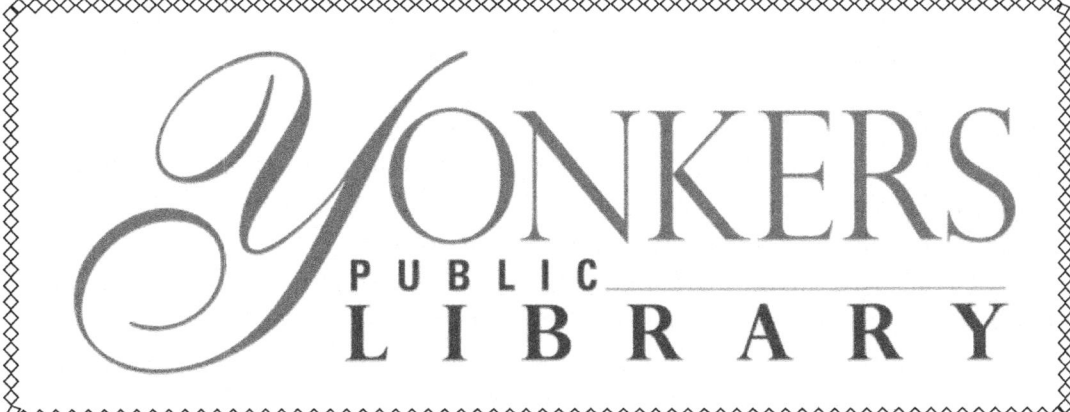

Yonkers Public Library Reading Series

- Phil Poggiali, Librarian, Yonkers Public Library, Crestwood
- Z. Baird, Branch Librarian, Yonkers Public Library, Crestwood
- Mary Ann Penzero, Penzero Productions

FEATURING

- Betty, Chris S., Leonard, Theodora, Ann Marie, Ann, Chris, Eileen, Frank, Gabby, Gina, Sarah, Sue, Sumie, Tammy, Tim, Wale, and Jan

BACKGROUND

I'm a writer, still striving to finish *The Red-Headed Kid,* my Great American Novel. Since I retired, however, I've become heavily involved in the theater, resulting in this **Ewing Reviewing** yearbook series. Since we felt these volumes should, essentially, be reference works, not to mention that a good part of our intended customer base had just gone broke, we decided to contact libraries. Giving the enormous reach Zoom now gives us, this led to some fascinating conversations as far away as London. But, none of them as much fun, or as encouraging, as the reading series I wound up joining at the Yonkers Public Library.

THE READING CIRCLE

Well before the Pandemic, Phil Poggiali, the Yonkers librarian, organized a play-reading circle. One of his degrees is in Drama, so it was a natural fit. He knows the literature, he knows its history and pedigree, and he loves the theater. Somewhere along the way, I'm not sure when, his associate librarian, Z. Baird, and Mary Ann Penzero of Penzero Productions, became involved. By the time I met them, the Pandemic was already screaming, and the meetings were being held on Zoom, an almost perfect platform for such an activity.

On the last two Thursdays of each month, the group (basically, anyone who wants to log in) gathers to read a play Phil has chosen in advance. Some take parts and some just watch and listen. The parts are handed out more or less at random, allowing anyone to take on anything they wish. It allows one to play roles they could never do onstage. So far, I've played an elderly British colonel, a middle-age lesbian, and a bat.

The main thing, however, is the camaraderie everyone experiences, which, after almost a year of staying home, is one of the most important things I can think of. It provides company, conversation, and a chance to get out of one's own head. Phil's intelligent, knowledgeable, commentary on the material is always well-focused and helpful, and his patience is remarkable. The acting abilities of the participants vary, but that doesn't matter in the slightest. Everyone makes it up as they go along, reading from a script shared on the screen by Ms. Baird, and there's laughter and frequently surprising reactions all around.

THE LIBRARY

As I got to know the people in Yonkers, I was reminded of my own time in regional theater. Before moving to New York City, I directed groups all over the country, in Virginia, Michigan, Wisconsin, and upper New York State. I worked in communities like Yonkers, where the libraries and other educational institutions were closely involved in fostering and supporting the arts. In every case it was an absolute joy; more fun than it ever was in NYC, where it is a deadly earnest, life-altering obsession.

Institutions like the Yonkers Public Library, with their intelligent, interactive programs, train our audiences as well as our future players and stars. Far beyond just checking out books, they provide activities that lift and nourish our souls. Without what Yonkers does, Broadway and Off-Off-Broadway would not exist, and reading with Phil and his group reminded me of that. We're lucky to have them. If this was a theatrical review, I'd give them a **HAPPY FACE PLUS**.

READING INFORMATION

- www.ypl.org / Click "Virtual Events"

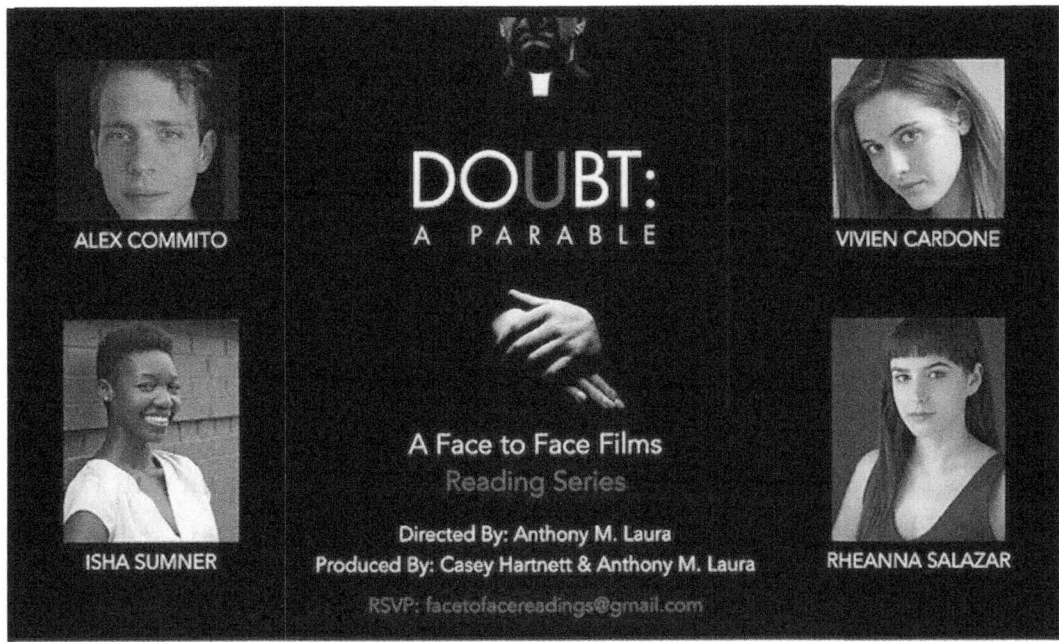

Doubt: A Parable

Reviewed online by William J. Cataldi on June 27th, 2020

- A ZOOM Production
- Produced by **Face to Face Films** in association with Casey Hartnett & Anthony M. Laura
- Playwright: John Patrick Shanley
- Director: Anthony M. Laura
- Press: Jay Michaels Arts & Entertainment

THE CAST

- Narrator: Anthony M. Laura
- Sister Aloysius: Vivien Cardone
- Sister James: Rheanna Salazar
- Father Flynn: Alex Commito
- Ms. Muller: Isha Sumner

THE PLAY

John Patrick Shanley's *Doubt: A Parable* explores suspicion in the absence of proof or a confession of guilt, which results in a state of eternal doubt. Sister Aloysius runs a Bronx, Catholic elementary school in 1964, during a dark period, during which, we now know, some priests were sexually molesting children. Mr. Shanley wrote the play amidst allegations of priest misconduct, which seems to have stretched back for decades. The audience is necessarily aware of the problem, but in 1964, there was no such awareness. During conversations with Sister James, a teacher, Sister Aloysius develops a nagging suspicion that Father Flynn, a priest at the school, may have an improper relationship with Donald Muller, a prepubescent male student, and the school's only black ward. Her suspicion develops a self-generating momentum, fueled by her strident nature. Sister Aloysius interviews Ms. Muller, Donald's mother, who obviously fears that Donald will be punished (because of his race), if she allows the Sister to rock the boat. Ultimately, Sister Aloysius confronts Father Flynn, who denies the allegation; but Sister Aloysius tells him she enquired about him with a Sister at his previous post. Father Flynn allows himself to be transferred out of her school. In the absence of a confession, Sister Aloysius, Sister James, and any reasonable audience member, are left with a nauseating doubt as to whether Flynn is a monster or a loving pastor.

Mr. Shanley's play is a masterpiece. If it's performed intelligently, it is impossible to decide what actually transpired between Donald Muller and Father Flynn. On the one hand, we have an audience trained by current events to eye all priests, indeed all males in charge of boys, with suspicion. On the other hand, we have an accuser who seems to conjure the allegations with little evidence, and who seems to have possible unconscious motivations. Father Flynn is written so well, that the audience is invited to believe that his interactions with the boy were pure of heart, coming from a place of great spiritual love for a vulnerable youngster. Priests are trained to keep sacred privacy between themselves and individuals to which they minister, so we know there could have been a thousand reasons why Flynn couldn't betray their confidences. If the priest really was a vehicle of salvation for Muller, helping a troubled boy navigate an all-white school, Aloysius' allegations destroyed a sacred relationship. This is something every Catholic takes seriously. Hence, *Doubt* is a tragedy any way you look at it.

Primarily, *Doubt* is about its two main characters—Sister Aloysius and Father Flynn, but its other two characters—Sister James and Ms. Muller—play essential roles in the unfolding drama. Sister James is innocent and naive, a woman who looks at the world always assuming the best of everyone. By the end of the play, Aloysius has demolished James' innocence. In Christian terms, she has dragged James away from purity into darkness, a major sin. Ms. Muller, not naive, but desperately struggling to raise her son amidst racism and economic vulnerability, sees her son's tremendous opportunity in attending this school, slipping away. We are led to believe that Ms. Muller could excuse impropriety, as long as Father Flynn seemed to be such a positive influence otherwise. And we feel for her. We might be inclined to look the other way, depending on the severity of the possible infraction. But we will never know the details. A well-rounded audience member is left with an even larger doubt. Is sexual impropriety with a minor always dark and sinister?

THE READING

Any actors performing *Doubt* have a difficult row to hoe. They cannot exceed the script by letting body movements, or voice inflections destroy the delicate balance that allows the audience to suffer that awesome, nauseating doubt. Father Flynn can't look guilty, and Sister Aloysius can't look excessively vigorous or implacable. Aloysius may be unlikeable, but she cannot be seen as insincere or having ulterior motives. Sister James can't be imbecilic, and Ms. Muller can't be so attached to her son's opportunities, that she doesn't care about possible sexual abuse. These are all risks for *Doubt* actors. All four actors in Face to Face's reading were astonishingly impeccable.

Isha Sumner, who played Ms. Muller, had a slight accent, which added an extra dimension to her vulnerability. She made palpable her fears that her son might be punished for testifying against a white priest; that Donald might lose a tremendous opportunity; that an important man, who had taken an interest in helping her troubled boy, might be forced to abandon him. These concerns seemed out of the blue to me, until I empathized with the Mullers' situation. Her concerns definitely shocked Sister Aloysius, who becomes aware of them at the same time as the audience. And Ms. Sumner depicted the pain of having to overlook bad things perfectly.

Rheanna Salazar, who played Sister James, did a similarly great job with her role. Not overly wide-eyed, Ms. Salazar portrayed innocence believably, with aplomb. Her naivete wasn't funny, and her fall from grace, at the hands of her fellow Sister and boss, certainly wasn't funny. She also had a knack for depicting Christian love, an extremely rare commodity in America today. By the end of the play, she has become much more complex and scarred with trouble. Ms. Salazar showed us that transformation perfectly.

It may be inappropriate for me to say this, but Alex Commito, who played Father Flynn, exceeded Philip Seymour Hoffman's brilliant performance in the 2008 film. Mr. Commito was so perfect in this role, that I guess his was one of the top performances I've seen since I've been reviewing theater. If Mr. Commito is not a Catholic, I do not understand how he could have rendered a loving, sincere priest so effortlessly. I could see in his face and comportment, how he struggled to negotiate the accusation, while being strictly compelled to keep his interactions with Donald confidential. He was so earnest. But when Aloysius outmaneuvered him, he caved. Was that a tacit admission of guilt? Was his earnest, loving nature concealing sinister events? Mr. Commito played it impossible to tell. This fine, young actor deserves an award.

Just as perfect was Vivien Cardone's portrayal of Sister Aloysius. Again, if Ms. Cardone isn't Catholic, I can't understand how she was able to render the suspicious nun to such great effect. Aloysius loved her students just as much as Sister James loved them, but her love was harsh and tough. She assumed others were up to no good, and she felt it her duty to head them off at the pass. She represents a

Machiavellian attitude that people are likely to be bad if given the chance, and that it is better to be feared than loved. But Ms. Cardone was careful not to portray a maniac. Her depiction was strident but always kept fairness in mind. There wasn't an inkling of vulnerability in her performance, until the end when she confesses tortured doubt. As with Mr. Commito, Ms. Cardone's sweet perfection was one of the best performances I've seen since I've been working with HI! DRAMA.

CONCLUSION

Boy, would I love to see this cast on stage. The play is magical, and these performances were otherworldly. I can't think of anything at all that might have detracted from this presentation: not one dropped line, not one missed opportunity. I just have one piece of important advice for the folks involved with this reading. It's a bad idea for artists to create perfect art: they run the risk of making God jealous. **HAPPY FACE PLUS**

PERFORMANCE INFORMATION

- facetofacereadings@gmail.com

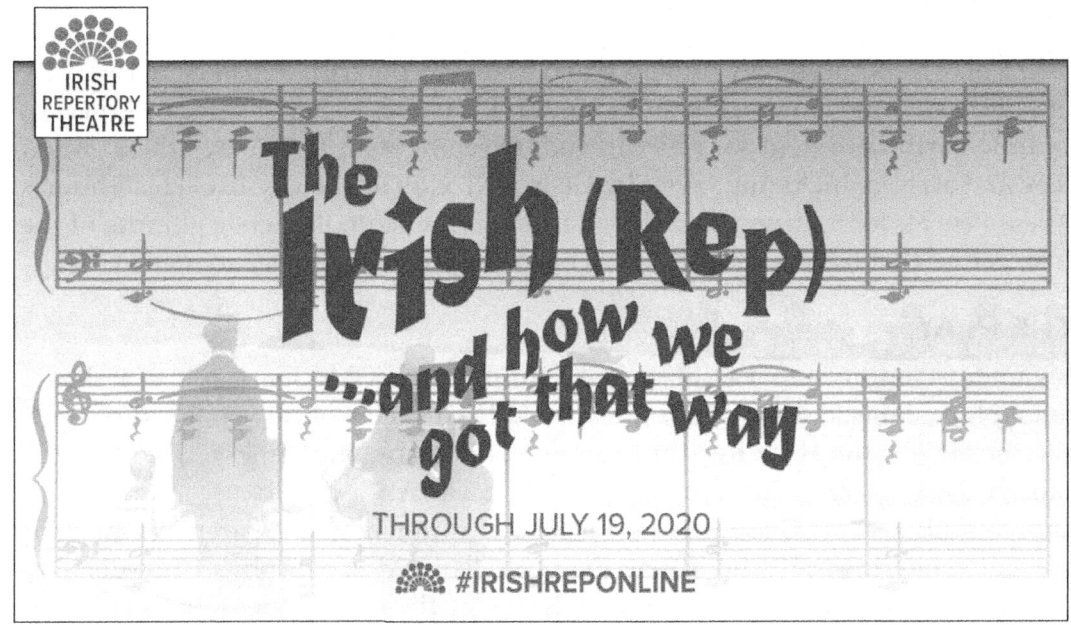

THROUGH JULY 19, 2020

#IRISHREPONLINE

The Irish (Rep) ... and how we got that way

Reviewed online July 13th, 2020

- Based on *The Irish ... and how they got that way* by Frank McCourt
- Produced by the **Irish Repertory Theatre** [#irishreponline]
- Artistic Director: Charlotte Moore
- Producing Director: Ciarán O'Reilly
- Musical Direction & Arrangements: Rusty Magee
- Scenic Design: Shawn Lewis
- Lighting Design: Dan Walker
- Costume Design: David Toser
- Choreography: Alexia Hess Sheehan

FEATURING

- Terry Donnelly
- Bob Green (On Fiddle)
- Marian Tomas Griffin
- Ciarán O'Reilly
- Rusty Magee
- Ciarán Sheehan

BACKGROUND

Unlike so many online presentations these days, this rousing celebration of (mostly) traditional Irish music is an actual, onstage performance. More a musical review than a play, it was originally produced and filmed by the Irish Rep in New York City in 1998, to remind a new generation how and why the Irish first came to America, and the harsh treatment they had to endure (along with too many others) when they first arrived. Including music by George M. Cohan, George L. Giefer, Thomas Allen, Pete St. John, Ernest R. Ball and Chauncey Olcott, it offers a glimpse of the Irish genius that has enriched the lives of countless millions over so many years.

THE PLAY

My understanding is that Pulitzer Prize winner, Frank McCourt, one of Ireland's finest playwrights, fashioned this piece, which he'd been working on for some time, specifically *for* **The Irish Rep,** an American company only nine-years-old at the time. Whatever the history, he couldn't have chosen a better cast. The warmth and commitment of these fine performers is immediately apparent, from their raucous rendering of "Who Threw the Overalls in Mrs. Murphy's Chowder?" to Ciarán Sheehan's heartbreaking "Danny Boy," one the most tender folk ballads ever written. Add in Cohan's "It's a Grand Old Flag," and "Over There," with some fine clog dancing and splendid vocalizations by everyone on the stage, and you have an entertainment for the ages that ends much too soon.

CONCLUSION

The Irish have supported civilization as far back as anyone can remember. Beginning with an enormous body of stunning erotic poetry, written by Gaelic royalty during their golden age, to their almost single-handed preservation of Christian art and thought in the Middle Ages, they have given us great literature, theater, and art, invariably created with imagination, intelligence, and love. Which leads me to one final comment. To the Irish, literature is so important that they are the only country in the world that does not charge their writers income tax. For that alone, the Irish truly belong at the feet of God. **HAPPY FACE**

PERFORMANCE INFORMATION

- Streamed online July 13th – 19th, 2020
- https://irishrep.org/

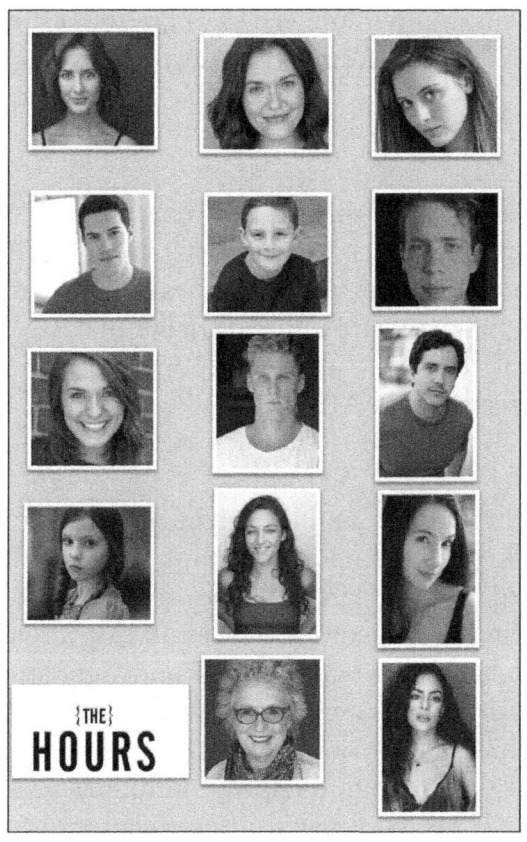

The Hours
Reviewed online live August 1st, 2020

- Produced by **Face to Face Films** in association with Anthony M Laura and Casey Hartnett
- Play by David Hare based on the novel by Michael Cunningham
- Directed by Anthony M. Laura
- Press: Jay Michaels Arts & Entertainment

THE CAST

- Virginia Wolff: Casey Hartnett
- Leonard Wolff: Gabe Calleja
- Vanessa Bell: Kristen Hasty
- Laura Brown: Samantha Yestrebsky
- Nellie/Mrs. Latch/Barbara: Candy Dato
- Richie (young Richard): Andrew Rosenbloom
- Richard: Alex Commito
- Clarissa Vaughn: Vivien Cardone
- Sally Lester: Rand Faris
- Kitty: Cebi Stough
- Louis Waters: Jose Duran
- Julia Vaughn: Amanda Kristin Cox
- Dan Brown: Henry Priest Miller
- Angelica Bell: Alexandra Rooney
- Narrator: Sofia Licata

BACKGROUND

Virginia Wolff's mental illness has been discussed many times. From all appearances, it appears to have been schizophrenia. Delusions, hallucinations, and inconsistent behavior — not to mention three suicide attempts, the last one having succeeded — are all symptoms she displayed during her lifetime. From everything we know, she was certainly difficult to deal with, in spite of the efforts of her husband, Leonard, who did everything he could at the time to assuage her frustration and depression.

In spite of this, she is considered one of the most important writers of the 20th Century, a feminist icon embraced by generations of women since the resurrection of her reputation in the 1960s.

THE PLAY

David Hare's *The Hours* examine the lives of three women linked by Wolff's 1925 novel, *Mrs Dalloway*. In carefully integrated segments, we see Virginia, in 1920s England, struggling with depression and mental illness as she finishes the novel in question; Laura Brown, a 1950s housewife, pregnant and unhappy in her marriage; and Clarissa Vaughan, preparing a party in 2001 for her friend, Richard (Laura Brown's now adult son, Richie), who is suffering from AIDS.

THE PERFORMANCE

The performances are consistently fine throughout, as one might expect from **Face-to-Face Films** after their superb rendering of John Patrick Shanley's *Doubt* in June (**https://bit.ly/HD_Doubt**). As Virginia, Casey Hartnett appears to be somewhat detached until one begins to appreciate the difficulty she faces playing a role as complicated as Virginia Wolff. Wolff's relationship with her husband, Leonard, well played by Gabe Calleja, is superbly written, reflecting the attitudes and concerns of a time when the basics of schizophrenia were not clearly understood, and there was virtually no way to treat it other than trying to apply "common sense," which, as we now know, is utterly futile. Both Ms. Hartnett and Mr. Calleja rise to the occasion, and their scenes together are stark and realistic.

Alex Commito, as Richard, was remarkable. Indeed, he is a remarkable talent. My colleague, William Cataldi, described his performance as Father Flynn in *Doubt* as "perfect," and I can imagine that it was. Richard is suffering from AIDS in 2001, a time when practically everyone who contracted that disease died horribly (something too many of us have forgotten as AIDS has become more and more manageable). His pain and despair were clearly evident in every word, and the resolution of his suffering at the end was heartbreaking. Kudos, Mr. Commito. We look forward to seeing more of you someday, hopefully, onstage.

Samantha Yestrebsky and Vivien Cardone, as Laura Brown and Clarissa Vaughn, were completely believable as women suffering from the feminist concerns that Virginia Wolff was, perhaps, the first to detail in *Mrs. Dalloway*. For Laura, they were almost fatal, for Clarissa, they led to confusion and guilt. Ms. Brown was particularly moving when she returned as an 80-year-old mother at the end of the play.

As Dan Brown, Laura's clueless husband, Henry Priest Miller was surprisingly sympathetic. His portrayal as a member of the World War II generation was almost poignant. He came back from the war expecting a certain sort of married life, and was totally perplexed when he was unable to find it. This was a considerable problem in the 1950s, when men were trying to regain the past after women had been given a taste of the future. Rosie the Riveter did not want to go back to the kitchen, which led to a conflict that has been developing ever since.

The supporting members of the cast were also quite engaging. Kristen Hasty as Vanessa Bell, Rand Faris as Sally Lester, Amanda Kristin Cox as Julia Vaughn, Cebi Stough as Kitty, and Jose Duran as Louis Waters, supported the principal characters with intelligence and skill. Candy Dato, the only member of the cast to play more than one role (Nellie, Mrs. Latch, and Barbara), moved easily from character to character, although her presentation was somewhat confused by the screen (Zoom) label that appeared as "Mrs. Latch" whenever she was onscreen.

And, finally, Andrew Rosenbloom as Richie and Alexandra Rooney as Angelica Bell, youngsters who do what children usually do in plays, steal scenes from the adults. Both read their lines with considerable charm. I'm sure they will have long careers if there are still onstage productions when they grow up.

THE PRODUCTION

Even in a theater, this is not an easy play to stage. There are many scene changes, time shifts, and complicated actions. It is a drama. It does not end happily. All of these are things are difficult to present onstage. On Zoom, some of them are almost impossible to visualize. The answer to this problem is to include a narration. In the Zoom world at the moment, the author's stage directions are generally spoken by another actor, sometimes appearing in a window, sometimes not. In this instance, Sofia Licata read the stage directions with intelligence and understanding. But, the narration itself, and the way it was presented, did not contribute to the flow of this otherwise excellent reading.

There is no reason *not* to rewrite the stage directions of a play. The lines are sacrosanct, the stage directions are not; they change with every new director. The first thing a director usually does when a work is presented onstage, is to rework the actions to suit his or her resources. As this pertains to *The Hours,* at least 80% of the narration is indicated in the dialogue and action. There is no reason to say "He blushed," or "She looked nervous" when these reactions are clear in the way the actors say their lines.

Nor is it necessary (or technically required) to put up a sign saying "Narrator" every time that person speaks. Too much of this production was interrupted by that and black screens with the character's names flashing on and off, sometimes making no sense at all. It caused inordinate delays in otherwise moving dialogue.

So, I would recommend that the narration be rewritten to make it shorter and succinct, including only those directions necessary to make sure the actions are clearly understood, and I would eliminate the black screens entirely, thus allowing the shortened narration to be read over the action. This can easily be done with the Zoom software, and it would have made an already excellent production really superb. Because of all that unnecessary stage direction, and those endless black screens, I have to give this play a **HAPPY FACE MINUS**.

PERFORMANCE INFORMATION

- Presented online live on August 1st, 2020
- https://www.facebook.com/FaceToFaceFilms/

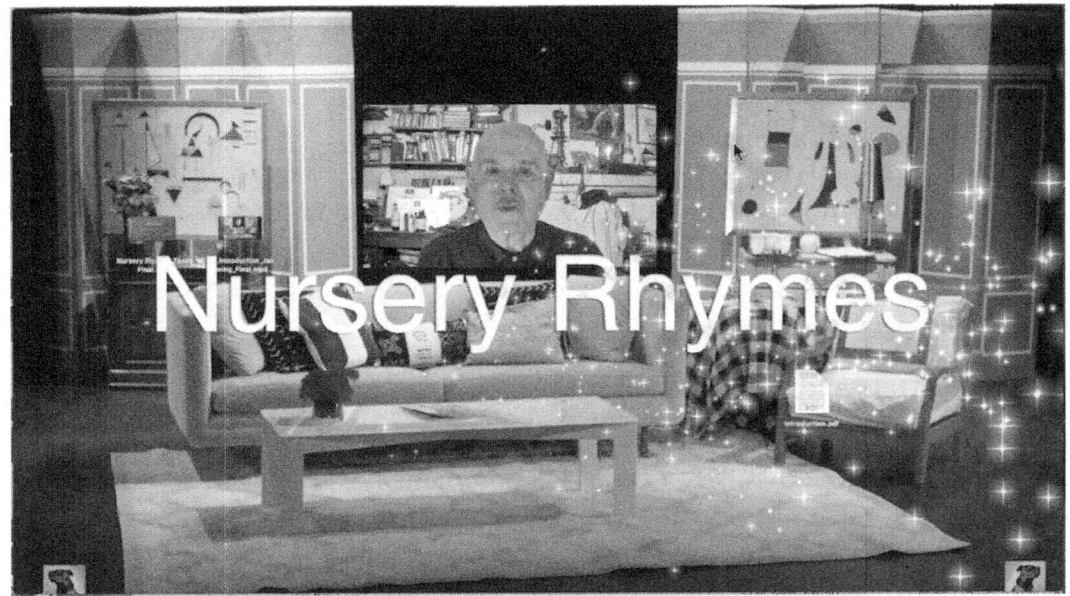

Jan Ewing / Nursery Rhymes

Nursery Rhymes
Reviewed for Arts Independent by Jen Bush

- Written & Directed by Jan Ewing
- Produced by Jan Ewing and Jay Michaels
- Set Design: Michael Mitchell
- Press: Jay Michaels Arts & Entertainment

CAST (in order of appearance)

- Irene Mangus: Colleen White
- Chip Mangus: Patrick Hamilton
- Marge Stevens: Kristyn Koczur*
- Frank Stevens: J Michael Baran

KIDDING AROUND

In *Nursery Rhymes,* Jill wants to go up the hill with Jack and do a lot more than fetch a pail of water. Mary wants to have a little lamb with Jack Sprat who eats no fat and is fitness obsessed. Irene and Chip are a couple in their mid to late thirties. Irene is a successful V.P. in advertising and Chip is a freelance writer working from home. Irene's biological clock and libido are out of control. She starts dropping some not so subtle hints around the house to encourage Chip toward parenthood. Chip is resistant. He's very happy to jog and do push-ups without a child underfoot and wonders why Irene wants a baby as opposed to an Equinox body. Unbeknownst to

Chip, Irene invites a couple in their 50's over for coffee and conversation. This was no social call. Marge and Frank were tasked with railroading Chip into fatherhood. After arguing about babies, birth control, money and the missionary position, the doorbell rings.

Marge and Frank have a twelve-year-old at home. They enter Chip and Irene's home bickering about leaving little Mikey alone. Marge appears disoriented and doesn't seem to know where she is. We find out that she's been hit hard by menopause. Chip is initially rude but the characters eventually find a way to discuss the very personal topic of parenthood.

THE PRODUCTION

Jan Ewing wrote, directed, and co-produced along with Jay Michaels a compelling and resonating piece that is accessible to all humans regardless of race, gender or sexual orientation. Unless the decision is made at the beginning of the union, all couples wrestle with when, how and where to bring an offspring into the world. Amid a lot of bickering and arguing among all four characters, there were some very funny and some very poignant moments.

This was a play presented on Zoom with a spot-on narration provided by Jan Ewing. It was executed so well that the viewer was able to concentrate on the content and forget they were seeing a play on Zoom. All the actors were well suited to their parts. Colleen White did a wonderful job bringing the baby obsessed, sex crazed Irene to life. She showed a wide range of emotion and did well with delivering humorous lines. Patrick Hamilton had good chemistry with Colleen White and gave the character of Chip some acerbic wit as well as effective humor. It is evident that he is a confident and experienced actor.

Kristyn Koczur gave an outstanding performance as Marge, who was struggling with menopause. Her character may have been forgetful, but her performance is hard to forget. She was funny one moment, and the next she was breaking your heart. J Michael Baran did a fine job as Marge's mercurial yet introspective husband Frank. He gave a very focused and even-keeled performance. His character was also the unassuming voice of reason in the show. If you are wondering if Chip and Irene decide to rock-a-bye baby, you'll have to see the show to find out.

PERFORMANCE INFORMATION
- First Streamed August 6th – 30th, 2020
- Still available on **JMC: Channel i** (jaymichaelsarts.com)
- Review first published by Jen Bush on
  https://artsindependent.wordpress.com/2021/01/26/kidding-around/

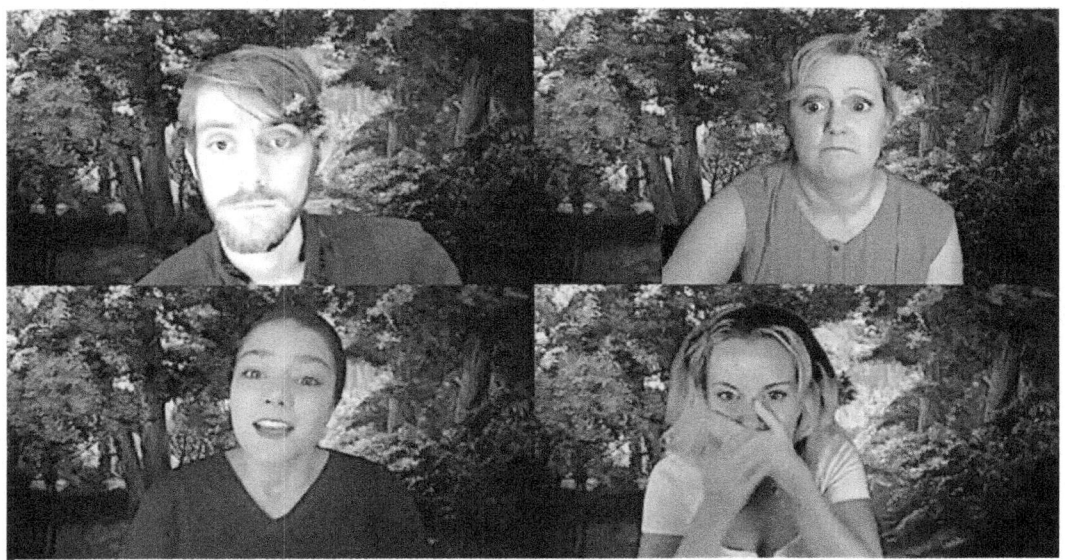

William Ketter, Erin Cronican, Weronika Helena Wozniak & Ellinor DiLorenzo

A Midsummer Night's Dream
Reviewed online live by William J. Cataldi August 30th, 2020

- A Zoom Production
- Play by William Shakespeare
- Presented by **The Seeing Place Theater**
- Producers: Erin Cronican* and Brandon Walker*
- Associate Producer — Outreach: William Ketter
- Executive Artistic Director: Erin Cronican*
- Co-Directors: Brandon Walker* and Erin Cronican*

CAST

- Theseus/Oberon: Brandon Walker*
- Hippolyta/Titania: Laura Clare Browne
- Egeus/Puck: Jon L. Peacock*
- Hermia/Snout/Cobweb: Ellinor DiLorenzo
- Lysander/Starvling/Moth: Weronika Helena Wozniak
- Demetrius/Flute/First Fairy: William Ketter
- Helena/Quince/Peaseblossom: Erin Cronican*
- Bottom/Second Fairy: Dan Mack

STAFF

- Original Music Composition: Randi Driscoll
- Stage Management: Shannon K. Formas

- House Managers: Robin Friend, Hailey Vest
- Graphic Design: Laura Clare Browne, Erin Cronican*
- Social Media Outreach: Weronika Helena Wozniak
- Digital Design: Ellinor DiLorenzo
- Marketing Support: Robin Friend
- Dramaturgy Program: Jon L. Peacock*
- Fundraising Support: Sandra Trullinger*, Olivia Hardin

The poet's eye, in fine frenzy rolling,
Doth glance from heaven to earth, from earth to heaven;
And as imagination bodies forth
The forms of things unknown, the poet's pen
Turns them to shapes and gives to airy nothing
A local habitation and a name.
— A Midsummer Night's Dream, Theseus, Act V, Scene 1

THE PLAY

My partner, Jan Ewing, reviewer at **HI! DRAMA** and the lead reviewer at **Ewing Reviewing**, remembered two recent productions by **The Seeing Place Theater** fondly: *The People vs. Antigone* (April/May 2018) and *Animal Farm* (February 2020). Those were both onstage productions, but **The Seeing Place Theater**'s Zoom production of *A Midsummer Night's Dream* this month makes it a cool trifecta. The two earlier shows stood out in Jan's mind so much, that he knew immediately what **The Seeing Place** was when *Midsummer Night's Dream* came up. I had high hopes, was looking forward to this show, and it far surpassed my expectations.

Egeus wants his daughter Hermia to marry Demetrius, but Hermia loves Lysander. King Theseus, preparing to marry his own bride, Hippolita, wants to please Egeus, so he orders Hermia to marry her father's choice or face death or a nunnery. Privately, Helena, Hermia's friend, offers to take Lysander and Hermia to a relative's house in another kingdom. They proceed into the forest, followed later by Demetrius, who has found out.

In the forest, Oberon and Titania, King and Queen of the Faeries, are squabbling about something or other. Oberon instructs his lead faerie, Puck, to acquire a flower, the juice of which will cause a sleeping person to fall instantly in love with the first creature they see upon awakening. Oberon tells Puck to squirt the juice onto Titania's sleeping eyes, and the "Athenian," meaning Demetrius, so that Demetrius will rekindle his love for Helena. Concurrently, a group of Athenian workers, practicing a play they plan to present at Theseus' and Hippolita's wedding, also get lost in the forest.

Soon folks fall asleep, and Puck, mistaking Lysander for Demetrius, squirts the love juice into Lysander's eyes, and also does so to the sleeping queen Titania. On a lark, he turns the most arrogant Athenian actor, Bottom's head into a donkey. When the rest of the cast of the pretend play see him, they scatter, and he wanders the forest aimlessly. Titania wakes and sees him first, and falls in love with the donkey-headed Bottom.

Meanwhile, Lysander wakes up to see Helena, who has found her friends asleep in the forest. Lysander renounces Hermia and declares his love for Helena. When Demetrius finds the other three, the four squabble. The two men are in love with Helena, with Hermia increasingly jealous. Finally, Oberon orders Puck to reverse all of the spells. Everyone stumbles out of the forest on the morning of Theseus' and Hippolita's wedding day. Theseus, having slept on it, reverses himself on Lysander's and Hermia's love, allowing them to marry, and everyone is basically happy. On the night of the weddings, the Athenian worker's put on their play. And Puck closes the play with a speech.

Shakespeare's play is irrational, self-consciously dreamlike, and full of a great affection for youthful, innocent, romantic love. We could probably fill a small office tower with individual books and papers on this play or partially about this play. So that's all I have to write about the playwright's work.

THE PRODUCTION

The Seeing Place's production brought this magical comedy to life with great depth and understanding. Billed as an LGBTQ-themed take, Lysander was played by a woman (Weronika Helena Wozniak), a few of the actors were non-binary (although they played their parts as written), and Puck seemed plainly queer (although aren't all faeries queer?). In fact, it seems as though Shakespeare's play is pretty queer-themed without any tinkering. It did not seem that **The Seeing Place** dug especially deep to present an LGBTQ slant.

That doesn't matter. The production gave us brilliant performances with out-standing digital effects and overall stellar direction. Not one of the eight actors came up short with their acting acumen, and notably, their awesome facility with the four hundred year old language. In almost all contemporary Shakespeare the-ater or film, at least one or some of the actors seem flat or stilted. But not here. All eight seemed to understand everything they were saying, and delivered their lines as if they were on a first name basis with The Bard. They also had such a deep understanding of the play, that they were able to communicate it to a twenty-first century audience easily. I just want to point out, that a late sixteenth century play about ancient Athens made itself at home in New York City in 2020. The humanity of that astounds me.

I'd like to mention three of the actors especially, although again, all were excel-lent. Ellinor DiLorenzo, who played Hermia, et. al., had that little extra something. I found her performance fascinating, my eyes gravitated toward her. She appeared perpetually understated and casual, which for a Shakespeare play is really saying something. She had a charisma that transcended her slight Swedish accent. Second, Dan Mack, who played Bottom, et. al., played the egocentric actor brilliantly. We didn't like Bottom, while at the same time finding him comically charming.

Finally, Brandon Walker, who played Theseus and Oberon, rendered the two kings with power, sexiness, and regal grace. Every time they were on screen, they dominated the space. Even when they weren't speaking, my eyes gravitated toward their panel. I see they also co-directed this production, and wrote and co-directed *Animal Farm* for **The Seeing Place**, which I indicated above, Jan Ewing raved about. They are a theatrical powerhouse in their own right.

Traditionally, directing is a one-person job. That's because it's the director's job to bring words on a page to life. Theater made by committee usually looks like it was made by committee—weak. Brandon Walker and Erin Cronican must have a very special working relationship. They co-directed this production, and Animal Farm, mentioned above. The direction of both productions was sharp and focused. There was no sense that anything was a compromise. From the actors' gestures to the special effects to the rehearsals which must have involved endless hours of struggle to understand and communicate every word of this play, Walker and Cronican generated a beautiful, singular vision for the entire cast and crew.

In addition to the great direction, Walker and Cronican also designed amazing special effects for the show. In a given scene, everyone had the same background in their panel, dually designed by both directors; a palace in Act 1, Scene 1; a mythological forest when the lovers were bickering in the forest; etc. These backgrounds were perfectly chosen. And the faeries' visages were painted with filters, giving them colorful, otherworldly masks, that moved as the actors moved; brilliantly designed and executed by Erin Cronican.

That brings us to the development and future of Zoom productions in general. When I first began viewing Zoom work last Spring, the production values were primitive. Folks were hoping we'd go back to theaters soon. When that didn't happen (and now we're looking at January), scintillating things began to happen with Zoom productions. Creative energy went into making them always better. People experiment. The COVID crisis is actually an exciting time in theater. An entirely new art form is being devised, that, hopefully, will outlast the virus. Since I produced a Zoom production of a play myself, I know it costs very little cash. The great charm of the Zoom production is the charm of old-time radio plays. Brain scans of folks listening to radio are much brighter than folks watching TV. That's because one has to actively imagine a lot to enjoy radio. Television and film, as great as they can be, imagine everything for the viewer up front. Radio and theater require the viewer to fill in the blanks. Jan Ewing and I both hope Zoom is here to stay. We were all there when a great new artform was born.

The Seeing Place Theater's Zoom production of *A Midsummer Night's Dream* is perhaps the best Zoom work I've seen so far. We've gone from actors sitting around in T-shirts reading the script, to actors acting their parts with movements and sets and special effects. What a dream to spend a Sunday afternoon watching a full phalanx of brilliant actors performing Shakespeare in a setting that invited me to imagine a lot of the details. **The Seeing Place Theater** will undoubtedly continue to hold a special fascination for the Ewing-Cataldi household team of reviewers. **HAPPY FACE PLUS**

PERFORMANCE INFORMATION

- www.seeingplacetheater.com

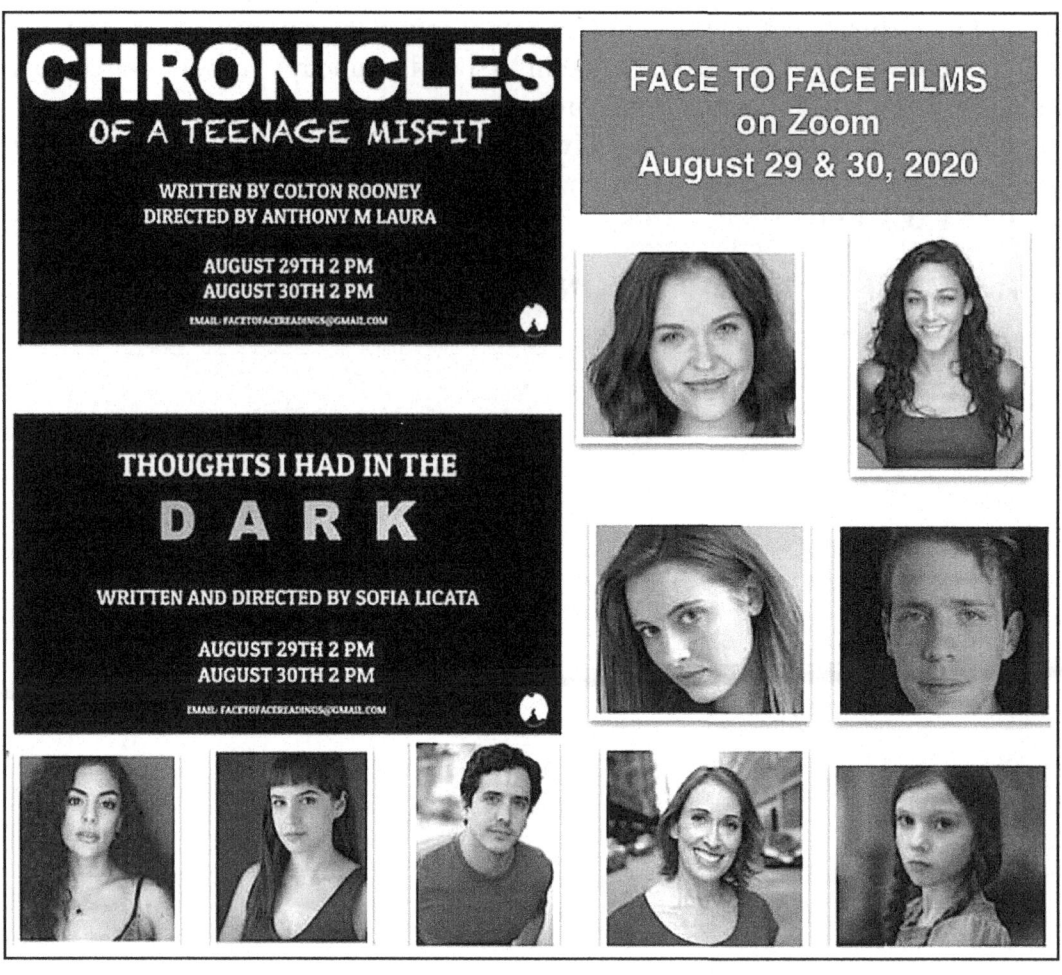

Two Original One-Act Plays
Reviewed online live August 30th, 2020

- Produced by **Face-to-Face Films**
- Press: Jay Michaels Arts & Entertainment

=========== CHRONICLES OF A TEENAGE MISFIT ===========

- Play by Colton Rooney
- Directed by Anthony M. Laura

THE CAST

- Arlo: Alex Commito
- Shelly: Rheanna Salazar

- Mother/Susan: Margie Foley
- Father/Frank: Jose Duran
- Claire: Alexandra Rooney
- Dr. Wright: Rand Faris

THE PLAY

Colton Rooney's *Chronicles of a Teenage Misfit* is a comprehensive look at the problems faced during adolescence. Since Mr. Rooney is actually an adolescent, we can be sure, for a change, that what we're hearing comes straight from a writer intimately involved in the process; alienation; the difficulties of communicating with parents who, we are convinced, cannot understand anything about us; sexual confusion, which inevitably affects us all, regardless of our ultimate sexual orientation. These are things *I* was worried about at his age and, since then, I have come to believe thay are almost universal concerns that affect us all.

Mr. Rooney has done a splendid job detailing the insecurities that can plague us as teenagers. Understanding what one is going through is very difficult when the world is new and we haven't yet developed the ability to weigh our reactions because we lack the analytical experience that can only come with age. When we're very young, we don't realize that, which sometimes makes what we're going through seem impossible to deal with. This is not to suggest that Arlo, skillfully played by Alex Commito, is not genuinely distressed. Teenage concerns can be devastating, frequently causing lasting harm when they are not recognized and dealt with.

Be that as it may, in most cases, understanding eventually comes and we move on. Teenage angst is seldom permanent, and, more importantly, not usually fatal. There are heart-breaking exceptions, of course, but, in Arlo's case, Mr. Rooney paints an optimistic picture. There seems to be hope at the end of his play, which I, personally, find extremely encouraging.

THE PERFORMANCE

Everyone in the cast did a fine job, with Jose Duran as Arlo's father, and Rheanna Salazar as the sympathetic Shelly being particularly effective. Indeed, the director, Anthony Laura, has assembled an excellent troupe. The **Face-to-Face** actors are skillful and committed. They consistently imbue their characters with charm and intelligence, not to mention that their agenda at the moment is extremely ambitious.

CONCLUSION

Mr. Rooney's dialogue is well written, engaging, and frequently moving. His narrative sense is already well developed, which suggests that his future work will be well worth a look. He provides a balanced picture of *all* of his characters, a surprisingly mature approach for a young playwright. Go to it, Mr. Rooney. You deserve a very **HAPPY FACE** all around.

============== **THOUGHTS I HAD IN THE DARK** ==============

- Written and Directed by Sofia Licata

THE CAST

- Diana: Samantha Yestrebsky
- Ariadne: Cebi Stough
- Pandora: Vivien Cardone

THE PLAY

Sofia Licata's reflective *Thoughts I Had in the Dark* is a series of monologues. They detail the alienation and emotional pain experienced by three middle-class women who have reached the point of despair. The level of that despair varies in each case. Diana and Pandora seem to be close to mental illness, while Ariadne appears at least slightly less desperate. The monologues are beautifully written, and delivered with great skill and intelligence. But, there is a sameness about them that makes listening to all three at one sitting a bit of a stretch.

All three women are suffering from loneliness and perceived rejection. They are bitter and estranged because of how "they" have treated them. It's never exactly clear who "they" are, which doesn't help to clarify their suffering. This is meant as a comment, not as a criticism. Ms. Licata is obviously a fine writer, with an excellent sense of dramatic style. If any one of these monologues were to be set into a comprehensive narrative, it would serve as a stunning tour de force for any lead actor. As stand-alone reflections, without back-stories to support them, they seem more like domestic complaints, but they are actually too well written for that.

THE PERFORMANCE

No reservations here. All three performers are first rate, and Zoom is almost designed for monologues. The dialogue is delivered with understanding, each character is unique and interesting, and, like most everyone in this fine company, they deal with the intricacies of playing to an audience that is two feet away and staring into their faces with aplomb. None of the actors in either one of these plays seemed to be reading. They were all acting, and that's one of the most positive things I can say about any Zoom performance.

So, in spite of my comments suggesting that these pieces would be more effective set into their own supporting narrative, I feel they were professionally presented and well conceived. Ms. Licata and her actors also deserve a **HAPPY FACE**.

PERFORMANCE INFORMATION

- Streamed twice on Zoom, August 29th & 30th, 2020
- https://www.facetofacefilms.net/

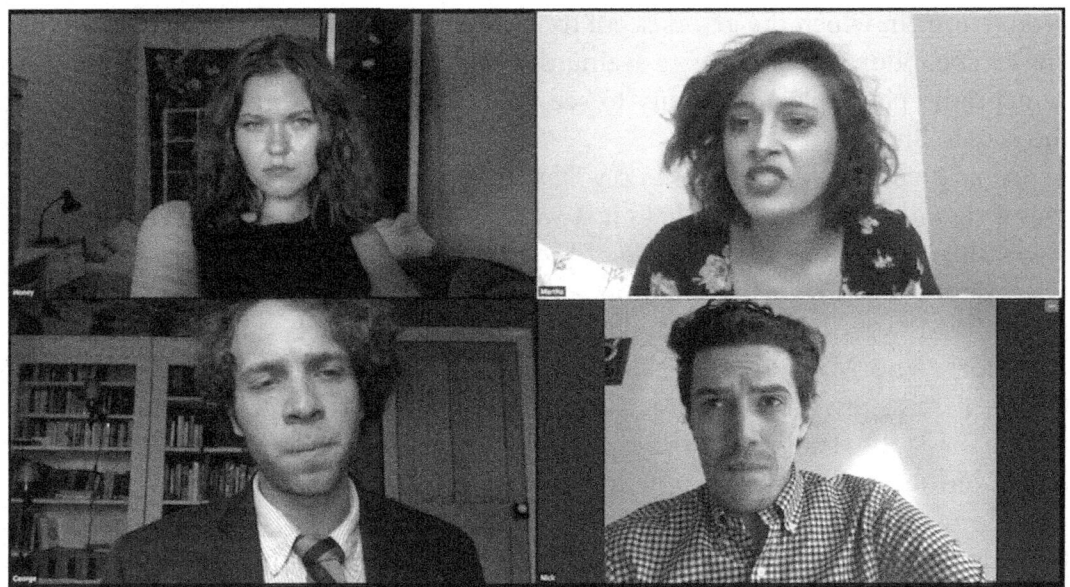

(L–R) Samantha Yestrebsky, Vivien Cardone, Alex Commito & Gabe Calleja

Who's Afraid of Virginia Woolf?
Reviewed online live by William J. Cataldi October 4th, 2020

- A Zoom Production
- Produced by **Face to Face Films**
- Playwright: Edward Albee
- Director: Anthony M. Laura
- Composer: Philip Lauto
- Press: Jay Michaels Arts & Entertainment

THE CAST

- Martha: Vivien Cardone
- George: Alex Commito
- Honey: Samantha Yestrebsky
- Nick: Gabe Calleja
- Narrator: Sofia Licata

THE PLAY

The best part about what Zoom productions have become is that the actors actually act. In the early days (last May and June), people got together for readings, read the script with little nuance, and most of the literature was left to the viewer's imagination. Since then, companies like **Face to Face Films** (featured here) or **The Seeing Place Theater** recognized the potential of Zoom technology and offered excellent productions in which the actors seem to know their lines, and are able to hold the viewer spellbound, as if we were seeing the play live on stage. It resembles professional radio plays, plus the ability to see the actors faces and torsos as they bring the play to life.

After giving us brilliant takes on *Doubt: A Parable* and *The Hours,* as well as *Two Original One-Act Plays* (that's just what **Ewing Reviewing** has seen), **Face to Face Films** brought us *Who's Afraid of Virginia Woolf?* at the beginning of October. My experience with this presentation resembled that of my experience with *Doubt: A Parable.* The acting was breathtaking. The production slick.

George and Martha, an old-line couple at a New England university, where George is Assistant Professor of History, come home at 2AM from a university party. Martha is the daughter of the college president, and, on instructions from her father, has invited another couple for drinks. Soon, twenty-somethings Nick and wife Honey arrive. They are taken aback by George's and Martha's hostile attitudes towards one another. The alcohol-fueled sparring goes on until dawn.

One telling way Edward Albee's masterpiece reveals itself is the fact that "George and Martha" recall the most famous couple in American History: George and Martha Washington. I mention this only because when I've pointed that out to a number of well-read people in the past, they hadn't made the connection. The fact suggests that once peaceful, loving Americans had devolved into warring factions that infect and destroy everyone they encounter. Little did Edward Albee know, in 1962, what our public life would become by 2020.

THE PRESENTATION

When I saw that fairly young actors would be playing the late-forty-somethings George and Martha, I wondered how this would go. Can young people know what it's like to be nearing fifty? Can they know what it's like to be bitter and angry at life? Vivien Cardone and Alex Commito, as Martha and George respectively, seemed to understand implicitly. I should get over being surprised by young people's acting acumen, since, as I am told: It's called "acting." Nevertheless, both actors seemed to be able to plumb the depths of George's and Martha's souls, which are somewhat tangled and damaged by a life that didn't go their way. I have seen both Ms. Cardone and Mr. Commito in *Doubt: A Parable,* where they were brilliant. Those weren't one-off, accidental performances. Their ability to take on radically different characterizations for this Albee play is a testament to their versatility. Clearly, these actors have a sophistication that will propel them far, if we ever get back to live theater. I love their Zoom personas, but Zoom will never give them the recognition they deserve. Their performances lacked nothing.

Samantha Yestrebsky as Honey had all the requisite shallowness and her own indicators of mental illness. Her role is the least consequential; she serves as a vehicle to reflect on the other three characters. Nonetheless, Ms. Yestrebsky did a great job doing that. Gabe Calleja as Nick is also a cypher of sorts (the play revolves around George's and Martha's marriage), but he interacts more consequentially with the central couple than Honey does. Mr. Calleja sported just as much professionalism and verve as all the others, but he may have been distractingly miscast as Nick. Now, this might just be my own prejudices coming to play, as well as my memory of George Segal in the role in the famous 1966 film. Mr. Calleja just didn't seem like a biology professor at a New England university. There's no reason to type cast, but if a production team isn't going to type cast, it creates aesthetic problems that potentially existed here. Whatever the case, all four actors surprised me with their command of the play's themes, rooted as they are in another era.

The Zoom presentation went without any technological glitches. The narration was kept to a minimum, which is always good. The viewer can imagine sets and interactions without very much help from superfluous narration. This production exceeded my expectations, and I am aware of the high quality of **Face to Face Films**' work this season. While I am eager to return to live theater, I sincerely hope **Face to Face Films** will continue creating Zoom productions beyond COVID. It's a new artform, created out of necessity, that deserves to be permanently ensconced in American art. **HAPPY FACE PLUS**

PERFORMANCE INFORMATION

- Streamed twice on Zoom, October 3rd & 4th, 2020
- https://www.facetofacefilms.net/

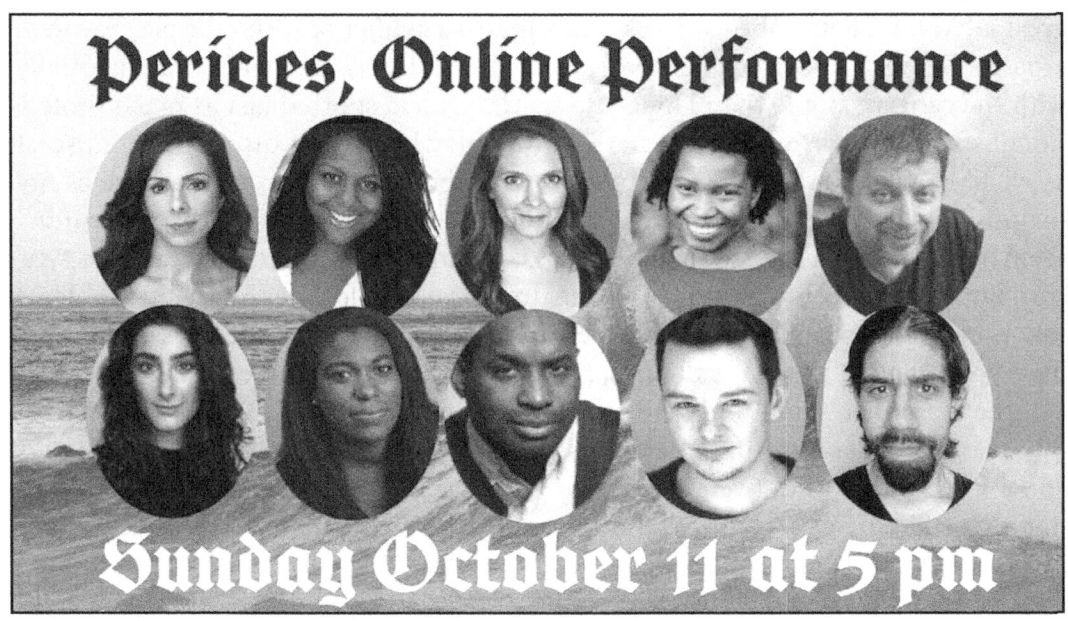

Pericles: Prince of Tyre
Reviewed onlive live October 11th, 2020

- Play by William Shakespeare and George Wilkins
- Produced by **Shakespeare Sports**
- Directed by Carrie Isaacman
- Press: Jay Michaels Arts & Entertainment

THE CAST

- Gower, Philemon: Nettie Chickering
- Pericles: Michael Hagins
- Thaliard, Leojnine, Pandar: Kristoffer Infante
- Fisherman, Pirate, King Simonides, Ceremon: Megan Khaziran
- Knight, Pirate, Cleon, Lysimachus: Dave Marr
- Fisherman, Lychorida, Bawd: Kitty Mortland
- Helecanus, Dionyza, Diana: Diana Nam
- Daughter, Thaisa: Mary J. Price
- Marina: Stepahany Slade
- King Antiochus, Escanes, Knight, Pirate, Bolt: Roger Stude

BACKGROUND (paraphrased from Wikipedia)

Pericles, Prince of Tyre is a Jacobean play written at least partly by William Shakespeare and included in modern editions of his collected works despite questions over its authorship (it was *not* included in the First Folio). While various arguments support that Shakespeare is the sole author of the play (notably DelVecchio and Hammond's Cambridge edition), modern editors generally agree that Shakespeare wrote the last half of the play, and that the first two acts, detailing the many voyages of Pericles, were written by a collaborator, which strong evidence suggests to have been the dramatist George Wilkins.

Shakespeare is difficult to perform on Zoom. The plays are complicated, long, and rife with arcane references. The poetry is exquisite, but it is sometimes difficult for modern audiences to appreciate. Pericles, Prince of Tyre is one of those plays. Written in rhymed verse, it is thought of as Shakespeare's first romance, even though it was actually written during what is considered to be the final period of his career.

THE PLAY

The play begins in the court of King Antiochus of Syria, where Pericles has entered a contest for the hand of the King's daughter. As is common in such fables, if he fails to answer an "impossible" riddle correctly, he will die. As one might expect, he does solve the riddle, which reveals an incestuous relationship between King Antiochus and his daughter. Enraged, the king sentences Pericles to death, causing him to flee back to Tyre. But, Antiochus is determined to see him dead, so he sends the assassin Thaliard to Tyre to carry out his sentence.

Back in Tyre, Pericles is advised by his friend, Lord Helecanus, to go abroad in order to avoid King Antiochus' retribution. As a result, Pericles embarks on a series of sea voyages which include his saving Tarsus from famine, and being shipwrecked in a strange land where he is honored by King Simonides, enters a jousting contest, and wins the hand of Simonides' daughter, Thaisa. After living happily with her for several months, and siring a daughter named Marina, Pericles learns that King Antiochus is dead, and sets sail with his new family for home. On the way, as the result of another shipwreck (another device frequently used by Elizabethan Theater, as is the "contest" for a Princess' hand), Pericles is separated from his family and thinks them dead. Fifteen years later, he discovers he was mistaken, finds his daughter, and reunites with his wife. Thus, the play ends happily.

THE PERFORMANCE

Director Carrie Isaacman, the founder of **Shakespeare Sports** is to be commended for taking on this complicated play. My understanding is that this work, as is the Hamlet they performed online in June, is intended to be done onstage next year. We all hope that will happen, as the "scroll" acting style they espouse is quite interesting and best experienced when one can see it happening.

The cast was committed and well prepared. Each actor had his or her moment, although, as might be expected, they varied somewhat in their expertise with the language from superb to just acceptable. But, I didn't find this to be a problem. This was a reading, after all. The poetry was clearly and intelligently presented, and Shakesperean English is something all actors must master as they develop. Kudos to everyone in this cast for taking on the challenge.

As Gower, the narrator who opens and closes the play, Nettie Chickering was particularly effective. She has a lovely speaking voice and read with great charm. Michael Hagins, who played Pericles, was appropriately strong and masculine, while Diana Nam moved easily between Lord Helecanus, Dionyza of Tarsus, and the goddess Diana.

Indeed, everyone in the cast except Mr. Hagins and Stepahany Slade, who played Pericles' daughter, Marina, with great sympathy, successfully negotiated multiple roles (see above). Roger Stude played King Antiochus with sharp humor, and was a real treat as he used clever props and costumes to play four other parts. As King Antiochus' daughter and Thaisa, Pericles' wife, Mary J. Price was gentle and retiring, while Kristoffer Infante presented the assassin Thaliard as a dark, looming presence. He has a remarkable speaking voice, and his reading of the Elizabethan dialogue was, perhaps, the most effective in the play.

Dave Marr, as Cleon of Tarsus, showed considerable promise, moving intelligently between several diverse roles, while Megan Khaziran and Kitty Mortland were great fun to watch, delineating their characters with shrewd insight and delightfully energetic humor.

CONCLUSION

The Zoom work was a bit confusing at times. The characters' names appeared in their windows whenever they spoke, but they didn't always change in sync with the actors' different roles. At first, I thought there were two princesses in the play named Thaisa, until I realized that Ms. Price, who played both, was incorrectly identified by that name when she first appeared as King Antiochus' (nameless) daughter. But, that's a small thing. Errors of that sort are almost inevitable when readings are presented *live* using a new technology we're all learning about. Given all the positive elements in *Pericles, Prince of Tyre,* I think Ms. Isaacman and her company have earned a very **HAPPY FACE** for their efforts.

PERFORMANCE INFORMATION
- Performed online live October 11, 2020
- https://www.shakespearesportstheatrecompany.com/

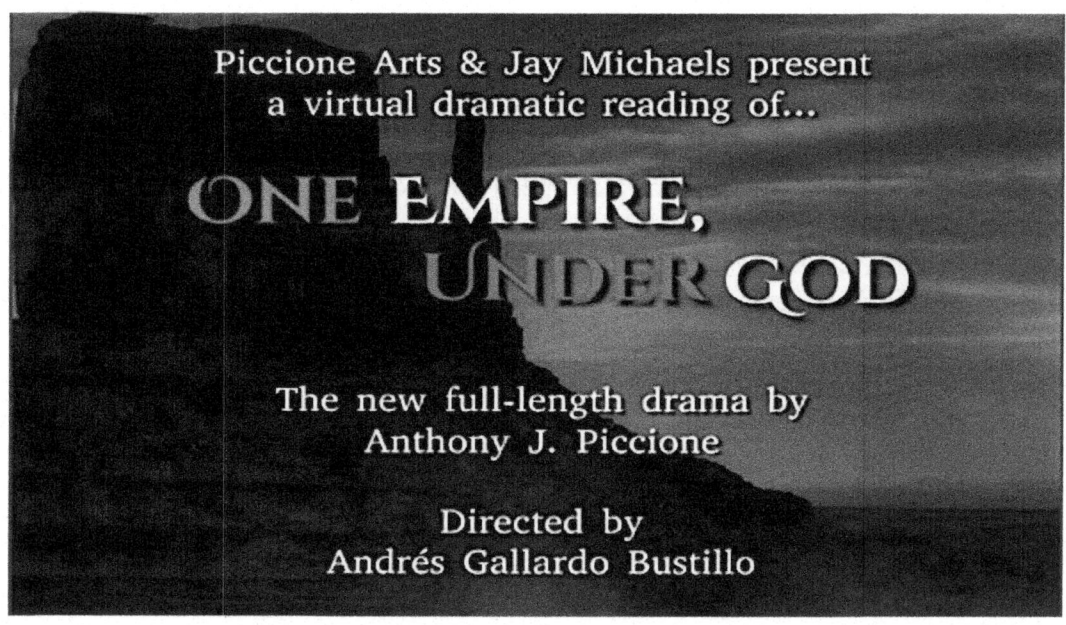

Piccione Arts & Jay Michaels present a virtual dramatic reading of...

ONE EMPIRE, UNDER GOD

The new full-length drama by Anthony J. Piccione

Directed by Andrés Gallardo Bustillo

One Empire, Under God
Reviewed online live by William J. Cataldi October 16th, 2020

- A Zoom Reading
- Playwright/Producer: Anthony J. Piccione
- Director: Andrés Gallardo Bustillo
- Assistant Director/Stage Manager: Charlotte J. Bradshaw
- Production Assistant: Hannah Cohen
- Co-Producer/Press: Jay Michaels Arts & Entertainment

THE CAST
- Damian Cunningham: Matthew Hagen
- Reverand Ian MacDougal: Marc Verzatt
- Jessa Barclay: Emily Brady
- Josh Garcia: Luke Hodgson
- Joshua Cunningham: John Blaylock
- President Darren Cunningham: Eric James Dino
- General River Kalvin J'Quay: Lamonte Gibbs
- President Armani Bakali: Raluca Georgianna
- Vice President Zaine Thompson: Lisa Boyett
- Senator Jane Harvey: Ellen Williams
- Ensemble: Louise Heller, Andrew J. Koehler, Beatrice Manfredi, Bill McAndrews, Sarah Nowik

THE PLAY AND THE PERFORMANCE

I have never seen anything by Anthony Piccione before *One Empire, Under God.* My partner saw and reviewed *A Therapy Session with Myself* quite a while ago. We discussed it thoroughly at the time, and it has become a staple in our household. It comes up now and again. That alone tells you how intriguing Piccione is as a playwright.

One Empire, Under God is a polished play about political theory. Specifically, it explores a fairly generic case of a fascist government coming to power and running the world. It offers details about the kinds of people and events involved in that "coming to power," and about predictable structures that come to exist in that "running of the world." It is anti-fascist.

It is also anti-religious. The fascists in this case are Christian Evangelicals. Piccione leaves zero doubt that he considers toxic religiosity to be dangerous, and probably all religion to be bunk. The heroes in this play, if there are any, are the secular humanists. The problem for Piccione is that humanism developed out of Christianity, between the Renaissance and the French Revolution, not independently of Christianity. Piccione suggests that religion has nothing of any value, which resembles Oedipus killing his father. Nevertheless, obviously Protestants in the United States have supplied a lot of fascist insurgence. Piccione is not wrong.

The Zoom technique excelled. Images, usually ominous, with quotes from important figures flashed on the screen frequently. They were accompanied by snippets of news reports which propelled the story. For our moment in the development of Zoom techniques, the values were excellent. Their virtues complemented the thorough and intelligent script. On the other hand, the acting was uniformly uninspired. Perhaps that had a lot to do with the material. The characters exhibited psychological shallowness because they are properly seen as ideals, or pieces in a grand political chess game. In order for Piccione to have time to elaborate on the grand politics, little time is left to explore the complexities on the ground. That's Piccione's choice, and what he does he does very well.

Indeed, this is a review about a play — not a performance. Piccione draws his science fiction directly from our headlines. It's a play about a specific political theory. The only drawback remains the fact that the ideas explored are unripe. This does not mean "shallow." It means that political science can only offer us a narrow field of tools to use to analyse a situation. Other considerations, like psychological or literary ones, get sidelined. For example, Damien Cunningham, hero of the first act, and driving force behind the fascist takeover of the United States, reveals in passing that he was once an alcoholic. What happens in an ex-alcoholic's head to turn him into a fascist? The detail goes nowhere. So Piccione's analysis comes from a narrow perspective. Isn't it only a matter of time before the revolution turns into the oppressor? What kind of person, with what kinds of thinking, becomes a fascist? Becomes a revolutionary? In order for Piccione's analysis to ripen, he needs to explore these kinds of questions too. He will undoubtedly do that, since, from what I can tell, he's come miles in a very short time. He is ambitious and confident, and he will no doubt continue to be a factor in Off-Broadway theater.

Not long after Damien begins his radio show, discussion between Damien and his priest devolves into the assertion that they're doing God's will. God's will is not a reason to do anything. If you hear people talking this way, run in the other direction. God is love. The reason to do anything and everything is that love requires it of us. God is a signpost, love is the destination. **HAPPY FACE**

PERFORMANCE INFORMATION

- Performed Live on Zoom October 16th @ 7pm
- YouTube: https://youtu.be/ml5woNra6uw

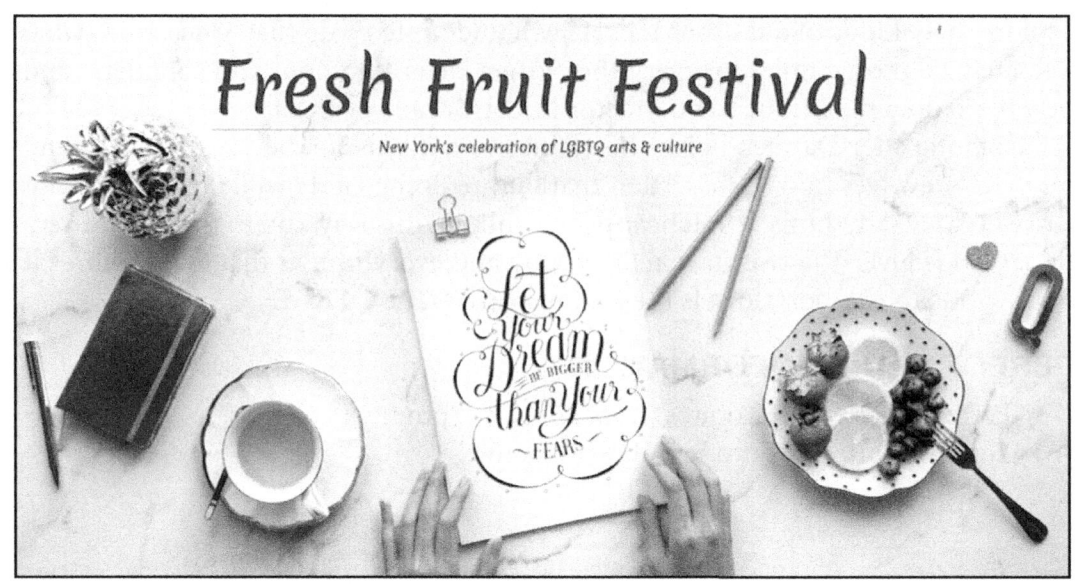

LGBTQ Monologues Project 2020
Reviewed online by William J. Cataldi October 22nd, 2020

- A video project in October 2020
- Produced by **Fresh Fruit Festival**
- Curated by Rachel Kara Perez
- Artistic Director: Dennis Corsi
- Executive Director: Louis Lopardi
- Press: Jay Michaels Arts & Entertainment
- Playwright: Various
  - *ado (a remix of my name):* olaiya olayemi
  - *Christmas Cantata:* Craig Winberry
  - *How Cold is the Snow:* Nathaniel Foster
  - *Nigel, Guys, and Dolls:* Doug DeVita
  - *One Night in Lisbon:* Manuel Igrejas
  - *Red or White:* Rachel Herron
  - *Stay as Long as You Like:* Sebastian Timpe
  - *Uncovered:* Sydney Haas
- Directors: Various:
  - *ado (a remix of my name):* an Chen
  - *Christmas Cantata:* Craig Winberry
  - *How Cold is the Snow:* Carly Nazaryk
  - *Nigel, Guys, and Dolls:* Jay Michaels
  - *One Night in Lisbon:* Cheryl Katz

- *Red or White:* Rachel Herron
- *Stay as Long as You Like:* Alex Mayben
- *Uncovered:* Jasmine Ritter
- Titles and Performers
  - *ado (a remix of my name):* olaiya olayemi
  - *Christmas Cantata:* Craig Winberry
  - *How Cold is the Snow:* Nathaniel Foster
  - *Nigel, Guys, and Dolls:* Joe Moe
  - *One Night in Lisbon:* Gary Martins
  - *Red or White:* Rachel Herron
  - *Stay as Long as You Like:* Alex Mayben
  - *Uncovered:* Becca Silva

MONOLOGUES PROJECT 2020

I love monologues. I love speeches in plays and film; I love soliloquies; I love story narration. As a young man, I happened upon videos of Spalding Grey's *Monster in a Box* and *Swimming to Cambodia.* I was transfixed for what seemed like hours. Marlon Brando's Pipe Speech in *Last Tango in Paris* blows my mind every time I see it. Frannie Liebowitz' *Public Speaking* (A film by Martin Scorcese) makes me shudder, it's so good. These are just a few relatively contemporary examples of an exciting art form.

Notice how hard it is to truly empathize with a character in a big musical. What's exciting is the ensemble. Then there are plays with four characters, like *Long Days Journey into Night.* At almost four hours, O'Neill has plenty of time to explore all four characters. It's an intense psychological drama. Finally, there are monologues. Here, the work focuses exclusively on one person. What's exciting is the miracle of dramatic empathy that the viewer can find with the single character and their story. Monologues are multi-dimensional. We have the story the character is telling. We're told how the character thinks and feels about the story, and how the character was transformed by the story … and we ideally have larger themes that the monologue explores by implication. If we're lucky, the narrow focus intensifies the power the monologue can have.

Fresh Fruit Festival, which specializes in LGBTQ theater and film from its home in New York City, sponsored their *Monologues Project 2020.* They opened to submissions of monologues on the theme of "The Ache for Home." They offered technical help and support to produce final video versions within an arbitrarily imposed limit of eight minutes. Eventually, they whittled their way down to eight submissions which they published, encouraging folks to vote for favorites. It was easy to see why these eight were chosen. All of them had something to be said on their behalf. I'm going to briefly discuss each one in turn, saving two stand-outs for last.

THE VIDEOS

ado (a remix of my name) by olaiya olayemi poetically surveyed a visit to her Mississippi home by a young, black, trans-woman. The writer dancing on a beach in a white tunic with symbolic props accompanied the reading of the poem. The poetry is intelligent, wise and stirring, but there were no surprises here.

Christmas Cantata by Craig Winberry told the story of a pubescent boy who stole the fire beneath his mother's participation in a community Christmas pageant. The story was interesting for a lot of reasons, but I couldn't get behind it, because of the editing. The team filmed every sentence or two separately, and then strung them together. In my humble view, this was a disasterious choice. I didn't care about the story, because the editing was so disjointed.

Nigel, Guys, and Dolls by Doug DeVita, performed by Joe Moe (the character is now 50), tells the story of his home life as a youth. The film has creepy overtones, and a disagreeable twist, that makes this one of the most impactful of the eight submissions. In fact, this piece has the most cinematic overarching theme of any of the videos. Jay Michaels, the director, specializes in art-house horror technique, and it showed.

One Night in Lisbon by Manuel Igrejas, performed by Gary Martin, describes a trip to Lisbon, won by a gay, restaurant supply salesman from New Jersey. Igrejas' writing is compelling, but as is the case with many monologues, the performer and the virtues of the writing must match. Unfortunately, Mr. Martin didn't do that. (I have seen monologues in which the performer exceeded the script. That's disappointing in a different way.)

Uncovered by Sydney Haas, performed by Becca Silva was one of two New York transplant stories. She tells the story of how her coming to see her adoptive home in the city, where she can be open and free, will have to supplant the home of her youth. I enjoyed the heavy emphasis on metaphor. (To me, metaphor is everything). Haas' technique is underdeveloped, but she uses metaphor profusely in this piece. That's significant.

Stay as Long as You Like by Sebastian Timpe, performed by Alex Mayben, describes a change of heart in a young man, when his buddy moves in with him. At first, he doesn't want a partnership. It's tender and sweet, and an extremely tight monologue. I shed a tear at the end. Unfortunately, Mayben seemed out of breath during the first half. Why? I cannot figure that out. Whatever the reason, it was ineffective and led to lack of enunciation and crashing words. An actor can speak casually and clearly.

As art goes, the next two entries were the most fully-formed and even jaw-dropping.

Red or White by Rachel Herron is the bar musings of a young, bisexual woman, who has been studying wine and has become a young connoisseur. Her comparison of bisexuality to wine drinking, in which folks like white or red depending on the situation struck me as obvious—yet I'd never heard it before. It was a conversational stroke of genius. Herron's acting was marvelous. It felt like we were really having drinks at an upscale bar in Manhattan. Herron had conviction, skill. The video was a beautiful aesthetic confection, that had a simple point, and didn't color outside the lines. The art had magnificent economy.

How Cold is the Snow by Nathaniel Foster is near perfection. It involves a pay-phone phone call by a young man in New York, back home to his mother. That's all. Again we have a piece with extraordinary focus and economy. Foster acts beautifully. The directing is fine except for a moment when the boom comes into the frame. It's good that happened, because the piece would have broken my heart otherwise. The boy has no money; no place to stay, yet; and no job, yet. Still, New York is the most exciting thing he's ever experienced. This is the jaw-dropping piece of the collection. It moved me to tears.

CONCLUSION

Fresh Fruit Festival has yet another interesting accomplishment under its belt. The videos can be seen until November 1. Audience choices for best video will be posted November 2. The videos take about an hour to watch. It's well worth a look. **HAPPY FACE**

PERFORMANCE INFORMATION

- http://www.freshfruitfestival.com/

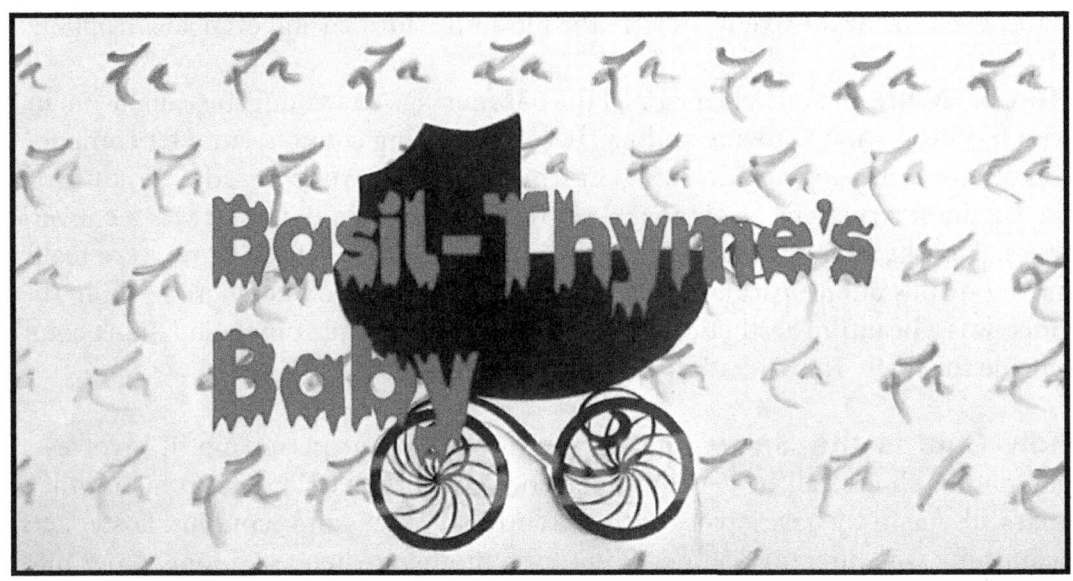

Basil-Thyme's Baby
Reviewed online live October 26th, 2020

- Written, Directed & Presented by the **Bargain Basement Players**
- Editing by Colleen White

THE CAST
- Basil-Thyme: Eben Moore
- Grant Wooden: Colleen White
- Sadie Satani: Kirby Cernosek
- Samwell Satani: Brendt Reil
- Voice Overs: Joshua Miles Fetner, Maria Mallardi Stewart, Trevor Van Uden

BACKGROUND

The number of theatrical events being produced online has increased exponentially since the world stopped at the beginning of March. Suddenly, a sea of actors, musicians, dancers, directors, and writers were out of work and bereft of attention, something vitally necessary when one is building a performing career. Thank God, there was an alternative. The Zoom software, originally intended to allow for online business meetings, offered a readily available medium for viewing at a distance. Indeed, what would we have done during the Pandemic without it?

Almost immediately, artists of all sorts took advantage of this technology and began turning out remarkable works of art, taking advantage of its limitations to conceive and build fantastic and fantastical structures totally unique in the way they are presented and perceived. During the past seven months, I've seen Zoom plays, musicals, operas, ballets, and films get better and better; some adapted from existing works, more and more conceived specifically for this new medium.

THE PLAY

So, it was no surprise when I almost accidentally came across an absolute gem. *Basil-Thyme's Baby* from the **Bargain Basement Players**, offered as a Halloween spectacular, is a real stitch. Based on Roman Polanski's 1968 film, *Rosemary's Baby*, it's funny, intelligent, and beautifully put together. I haven't laughed so hard for months. For those who have been living in a cave since 1968, or, more likely, who weren't born yet, it concerns a young couple, Basil-Thyme and Grant Wooden, who rent an apartment in a building dominated by a coven of witches. Taking advantage of their innocence, an evil older couple, Sadie and Samwell Satani, manipulate the pair, resulting in Basil-Thyme being impregnated by Satan.

THE PERFORMANCE

Everyone in the cast made me laugh. As Basil-Thyme, Eben Moore was shy and petite. He and Colleen White, who played Grant, switched genders for their roles, and the result was hysterically funny. Both are fine actors, and their interactions were given a great deal of comedic depth by this simple device. Ms. White evidenced bluster and male bravado, while Mr. Moore was exquisitely fragile and more than delicate. As Sadie and Samwell, Kirby Cernosek and Brendt Reil were evil incarnate. Cackling and broadcasting hysterical laughter as they did their dire duty, they were intense and well focused. Once they turned Grant's professional ambitions to suit their needs, Basil-Thyme didn't have a chance.

THE PRODUCTION

This was one of the most cleverly thought-out Zoom productions I've seen. The music, secondary graphics, visual effects, and animations were all smooth and well-executed. The acting was first rate. The play was not done live, which many companies seem to think makes up for the fact that we can't see things onstage at the moment, but that's not always a good idea. Zoom, or something like it, is becoming an independent arts medium. For many reasons — that it's inexpensive and easily accessible being among them — Zoom is not going to go away once the Pandemic ends.

CONCLUSION

From what I can gather, it seems the **Bargain Basement Players** are a collective in the best sense of the word. Everyone worked on the script and everyone contributed to the execution. But, I believe Ms. White deserves some extra credit for her editing. She has a real talent there. Her manipulation of the Zoom images was imaginative and remarkably clever. For that, for the laughs, for the intelligent approach everyone in the play brought to this small Halloween treat, I'm delighted to say that Basil-Thyme's Baby deserves a **HAPPY FACE PLUS**. The link to this thirty-nine minute joy is listed below. Take a look. You won't regret it.

PERFORMANCE INFORMATION

- *View:* https://youtu.be/rqzH--8qKSg
- *Info:* www.thebbplayers.com

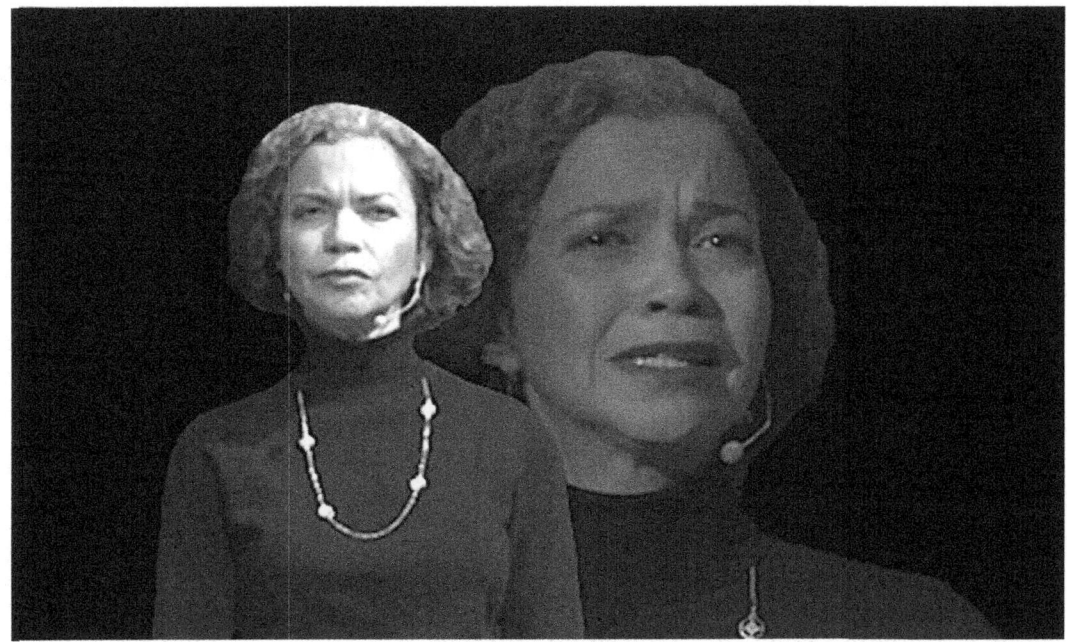

Roberta Gumbel

Driving While Black (DWB) An Opera
Reviewed online October 28th, 2020

- Presented by **Baruch Performing Arts Center** & **Opera Omaha**
- Video conceived by Ted Altschuler, Director **Baruch Performing Arts**
- Libretto by Roberta Gumbel
- Music by Susan Kander
- Directed by Chip Miller
- Developed at **University of Kansas School of Music**
- Filmed at **Lawrence Arts Center**, Lawrence, KS
- Audio: **The Post Haus**, Brock Babcock & P.J. Kelley;
  Oktaven Audio, Ryan Streber
- Video: **Four/Ten Media**, Kevin Eikenberg & Evan Chapman
- Press: Michelle Tabnick PR
- Photos courtsey of Susan Kander

CAST

- Roberta Gumbel: Soprano

MUSICIANS (New Morse Code)

- Cello: Hannah Collins
- Percussion: Michael Compitello

BACKGROUND

Racism is perhaps the most inflammatory subject in the United States. Wherever it's coming from, long standing prejudice or possible Russian manipulation of our social media, it has become clear that it's as big a problem as it always was, in spite of the progress we thought had been made since the passing of the Civil Rights Acts of 1964 and 1968. Like far too many people, I was under the impression that things had improved. Rights for blacks, Latinos, gays, and so many other social minorities seemed to be getting better.

Then, the Pandemic hit, and we all began to see what was actually going on. George Floyd, Breonna Taylor, Michael Brown; again and again, the murder of innocent African-Americans for no reason at all. Say what you will about the Pandemic, or that disaster in the White House, these things have made it obvious that the time has come. This must be stopped. It's as clear as day.

THE PLAY

Make no mistake, *Driving While Black* is an opera. Through-composed in the 21st-century academic style, it's a dazzling musical structure that requires trained musicians and psychological insight. The story of an African-American mother's journey, from the birth of her son to the day he drives off into a world rife with threats and violence, it's the story of every mother who has ever sent her son to war. The only difference being that this son is not traveling to a foreign country. He's driving to a mini-mart to buy milk.

The moving narrative of this work does not specify *where* the son is driving, just that he *is* driving. The mini-mart is my take on it. For many years, I've opined that the moment a child gets a driver's license must be one of the most frightening in a parent's life. Think how it must be for any mother who must deal with the threatening aspects so prevalent in modern day America. That is the subject of this brilliant musical work.

THE PERFORMANCE

Susan Kander's music is stunning; an intimate conversation between a soprano, a cellist and a percussionist. Michael Compitello, a true percussionist (as opposed to a mere drummer) was exceptional. A master of the xylophone, he used every percussion instrument at his disposal as the musical lines moved back and forth, adding his voice at key moments to emphasize and clarify the text. He and cellist, Hannah Collins, together, comprise a superb ensemble they call **New Morse Code**. Ms. Collins is equally as skilled and her vocal interjections were gently engaging while her cello, at times, brought me to tears.

Soprano Roberta Gumbel, who also collaborated on the music and text, was remarkable. Possessing a beautifully produced voice with a stunning range, her every word was clear and incredibly effective; the pain and worry she evidenced as she guided her son through the inevitable difficulties of growing up black in America were evident in every note. Her nuanced singing interacted with the other instruments with skill and enormous heart. When she had to let him go, it was heartbreaking; a first class performance in every way.

CONCLUSION

This is an opera and not for everyone. The music is dissonant and, therefore, requires thoughtful attention and intelligence. But, every minute is worth it. At forty minutes, DWB is the perfect length. Ms. Kander is a brilliant composer and Ms. Gumbel absolutely top notch. This work, both its performance and message demands a **HAPPY FACE PLUS**. See it if you can.

PERFORMANCE INFORMATION

- Information: https://bit.ly/BPACd

Through a Glass Darkly

Reviewed online live October 31st, 2020

- Play by Jenny Worton based on the screenplay by Ingmar Bergman
- Produced by **Face to Face Films**
- Director: Anthony M. Laura
- Press: Jay Michaels Arts & Entertainment

THE CAST

- Karin: Rand Faris
- Max: Dan Kelly
- David: Gabe Calleja
- Martine: Emily Tolnay
- Narrator: Sofia Licata

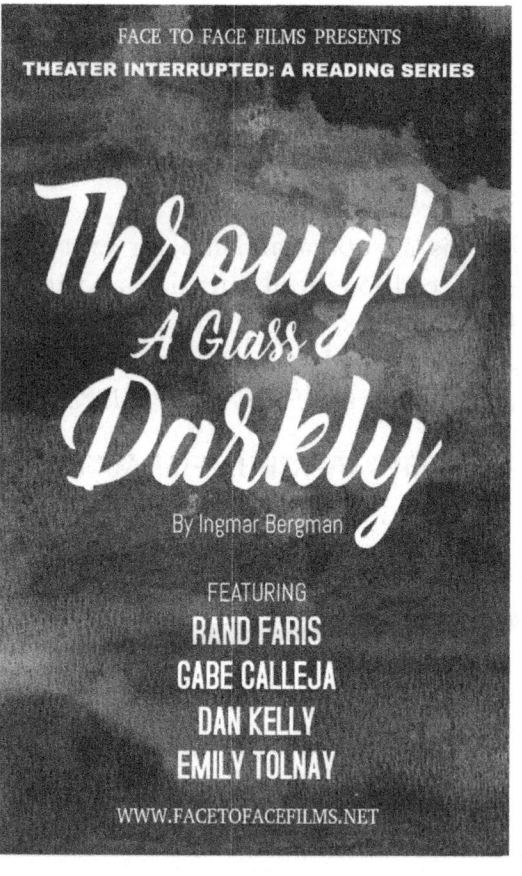

BACKGROUND

Mental illness and its treatment have changed a great deal since 1961 when Ingmar Bergman released his famed film *Through a Glass Darkly.* Back then, it seemed to most of us that all one had to do to was "get a grip" and everything would be fine. Mental afflictions were not often discussed, and there was a general feeling that those who sought psychological help were somehow "different." Librium, introduced by Hoffman-LaRoche in 1960, was one of the first medications developed to treat mental problems, but it was prescribed willy-nilly for practically everything and, along with Valium, which came soon after, it was widely abused, becoming a social problem that led to dependence and addiction. Since then, of course, as we have come to understand and appreciate the nature of mental illness, some excellent medications have been developed; Lithium and Resperidal immediately come to mind. As far as I can remember, however, I didn't even *hear* the term "bipolar" before 1992.

THE PLAY

Face to Face Films' reading of *Through a Glass Darkly* was based on Jenny Worton's English stage adaptation of Bergman's film. It chronicles a woman's descent into madness, the confusion of her spouse and brother, and the inability of her father to relate and offer aid. Set on a remote island at her family's cottage during what is intended as a rehabilitative vacation, Karin has just been released from a mental hospital. Her spouse, Martine, is extremely worried, as Karin cannot shake her depression and is suffering from hallucinations that seem to be getting worse. Her brother, Max, still a teenager, is going through problems of his own. His gender confusion is causing anxiety, and neither sister or brother is able to get help from their father, David, who is a published author so wrapped up in his own inadequacies that he is scarcely able to function.

THE PERFORMANCE

As we have come to expect, director Anthony Laura has done a fine job guiding his excellent actors through this complicated reading. Indeed, I found it to be more clearly defined and, thus, more engaging that I did Bergman's film. Admittedly, this version was read in English, while the film was presented in subtitled Swedish, and it's been many years since I saw it. Nonetheless, Mr. Laura's fine troupe read it with intelligence and understanding. Every moment of the narrative was beautifully defined and the progression of Karin's illness was sharp and focused.

Rand Faris, as Karin, moved flawlessly between sanity and madness. Every word was spoken with a clear understanding of the nature of bipolarity. As her spouse, Martine, Emily Tolnay gave a skillfully honed picture of the lack of understanding we all experienced when we first began dealing with the sort of symptoms Karin displayed. After trying every possible treatment available at the time, she lived in constant fear of Karin's relapse. As Max, Dan Kelly was the epitome of adolescent sexual confusion in a role written at a time when homosexuality was still considered an almost fatal aberration. All this while their father David, an aloof, troubled author unable to complete his great novel, was played by Gabe Calleja with narcissistic tendencies that made it next to impossible for him appreciate or adequately respond to his children's needs.

CONCLUSION

The **Face to Face Film** troupe is becoming extremely adept at presenting Zoom readings. They are one of the most persistent and active groups currently working online. Their readings are intelligent and nuanced, with well-delivered dialogue, intriguing characterizations, and meaningful narration offered by their colleague and playwright, Sofia Licata. Mr. Laura seems to have an uncanny ability to pick works that play well on Zoom. Everything I've seen so far has offered a clear glimpse into the depth of the piece involved. For that, and for the excellent take on Bergman's highly intellectual narrative, we give them another **HAPPY FACE**.

PERFORMANCE INFORMATION
- Performed live online October 31st, 2020 @ 7:30pm
- *Request access:* facetofacereadings@gmail.com

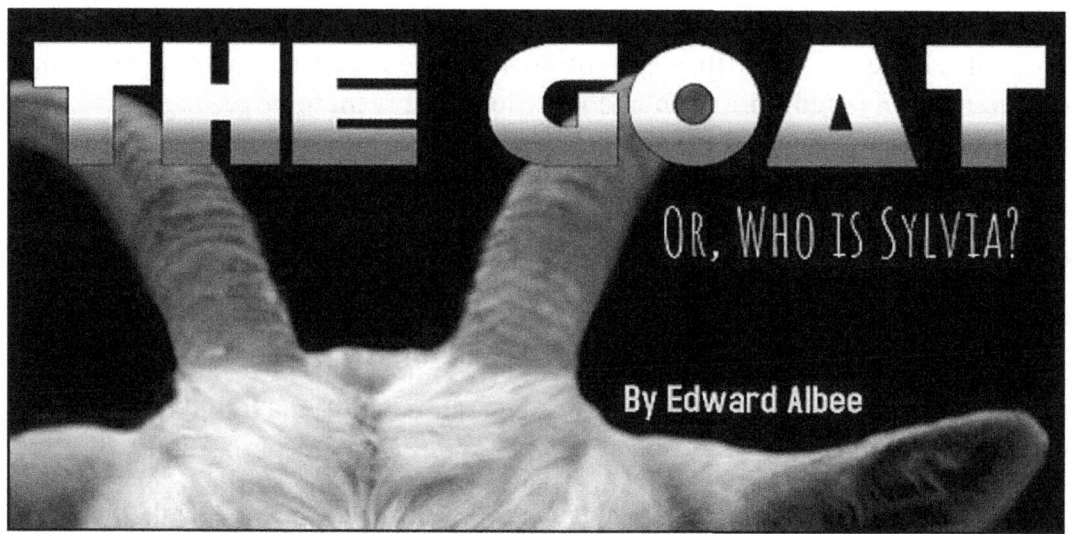

The Goat or, Who Is Sylvia?
Reviewed online live by William J. Cataldi November 1st, 2020

- Presented by **Face to Face Films**
- Playwright: Edward Albee
- Director: Anthony M. Laura
- Press: Jay Michaels Arts and Entertainment

THE CAST

- Martin: Alex Commito
- Stevie: Samantha Yestrebsky
- Ross: Jose Duran
- Billy: Tom Arrowsmith

THE PLAY

Jeffrey Dahmer seemed like an alien monster, who ate the internal organs of young gay men lured to his apartment for sex. As a homosexual man, being drugged or restrained by a serial killer after going to his apartment for sex remains one of the nightmares of urban lore. And it does happen — Jeffrey Dahmer was the real deal. Then, my partner and I watched a lengthy documentary about the man, which explored his history and mind in detail. It became clear to us that Dahmer was plagued by the same sexual compulsions we all are. The only difference being that our compulsions were for routine sex acts, while Dahmer's compulsions were for the consumption of human flesh. Our inclination to compassion made us sympathize with him. How awful it must be to feel that same compulsion that makes us need to engage in oral sex, for something so taboo, something that *must* be taboo — murder and cannibalism. Dahmer begged the judge never to let him out of prison. He knew his compulsion made him powerless, and he knew how much harm he had done. It turned out Dahmer had compassion too, and on the day he was murdered in prison, I wept.

In *The Goat or, Who Is Sylvia?*, Edward Albee explores the violation of a taboo, bestiality in this case, and the response of loved ones. Martin, an award-winning architect, reveals to his best friend, Ross, that he has encountered and fallen in love with a goat on a rural farm. Indeed, he's had sex with the goat, who he named "Sylvia." In a written letter, Ross reveals Martin's secret to his wife, Stevie, who subsequently confronts her husband about it in a lengthy, awesome scene, one of the finest Albee ever wrote. I won't reveal the ending, but except for doubtful sympathy from 17-year-old gay son Billy, Martin faces harsh condemnation from Stevie and Ross.

I have heard a case made against bestiality that the animal is a vulnerable being, who doesn't want the advances of a human being. My acquaintance argued that all bestiality is rape; rape is wrong; and therefore, bestiality is wrong. This argument, logical as it may be, never did persuade me. And, Albee ignores it too, since his play is not about that argument, but about the responses of people when someone in their midst is found to have violated a taboo. Albee wrote Martin with the utmost sympathy and compassion; he practically begs us to root for Martin, and that's definitely how Alex Commito played him. Ross responds with adolescent aspersions, but Stevie has a more complex row to hoe. Not only has her husband cheated on her in, as everyone admits, an otherwise faithful, strong marriage, but he has violated her entire moral framework, such that everything good about life has been utterly destroyed. The affair annihilated her.

My partner and I are not the loved ones of Jeffrey Dahmer or his victims. We don't know anyone involved in the story. So it's easier for us to have compassion and understanding. (Anglo-American law requires unaffected parties to serve on juries for this very reason). Stevie, however, does not see past her predicament, and how it affects her, to find any understanding for Martin's plight. She feels attacked, and she fights back. Martin is blindly her enemy. But, by watching this play, we become involved in the drama as bystanders, as potential jury members. I felt that it was too much to ask for Stevie to feel for Martin, despite Martin's trying his best to argue his case; but obviously I did.

Albee wrote this play in 2000. Had it been written in 1950, he would merely have had to change Sylvia from a goat to a human man, and the entire play could have remained intact. In 1950 people widely felt about homosexuality just like people today feel about bestiality — it crosses a line. Hence, the presence of Billy, Martin's and Stevie's teen-aged gay son, reminds the audience both of the unjust persecution of homosexuals for 1,400 years before Stonewall, and the fact that we need to approach violators of taboos like bestiality with caution, lest we engage in unjust persecution. This applies to BDSM, other forms of Leathersexuality, sex with minors, and even sexual killing like Jeffrey Dahmer. The play asks for more understanding for all violators of taboos, even if, in the end, we vote to send the violator to prison or worse.

THE READING

Face to Face Films has assembled a spectacular stable of actors for their numerous Zoom readings. Alex Commito has become a star of the company, and he works his magic portraying Martin here. Samantha Yestrebsky played Honey in *Who's Afraid of Virginia Wolff?* which did not provide an accurate picture of the depth of her acting. Here, she almost dominated Commito as Stevie. Both of these actors dug deep to comprehend their characters. They *became* their roles. They felt what Martin and Stevie were feeling. It's difficult for me to imagine what the dialogue looked like on Albee's page. The actors delivered the lines with a casual fierceness, no trace of recitation. Commito's and Yestrebsky's stellar performances reminded me that plays are meant to be seen (that's how the art comes alive), and not merely to be read.

Jose Duran as Ross, and Tom Arrowsmith as Billy, gave superlative supporting performances. Ross is something of a villain, and Duran captured his immature casuistry with every inflection. Arrowsmith had the smallest role, but he managed to depict a vulnerable, 17-year-old boy, who is losing his picture-perfect life through no fault of his own, beautifully. Anthony Laura, who directed this venture, and seems to be curator and artistic director of the company, can be proud of his accomplishments this year in the face of COVID. One thing is for sure, Laura has excellent taste.

CONCLUSION

Everyone involved in **Face to Face Films**' two Edward Albee readings reminded me that Albee is one of the finest playwrights America ever produced. He's won plenty of awards, and I am not saying anything controversial. He's able to suggest philosophical implications with dialogue, both what *is* said and what is *not* said. That effluence of intendence going on in an Albee play, often leaving questions open, makes his plays amongst the best of our age. **Face to Face Films** stood strong in capturing every nuance in Albee's writing, and they did so with *Doubt: A Parable,* I can attest. I've heard other productions were equal. **Face to Face Films** has taken advantage of the pandemic to make themselves a household name in our world. If you see a reading by this company, you can be sure it'll be excellent. **HAPPY FACE**

PRODUCTION INFORMATION

- Performed live online on Sunday, November 1, 2020 @ 2pm
- *Request access:* facetofacereadings@gmail.com

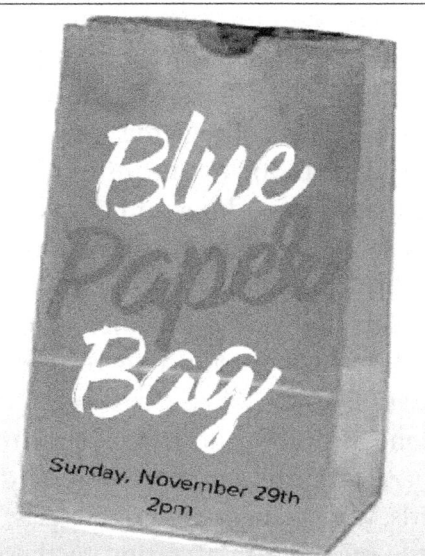

Blue Paper Bag

Reviewed online by William J. Cataldi November 29th, 2020

- Presented by **Face to Face Films**
- Playwright: Kristen Hasty
- Director: Anthony M. Laura
- Press: Jay Michaels Arts & Entertainment

THE CAST

- Mr. Aaron Morris: Gabe Calleja
- Gloria: Candy Dato
- Alice: Kristen Hasty
- Daisy: Alexandra Rooney
- Charlie (Charlotte): Rheanna Salazar
- B (Beatrice): Samantha Yestrebsky

THE PLAY

Alice, mother to young Daisy, lives with sisters B and Charlie, for whom she is guardian, in their parents' large home. Their father died too young, which sent their mother into alcoholism and ultimately mental illness. Alice, having succeeded with a book of poetry, struggles to write a second book, but she has been taking too long. Her editor, Gloria, begins to pressure her to finish and threatens to cancel her contract if she doesn't produce. When Charlie suffers from bullying in high school, Alice intervenes by contacting the very sane guidance councilor, Mr. Morris. The play gets its title from a blue paper bag Alice picked up off the street. The final poem in her book is to be about that bag.

Elsewhere I have written that one of the most important things a playwright must do is encourage the viewer to care about her characters. Usually, she can do this by introducing meaningful tension in the script. The tension doesn't have to be grand, like a king and a duke going toe-to-toe over control of a kingdom. An awesome thing about modern theater (theater of the last hundred years) is that it finds meaningful tension in the mundane, often in the psychological significances of daily life. Modern theater is democratic.

The only tension that resonated with me in the first hour and a half of *Blue Paper Bag* was Alice's frustration at not being able to finish her book. Frustration alone, however, did not capture this viewer's mind and make me care about the characters. The situations here, and the interactions between these four women and girls, were actually mundane. Why should we care? Playwright Kristen Hasty gives little meaningful attention to these women's feelings about the absent characters (father, mother, ex-boyfriend) until very late in the two hour production. Perhaps she tried, but I didn't find the attempts engaging enough. Now, quite possibly, a female reviewer might identify with the characters more. I am a man with little exposure to women and children. But I think, if Ms. Hasty doesn't want to irritate her audience with Alice's frustration, then she might need to add more weighty complications, flesh out B and Charlie more, or sharpen some of the psychological tensions earlier. Audiences need drama to invest in a play and its characters.

Alternatively, this play could be shortened dramatically. Pinteresque pauses and hesitations only work if there's something substantive to think about while the characters are stumbling over their words. No one wants the viewer ever to think, "Get on with it." Economy is a great thing in art. *Blue Paper Bag* might have made a powerful hour long play.

THE PERFORMANCES

It's difficult, with this particular play, to differentiate between the performances and the characters the actors represented. As usual, with a **Face to Face** production, the quality of the performances was excellent. Samantha Yestrebsky and Rheanna Salazar did great jobs with B and Charlie. They seemed like relatively *together* personalities, who were dealing with a troubled life as adults. And they were likeable, even if it was hard to invest in their lives. We don't know that much about them to love them.

Daisy, played by Alexandra Rooney, would have charmed the pants off any audience in anything. Candy Dato as Gloria was fairly lackluster, but then, her character was nothing more than functionary. Gabe Calleja as Mr. Morris reminds the audience that some people have their shit together. His work on this was terrific. Mr. Morris' brief discussion of how he sees his job as guidance councilor, and the fact that he doesn't emotionally invest in his students, surprised and gratified me. Playwright Kristen Hasty played Alice. My experience dictates against playwrights acting in (or directing) their own productions. That's almost always a bad idea. I don't know if it was a mistake here. It just seems that Alice was very annoying and frustrating, and I wanted to be as far away from her as possible. I think that was intended, but I'm not sure.

Perhaps I was not the man for this very female play. I have to confess, when Alice read her final poem at the end, I teared up. I think reworking the script with a lot more economy, so that Alice reads her poem after 50 minutes or so wouldn't have left me feeling so underutilized as an audience member. I might have cared about Alice instead of wanting to ostracize her from my world. It will be interesting to see what happens next with Kristen Hasty's career. **MIXED FACE**

FURTHER INFORMATION

- Presented live online on Sunday, November 29th, 2020
- Request access at facetofacereadings@gmail.com
- www.facetofacefilms.net

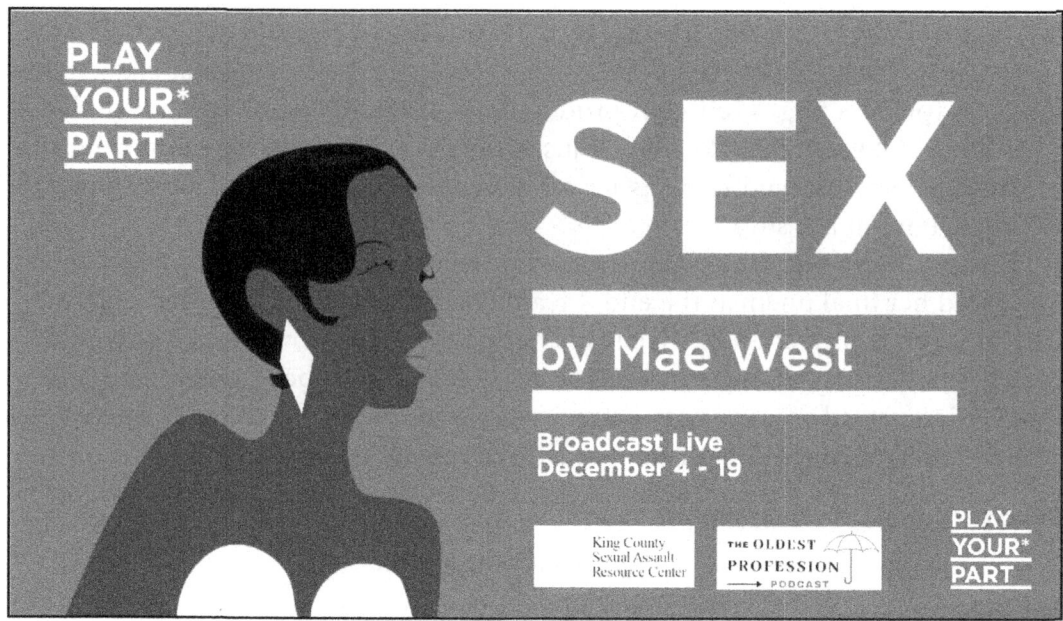

Sex

Reviewed online live December 4th, 2020

- Presented by **Play Your Part Seattle**
- Play by Mae West
- Direction: Isabella Price
- Original Music & Music Direction: Perice Pope
- Choreography: Sailor St. Claire
- Costume Design: Michael Notestine
- Production Design: Isabella Rivera
- Sound Design: Kayla Sierra-Lee
- Stage Manager: Dionne Wardrop
- Assistant Stage Manager: Alexandra Angelova
- Broadcast Engineer: Russell Hay
- Videographer: L. Fried
- Production Manager: Kevin Mikolajczak
- Marketing Coordinator: Rachael Langton

THE CAST

- Amariss Harris: Margy
- Michael Malanga: Rocky
- Dash Williams: Gregg
- Gloria Tsai: Clara

- Nicholas Ramsay: Jimmy
- Christina Brewington: Flossie/Marie
- Kyle Connors: Curley
- James Grice: Jones
- Gregg Mess: Robert Stanton
- Shan Moreno: Red
- Amr Nabeel: Agnes
- Ian Waters: Dawson
- Christian Ortiz: Condez
- Tony White: Waiter
- Carter Randolph Wright: Captain
- Kenon Veno: Manly/2nd Man/Policeman
- Nathaniel Kiss: Jenkins/1st Man

BACKGROUND

In 1926, May West wrote, produced, and directed a new Broadway play called *Sex,* about a prostitute with a heart of gold. Back then, even the word "sex" wasn't said out loud, especially in polite society of the sort that attended Broadway plays. Nor were prostitutes and other sex workers considered to be suitable subjects for the performing arts. In spite of that, the play, described by **The New York Times** as "crude and inept" was quite successful, with healthy ticket sales and a decent run, for a while, anyway.

Then, various religious groups and **The New York Society for the Suppression of Vice** complained to city officials about the immorality in this play that *most* of them hadn't even seen. This resulted in a police raid that closed it, and led to the arrest of its star, Mae West, who received a ten-day sentence for "corrupting the morals of youth." Although quite able to pay the fine leveled against her, Ms. West chose to serve her sentence, which led to an enormous amount of publicity (notoriety) that she was later able to finesse into life-long fame and a career that lasted until she died in 1980.

THE PLAY

First off, I more or less agree with **The New York Times**. *Sex,* as originally written, appears to have been dramatically "crude and inept." With three acts that run for two-hours-and-forty minutes, it certainly challenges the vastly shortened attention spans that TV has forced upon *us.* That said, I must confess that I was enchanted with the elan and charm brought to this historical piece by our colleagues in Seattle. Adapted for more modern viewers, the **Play Your Part** website describes it as the story of a "particularly successful lady of the night (originally played by Mae West)" that "explores the Canadian red-light district through a uniquely feminine lens, where sex workers navigate how to move up in a world dominated by men."

THE PRODUCTION

This is a very ambitious Zoom presentation, one of the most complicated I've yet seen. With seventeen actors and many, many, many scenes, ranging from Toronto to Trinidad and back again (the last act wasn't specific as to its location, except that it was an estate located within three hours of Toronto) being performed live by so many actors, all isolated in their own spaces by the pandemic, it's almost axiomatic that technical issues will arise. To the credit of the company and cast, that happened only once. During Act III, the audio for one of the actors went silent. But, it was handled well, obviously planned for in case it happened, and the play subsequently concluded with no other problems.

The production values, given the problems inherent in Zoom productions, were remarkable. The costumes, designed by Michael Notestine, were well thought out and attractive. A great deal of thought was also given to the settings. Since Production Designer Isabella Rivera had to coordinate everything between seventeen different locations, the fact that they were basically coherent was almost miraculous. The music, both original works composed by Musical Director Perice Pope, and drawn from historical sources by Sound Designer Kayla Sierra-Lee, was always appropriate and entertaining. I particularly enjoyed the Mae West originals that were played between scenes, as well as the very effective solo dance numbers choreographed by Sailor St. Claire and performed by Amariss Harris and Amr Nabeel between the acts.

THE PERFORMANCE

In the lead role of Margy (originally played by Mae West), Amariss Harris was strong and ambitious. Determined to better herself at a time when opportunities for women were extremely limited, she presented an intriguing picture of what they had to do when men were in charge of everything. We can only be grateful (hopeful) that this has begun to change. As Agnes, Amr Nabeel was extraordinarily moving, a picture of destroyed innocence and despair.

Michael Malanga as Margy's pimp, Rocky, was alternately charming and dangerous. The way he manipulated and used the women in his life was a lesson in itself. As Gregg, at first Margy's customer, then her lover and saviour, Dash Williams was sympathetic and determined. He and James Grice, who played Jones, were more than funny as a couple of horny sailors.

CONCLUSION

With such a large cast, it's impossible to mention all the actors. But, I can observe that everyone in the play was focused and committed, and played their supporting roles with a great deal of panache. Director Isabella Price has assembled a gifted, multiracial and gender fluid company, and given us a valuable historical work, from which we can all learn about both theater and the evolving sexual relationships that have become so prevalent in our culture.

And, finally, thank you so much Seattle for joining our list of Off Broadway and Off-Off Broadway reviews. That's one good thing about the Zoom revolution, it's allowing us to get out of New York City and find out about other brilliant work going on all over the country. Seattle is about as Off-Off-Off Broadway as one can get, but their work is entirely professional, as good or better than any Zoom work I've seen from here, and certainly deserves to be included as part of the increasingly important Independent Theater Movement.

Sex is streaming live online through December 19th. It contains explicit language and deals with sexual assault, suicide, prostitution, extortion, and crime. Not recommended for audiences under the age of sixteen, it's still fun and a terrific take on our (fairly) recent past; well worth a look. See the link below for tickets. **HI! DRAMA** is happy to award this performance a very **HAPPY FACE**.

PLAY YOUR PART'S PARTNERSHIP (from their website)

Play Your Part's partnership with **King County Sexual Assault Resource Center** and **The Oldest Profession Podcast** connects audiences with resources for sexual assault survivors and sex workers, so that they may learn more about how they can support this vital work. For information, access the link below.

PERFORMANCE INFORMATION

- Running live from December 4th – 19th, 2020
- Partnership information: playyourpartseattle.org

A Streetcar Named Desire

Reviewed online live December 5th, 2020

- Presented by **Face to Face Films**
- Play by Tennessee Williams
- Director: Anthony M. Laura
- Composer: Philip Lauto
- Press: Jay Michaels Arts & Entertainment

THE CAST

- Blanche Dubois: Rand Faris
- Stanley Kowalski: Nakai Mirtenbaum
- Stella Kowalski: Emily Tolnay
- Mitch: Dan Kelly
- Eunice: Kristen Seavey
- Steve: Chapman Hyatt
- Matron: Rheanna Salazar
- Narrator: Colton Rooney

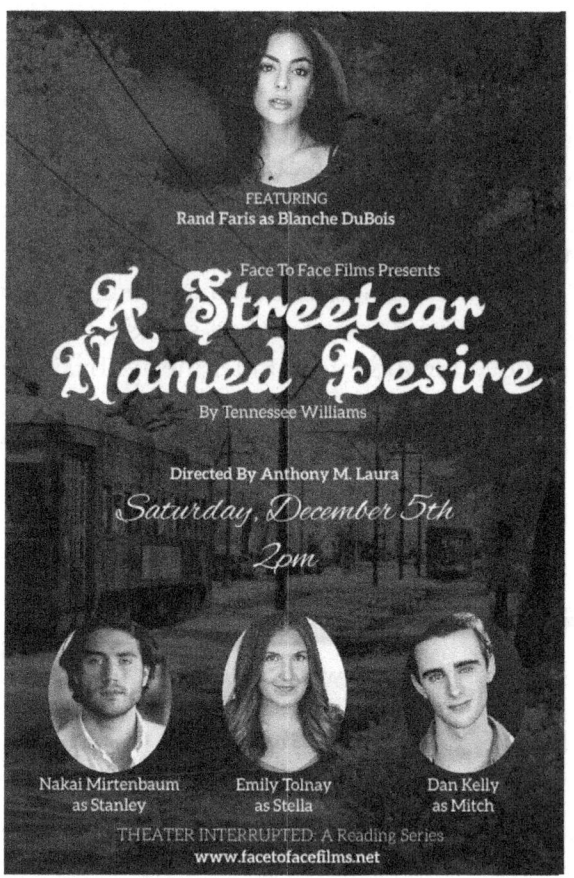

BACKGROUND

The first Tennessee Williams play I ever saw was *Glass Menagerie*. It's a perfect play. Four characters, basically paired off in succinct, individual scenes, with subtle exposition and dialogue that flows like music. Every since, I've held that a single work like *Glass Menagerie* is great enough to justify an artist's entire life. When you consider that it's only one of at least six masterpieces that immediately come to mind when one thinks of Tennessee Williams, it's not a stretch to suggest that Mr. Williams might possibly be the greatest playwright of the 20th Century.

A Streetcar Named Desire is certainly one of those six. For years, I thought that title was nothing but a metaphor. It wasn't until I visited New Orleans for Mardi Gras that I discovered an actual streetcar, charming, antique, a rattling relic running on a track with a brass plate proudly proclaiming its famous name.

That's gone now. Like so many of the best parts of our past, it's been replaced by a soulless machine that offers nothing but a cheap way to get from Point A to Point B. How sad it would have been if Williams had been forced to call his play *A*

Bus named Desire. But, that didn't happen, thank God, allowing for a title, a perfect metaphor as it happens, that describes a gentle woman's inevitable descent into madness.

THE PLAY

Stella Kowalski lives in the Elysian Fields section of New Orleans with her husband, Stanley. When her sister, Blanche Dubois, comes to visit, and subsequently moves in, her antebellum social affectations immediately offend Stanley, which leads to violence in the Kowalski household. The subsequent conflict is too famous for me to describe. Just let me observe that the Elysian Fields setting is, once again, a brilliant metaphor. The Elysian Fields enshrine the immortal souls of the heroic and virtuous in Greek mythology. Thus, they are entirely appropriate as the final resting place of the soul of Blanche Dubois, one of the most famous heroines in American literature.

THE PRODUCTION

In many ways, this "reading" of Tennessee Williams' play is one of the best productions I've seen from **Face to Face Films**. I put the word "reading" in quotes because this was definitely a performance. The actors weren't reading, they were acting, and the understanding and nuance drawn by Director Anthony Laura and his fine company from Williams' exquisite dialogue were truly first rate. Add to that, the improvements in the Zoom work, and the simplicity of Colton Rooney's understated narration, and one has as fine a rendition of this marvelous play as one can expect online, or, anywhere, for that matter.

THE PERFORMANCE

Rand Faris, as Blanche Dubois, was brilliant. From her first word to her last line, one so moving that it's become almost a cri de cœur in our social milieu, she was absolutely mesmerizing. I can't say I've ever seen a better Blanche Dubois, up to and including the unforgettable characterization of Vivien Leigh in the 1951 film with Marlon Brando. Fragile, delicate, and refined, it was horrifying to see her dismantled bit by bit by Nakai Mirtenbaum's strong, masculine Stanley Kowalski, as he thoughtlessly tore her defenses apart and scattered them like chaff around the French Quarter. Throughout, Mr. Mirtembaum exuded a sinister sensuality that suggested he might explode into violence at any moment, even when he was playing poker or begging Stella for forgiveness; a fine, memorable portrayal in every way.

    As Stella, Emily Tolnay was extremely sympathetic and clearly torn between her husband, who she loved passionately, and her sister, who she wanted to help and protect. When she finally had to choose between them, one could feel the pain and confusion that consumed her. In 1951, mental illness was a mysterious unknown.

There were only a few possible treatments available, most of which have since been discredited. Stella made the only choice she could, and it broke her heart.

Dan Kelly played Mitch with a great deal of warmth. Personally, I've never been able to forgive Mitch for deserting Blanche in her hour of need. Mr. Kelly did a fine job portraying his indecision, but his unwillingness to believe Blanche when she said what Stanley did was telling. As always, he took Stanley's side, leaving Blanche at the mercy of her inner demons.

Kristen Seavey and Chapman Hyatt as Eunice and Steve, the upstairs neighbors, were strong and supportive. The parts are small, but they were played with great sympathy, as was the Matron played by Rheanna Salazar. Kudos to everyone in the cast for their intelligent and emotionally engaging presentation of this great play. Tennessee Williams, himself, would have been proud. **HAPPY FACE PLUS**

FURTHER INFORMATION

- Presented live online on Saturday, December 5th, 2020
- Request access at facetofacereadings@gmail.com
- www.facetofacefilms.net

Anthony J. Piccione
presents

TALKING IT OUT

A VIRTUAL SHORT PLAY FESTIVAL
IN SUPPORT OF MENTAL HEALTH AWARENESS

Taking It Out Festival
Reviewed online live December 7th, 2020

- Produced by **Piccione Arts**
- Curated and Directed by Anthony J. Piccione
- Press: Jay Michaels Arts & Entertainment

BACKGROUND

Originally conceived in 2019 as a live reading of short plays exploring the difficulties experienced by those who suffer from mental illness, Taking it Out has morphed into a reoccurring festival of five dramas, staged online in one evening, presented on the third Saturday of every month (see below for upcoming events). While each of the plays is unique, they all highlight various aspects of mental illness, including anxiety, depression, autism, ADHD, PTSD, bipolar disorder, schizophrenia, and dementia. The screenings are free, but donations are encouraged and they will be shared equally by **Piccione Arts** and the **National Alliance on Mental Illness** (*www.nami.org*).

THE PLAYS

The first five plays, presented on November 21st at 7:30pm, were well written and informative, each one focusing on a specific mental illness. Mr. Piccione and his excellent actors, drawn from a wide range of ages and genders, have done a fine job detailing the pain and distress encountered not only by those suffering from the various disorders, but also those who support them. Following is a brief summary of each play. Each one contains a note on the sort of affliction being discussed.

BROAD DAYLIGHT
- Play by Alex Goldberg
- Max Berry as Jeremy
- Susan O'Doherty as Beverly

Jeremy's mother, Beverly, is beginning to suffer the effects of Alzheimers. This is a disturbing picture of a life-long relationship coming to an end. Exactly how it ends, however, is somewhat vague, leaving the denouement as an open question.

MEAN GIRL & BEST FRIEND
- Play by Monique Hebert
- Rayah Martin as Mean Girl
- Gemia Foo as Best Friend

Rayah Martin is definitely a mean girl. A high school bully (in the classic sense), she picks on her "best friend" who appears to be suffering from PTSD. By the end, however, Best Friend appears to be getting herself together, a hopeful development in any case.

EDDIE & EDNA
- Play by Donald Loftus
- Jamil Al-Chokhachi as Eddie
- Louise Heller as Edna
- Max Berry as Danny

Eddie appears to be suffering from hallucinations brought on by dementia. He has regular conversations with his wife, Edna, who, according to his son, Danny, passed away several years earlier. For me, however, the question remains, which entity was real, Edna or Danny?

AMYGDALA
- Play by Cassidy Tilden
- Scotty Corn as Nick
- Andres Gallardo Bustillo as Brain

Nick is experiencing a conflict over how to deal with a possible relationship, apparently caused by an imbalance in his mind; an argument, if you will, between the amygdalas located in the right and left hemispheres of everyone's Brain (there are two amygdalas in our brains that contribute to fear and anger, one in each hemisphere). I have to confess, I found this well acted narrative to be a bit confusing. The questionable emotions weren't exactly clear, a problem with the play, not the acting.

ANGELS OF THE MANSIONS OF THE MOON
- Play by Randy Gross
- Alexis Kurtz as Requiel
- Will Matus as Chubba Stone
- Haley Anderson as Kylie Stone
- Devon Lennon as Mikal Smythe
- Sarah Elizabeth Haga as Samantha Smythe
- Scotty Corn as Mike

Chubba and Mikal are plagued by PTSD (Post Traumatic Stress Disorder). Both served in the military and had experiences that led to hospitalizations, reoccurring nightmares, and other continuing emotional disturbances. This play is quite lovely at times, with good acting and well-written dialogue.

CONCLUSION

Like so many of us, I'm not exactly sure about many of the symptoms of different types of mental illness, so please bear with me if I misread some of them in my descriptions. Of course, that's why we need festivals like this. Anything we can do to achieve more understanding is in everyone's interest. Whatever, every work in this extremely interesting and well-done selection of plays piqued my curiosity and caused me to do research into the various manifestations of the afflictions. I learned a lot, and that's a great reason to watch any play. Below, is information about this continuing festival. Considering the quality of the material and Mr. Piccione's dedication to his subject, I highly recommend you take a look. **HAPPY FACE** all around.

FURTHER INFORMATION
- Five new plays every four months. Next festivals March 20th & July 17th, 2021.
- Tickets: https://www.eventbrite.com/e/talking-it-out-a-virtual-short-play-festival-tickets-111853867930.
- Information: www.facebook.com/talkingitoutfest.

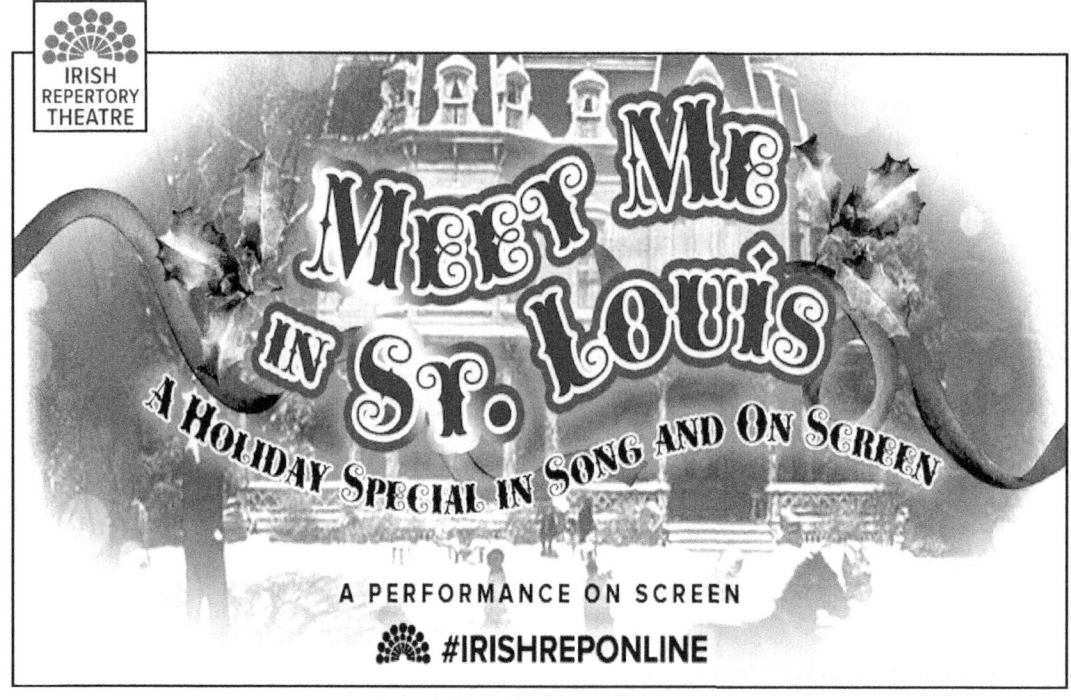

Meet Me in St. Louis
Reviewed online December 14th, 2020

- Presented online by the **Irish Repertory Theatre**
- Produced by Ciarán O'Reilly under the *2020 SAG -AFTRA New Media Agreement*
- Book by Hugh Wheeler
- Songs by Hugh Martin & Ralph Blane
- Based on *The Kensington Stories* by Sally Benson and the MGM Motion Picture *Meet Me in St. Louis*
- Adapted & Directed by Charlotte Moore
- Music Direction by John Bell
- Orchestrations by Josh Clayton
- Editor: Meridith Sommers
- Scenic Design: Charlie Corcoran
- Sound Design, Mix & Music: M. Florian Staab
- Lighting Design: Michael Gottlieb
- Costume Consultant: Tracy Christensen
- Production Manager: Brandon Cheney
- Production Coordinator: Pamela Brusoski
- General Manager: Lisa Fane
- Press: Matt Rose PR

THE CAST (in alphabetical order)

- Esther Smith: Shereen Ahmed
- Lon Smith: William Bellamy
- Alonzo Smith: Rufus Collins
- Lucille Ballard: Kerry Conte
- Anna Smith: Melissa Errico
- Rose Smith: Ali Ewoldt
- Katie: Kathy Fitzgerald
- Warren Sheffield: Ian Holcomb
- Agnes: Austyn Johnson
- Grandpa: Jay Aubrey Jones
- Tootie: Kylie Kuioka
- Postman/Trolley Man: Richard Ashley Robinson
- John Truitt: Max Von Essen

THE ORCHESTRA

- Piano/Conductor: John Bell
- Woodwinds: Jeremy Clayton
- Percussion: Joshua Mark Samuels
- Harp: Karen Lindquist
- Violin: Suzy Perelman
- Cello: Melanie Mason
- Bass: John Convertino
- Music Assistant: Adam Beskind

BACKGROUND

Long known as one of the foremost theatrical companies in New York City, **The Irish Repertory Theatre** has set a new standard for online productions. *Meet Me in St. Louis,* a exuberant musical based on Sally Benson's famous *Kensington Stories* (a series of short pieces published in **The New Yorker** in the early 1940s), and the 1944 MGM film of that name starring Judy Garland and directed by her future husband, Vincente Minnelli, is an incredible technical achievement. With a superb orchestral ensemble, masked and distanced as appropriate, and a cast of thirteen talented actors, who, as I understand it, were isolated in their studios and homes in several different states, the company made an upbeat contribution to everyone's holiday by taking us on a tuneful romp into early 20th Century America.

THE PLAY

Set in St. Louis, just before the famous 1904 St. Louis World's Fair, the play focuses on the activities of the Smith sisters, Rose, Agnes, Esther, and Tootie, as they stumble through childhood and late adolescence during a fabled time when parents were respected and democracy meant that those who got the most votes won. Featuring such American classics as *The Trolley Song, The Boy Next Door, Have Yourself a Merry Little Christmas,* and the wonderful title song itself, *Meet Me In St. Louis,* the MGM film was the most famous musical made during World War II, and maybe one of the most popular musicals of all times.

THE PRODUCTION

Producer Ciarán O'Reilly and director Charlotte Moore have done a remarkable job putting this all together, particularly considering that the lovers who kissed and danced together were standing in entirely different states. Zoom has become more and more important as the Pandemic has progressed, and, as is common in human artistic endeavors, it has improved immeasurably since the first, timid iterations of the softwear at the beginning of 2020.

To describe the technology, which is "indistinguishable from magic," would take more time than I have. So, I'm going to recommend this informative **New York Times** article by Melissa Errico who played the mother of the family, Anna Smith (*https://bit.ly/StLouisTech*). Her description of the process as she literally phones in her part is far more illuminating than anything I could say. Take a moment and read it. It was fascinating.

THE PERFORMANCE

It was also a great deal of fun. Like a sparkling plastic tree, it was too realistic to be real. It reminded one of a set of talented avatars, singing on a field drawn in 3D with Magic Markers and Sharpies. Detailed copies of human beings with beautiful singing voices, joie de vivre, hope and optimism; perfect and unchanging in an artificial world of highest definition. Which is why *Meet Me In St. Louis* was so much more than a performance. This lovely, old-fashioned work was not quite real. After all, it's a manipulated time-line, built out of episodes filmed in different places and assembled. History, frozen in numbers. Somehow, this seems to sum up the level of art in the 21st-Century.

That said, the performers all sang with skill and beauty. The ensembles were miraculous, seeing as how the voices were coming from many different places, accompanied by an orchestra that, I believe, was somewhere else in New York City. Professional and coordinated, musically uplifting in a way we seem to have forgotten how to do since 1944, it was a great holiday treat.

Shereen Ahmed as Esther, in the role made famous by Judy Garland, held her own on every count, up to and including her moving rendition of *The Boy Next Door*. Max Von Essen as John Truitt, the boy in question, was innocence itself. A fine, easy tenor. When the two of them kissed, touching lips from different states, the simplicity of the moment was breathtaking.

Austyn Johnson and Kylie Kuioka as Agnes and Tootie were appropriately adorable, and Ali Ewoldt played Rose with captivating charm. As Anna Smith, Melissa Errico painted a moving portrait with *You'll Hear a Bell,* a lovely bit of mother's advice not included in the film, about the moment when one first finds love. Add the comic *A Touch of the Irish,* sung by Kathy Fitzgerald as the intrepid Katie, and you have an absolutely first rate female ensemble singing some of the most optimistic music in the American canon.

Not that the men weren't engaging. But, at times, they felt more like props. Warren Sheffield, the "other" boyfriend, played by Ian Holcomb as a charming adolescent, was Rose's prop. As Alonzo Smith, everyone's doting father, Rufus Collins played the Smith Family's prop … and, the faux reality of the tech added to that impression. I believe this is a shortcoming of the script, not the performances.

Everyone in this cast was a trained singer, and when they sang together, wherever they were, it lifted your heart and spirits … and, it *is* about teenage girls falling in love with teenage boys. I remember from my own teens, how my sister and her friends (including mothers) manipulated every male they knew. I doubt I *ever* had a date that wasn't prearranged. That was clearly my sister's story, and everything that suggests. The point being that the men here are pawns being moved around, even the boy next door. This was revolutionary in 1944, a reversal of what had been done to women in theatrical works for centuries.

CONCLUSION

Admittedly, This is a strange review. The result, perhaps, of social isolation and digital overload. Still, the show had a happy ending and it made me feel good. Wonderful music, sweeping melodies, a fine, exuberant orchestra, conducted by pianist John Bell, period costumes exquisitely coordinated over three states, and everything else I said above. This happy, happy musical made me happy. For that, and all that technical magic, I can only give it a **HAPPY FACE PLUS**.

PERFORMANCE INFORMATION

- Support: https://irishrep.org/support
- Information: https://irishrep.org/meetmeonscreen

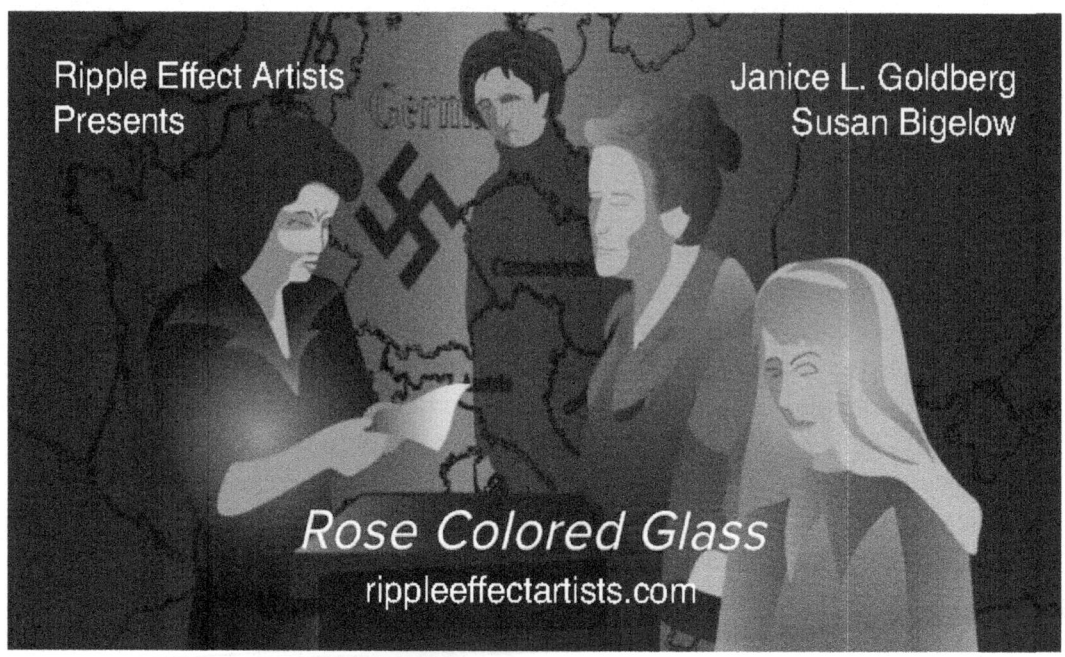

Rose Colored Glass
Podcast reviewed online December 18th, 2020

- Radio play by Janice L. Goldberg & Susan Bigelow
- Produced exclusively for WPKN Radio by **Ripple Effect Artists**
- Directed by Janice L. Goldberg
- Sound Engineering & Special Effects Coordination by Karl Custer
- Executive Producer: Bob Johnson
- Regional Music: Peter Yanka
- Press: Jay Michaels Arts & Entertainment

THE CAST
- Lady O'Riley: Jo Twiss*
- Rose Fleishman: Laura Gardner*
- Peg O'Riley: Story Moosa*
- Voice of the BBC: Gordon Cooper

BACKGROUND

I grew up listening to the radio. It was perhaps the single, most profound influence on my thinking and my development as an artist. Great music, soap operas, dramatized films, original plays, news and documentaries; the entire world coming out of a small AM radio by a little boy's bed. I was absolutely devastated when television usurped our popular culture and Rock 'n Roll took over everything. Not that TV doesn't offer magic of it's own, but it's a documented fact that *listening* stimulates more of the brain than *viewing*. It engages the imagination and creates mind-pictures that are absolutely unique to the listener. I'm happy to say that I was able to experience and recreate a great deal of that wonder as I listened to the two separate broadcasts of Acts One & Two of this excellent aural piece set in 1938 Chicago.

THE PLAY

Rose Colored Glass is a story of racial prejudice. The world in 1938 was awash in antisemitism. What was being done to the Jews in Europe at that time is a story that must *never* be forgotten. What is too often overlooked in that story is the attitude ingrained in all too many other cultures at that time; notably in this instance, in our own country, the United States, which by 1938 had all but closed its borders to the desperate immigrants trying to escape Hitler's tyranny.

As Act One opens, Peg O'Riley is thirteen years old. She lives with her grandmother, known as Lady O'Riley, who runs an Irish bar in Chicago. Across the alley is a Jewish delicatessen owned by a widow named Rose Fleishman. But, Peg can't understand why Mrs. Fleishman and her grandmother aren't better friends. Peg loves the delicacies Mrs. Fleishman offers in her deli, particularly on Friday when Lady O'Riley always insists they eat fish. So, Peg has vowed to bring these two women together, which is the basis of this excellent radio play by Janice L. Goldberg and Susan Bigelow.

In this instance, the reason the two older women are not already friends is more a matter of unfamiliarity than prejudice. Lady O'Riley is hesitant to accept Mrs. Fleishman, more because they don't understand one another than any undue prejudice on her part. When a letter arrives, telling Mrs. Fleishman that her eleven year old nephew, Abraham, is looking through "rose colored glass" as he escapes from Nazi occupied Vienna — a code phrase used on U.K. radio broadcasts to tell Jews all over the world that their relatives have escaped and are waiting for them to respond — Lady O'Reily begins to understand the incredible hostility facing the Jews. By of the end of Act One, Mrs. Fleishman has received letters from a myriad of organizations, including agencies of the United States government, all detailing why it is impossible for them to help her find her nephew.

At the beginning of Act Two, Abraham surfaces. He is in England, trying to find his aunt. But, whether or not Mrs. Fleischman, now willingly assisted by her new friend, Lady O'Riley and her Catholic church group, succeeds in her quest, I think I should leave to you to find out (see below). Suffice to say that during this act, two people, a Jew and a Catholic, bond in ways they had never before thought possible, as the author's paint a picture that's all too familiar, remarkably similar to the way families are now being torn apart at our borders. It's as egregious and reprehensible now as it was in 1938.

THE PERFORMANCE

It was a great joy to sit back with a glass of wine, close my eyes, and let my mind roam into the late 30s. The dialogue was well written, the characters sharply defined, and the narrative sadly familiar. Subtle sound effects and music appropriate to the period, skillfully put together by Karl Kuster, delineated the scenes, encouraging the imagination to move back and forth across that narrow alley as teenage Peg O'Reily, energetically played by Story Moosa, endeavored to foster the friendship between Mrs. Fleischman and her grandmother. It should be noted that Ms. Moosa's character also acted as a narrator, which kept the plot moving and crystal clear. Jo Twiss and Laura Gardner as Lady O'Riley and Rose Fleishman are also fine radio actresses, meaning that they use their voices to great effect; no lengthy pauses, excellent diction, and well spoken accents that always let the listener know who is speaking.

CONCLUSION

The only complaint I have about this radio broadcast is that the sound was too good, which isn't exactly a complaint, is it? We've come a long way, technologically, since the days of AM radio, when the frequency response was limited and actors were frequently overwhelmed by static. For me, it didn't "sound" exactly the same, which was a little bit disappointing. But, that's stupidly subjective. All in all, Susan Bigelow and Janice Goldberg (who also directed) have created a moving, engaging portrait of a lost time, one that can still teach us a lot about our country and our world.

Originally produced for WPKN Radio, the entire program can still be accessed on SoundCloud. The links are below. Pour yourself a drink, close your eyes, and travel into the distant past. *Rose Colored Glass* deserves a **HAPPY FACE** all around.

PERFORMANCE INFORMATION
- ACT 1: https://soundcloud.com/wpkn895/rose-colored-glass-act-one
- ACT 2: https://soundcloud.com/wpkn895/rose-colored-glass-act-ii

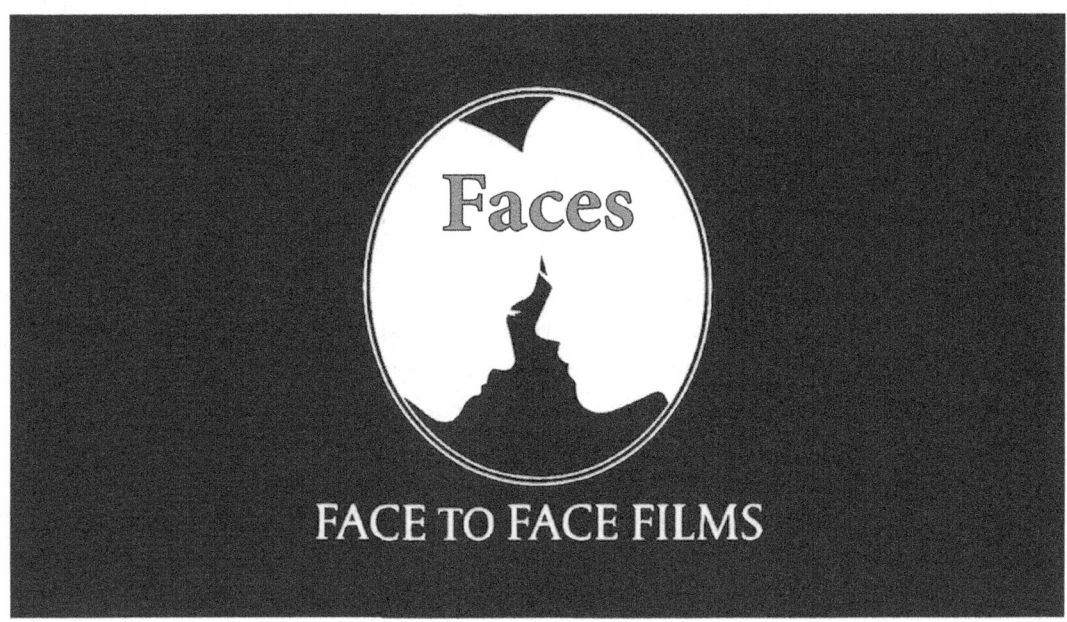

Faces

Reviewed online by William J. Cataldi December 27th, 2020

- Presented by **Face to Face Films**
- Part of the *2020 Theater Interrupted* series
- Writer and Director: Anthony M. Laura
- Press: Jay Michaels Arts & Entertainment

THE COMPANY (in order of appearance)

- Alexandra Rooney
- Kristen Hasty
- Jose Duran
- Dan Kelly
- Emily Tolney
- Emma Dubery
- Vivien Cardone
- Samantha Yestrebsky
- Kristen Seavey
- Alex Commito
- Kelsey O'Keefe
- Rheanna Salazar
- Tom Arrowsmith
- Josh Adwar
- Rand Faris
- Gabe Calleja

THE PERFORMANCE

Face to Face Films brought its *2020 Theater Interrupted* series of zoom productions of original and traditional plays to conclusion this week with *Faces,* a collection of original speeches and dialogues which managed to feature all or most of the actors in the company's stable. Artistic Director Anthony Laura, a brilliant, sleeves-rolled-up director; together with Executive Operations Director, Rand Faris; Producer Josh Adwar; and Production Executive Sophia Licata; created a thrilling end to a landmark season for the company. COVID provided an excuse, an impetus for compelling Zoom work with productions of everything from Albee classics to original work by Mr. Laura, as well as female associates of the company.

Face to Face's original work focuses on woman-oriented productions. Zoom productions are a hybrid of theater and film, under palpable restrictions, consistent with this company's mission. This led to a laser-focus on story and acting. *Faces* showcased the acting skill of the associate actors in the company — an awesome, fitting end to 2020's creative season.

At the risk of repeating myself (see past reviews), monologues, speeches, soliloquies concentrate theater in the persona of one actor. I assume it is the most difficult acting challenge of all to give a speech, within context or not, which traces a psychological process (the stuff going on in the character's head), revealing the intellectual, emotional and oft spiritual being of the character. The actor is not the character, which, if the speech is delivered well, is hard to believe. **Face to Face**'s actors are so sincere, so committed to understanding their characters deeply, that a speech can turn into a revelation, that makes this viewer weep with joy at the virtuosity of the art.

This is a report, not a full review, so I'm not going to explore every actor's performance. I'd like to discuss just two of the many wonderful examples of work in this collection. Jose Duran gave a stellar performance of a speech by a character called Barry, about his wife's suicide and its aftermath. Mr. Duran lived and breathed Barry for a couple of minutes that slammed me in the gut so hard, tears of pain rolled down my face. Duran conveyed all of Barry's casual language, complex feelings (notably anger and hurt), masculine reluctance to allow those feelings to take over, and confusion at the lack of answers and the need for practical resilience (he has to raise children alone). His speech was the quintessence of that one thing **Face to Face** does exceptionally well: the actors typically understand their characters deeply; they manage to portray that understanding in every gesture, every nuance of voice, which brings the character fully to life. This skill is what makes these productions so overwhelming. These actors are exciting. Mr. Duran gave yet another example of this in his portrayal of Barry, at sea over the love, anger and confusion he felt over his wife's suicide.

Similarly, Rand Faris gave an engrossing speech as Eve Craven, a young woman inclined repeatedly to cut her thigh with a razor blade until she bleeds. Now, the speech itself is brilliant, weaving unspecified SM credibility with a redemptive argument about Eve's hows and whys. Cutting is considered a symptom of mental illness, and it may be, but Eve manages to explain and to deliver herself from assumed professional mental health prejudice with a miraculous bout of self-exploration and understanding. Ms. Faris had a tough row to hoe. She performed it beautifully. She resembled Lisa Bonet (which Faris might have heard before) in her self-aware sensuality, her vulnerability, her nascent self-assurance, and her young-woman wisdom. She's comfortable with herself, and she defies others' inclination to judge her. Faris pulled all that off, which is unsurprising considering the rave review of her performance as Blanche Dubois in *Streetcar* written by my colleague Jan Ewing.

These two speeches were the best of the best. Every speech in *Faces* showcased a different actor, and featured this company's consummate acting skill. These people work hard in the days and weeks leading up to a performance. They take their roles seriously. They do not read. They act, which makes all the difference. Anthony Laura has assembled a team of professionals who outshined everything else going on in an exciting year of zoom productions in New York. Mr. Laura has good taste. That means he has a good mind. That means that we can look forward to years more outstanding theater films from this company. **Face to Face Films** is our discovery of the year. How much this makes us look forward to 2021! I'm giving the entire season, capped off by this wonderful collection of speeches, a big **HAPPY FACE PLUS.**

PERFORMANCE INFORMATION

- Presented live online on Sunday, December 5th, 2020
- Request access at facetofacereadings@gmail.com
- www.facetofacefilms.net

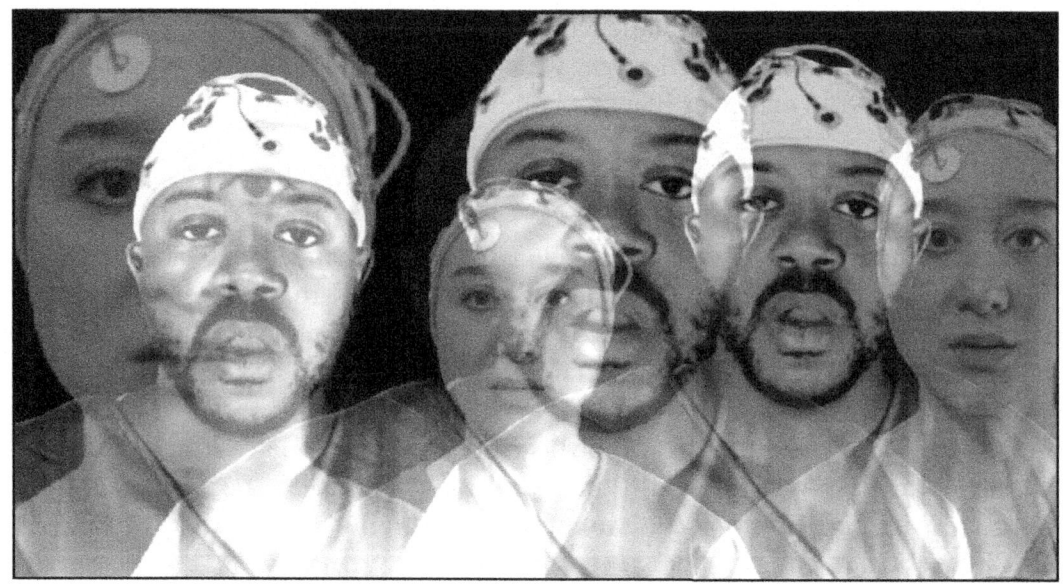
Hai-Ting Chinn & Jorell Williams

Only You Will Recognize the Signal
Reviewed onlive live December 27th, 2020

- Presented by the **HERE Arts Center**
- Composer: Kamala Sankaram
- Librettist: Rob Handel
- Director: Kristin Marting
- Press: Everyman Agency

CAST (in alphabetical order)

- Paul An
- Christopher Burchett
- Hai-Ting Chinn
- Adrienne Danrich
- Joy Jan Jones
- Joan La Barbara
- Jorell Williams

CREATIVE STAFF

- Video Design: David Bengali
- Virtual Stage Design: Liminal Entertainment Technologies
- Puppet Design: Hanne Tierney
- Costume Design: Normandy Sherwood

- Stage Management: Courteney Leggett
- Video Engineering: David Kunz
- Sound Engineering: Paul Pinto
- Lighting Design: Ayumu "Poe" Saegusa (Episode 6)

THE PLAY

The **Here Arts Center** has done it once again with a brilliant zoom-cast of Kamala Sankaram's new serial space opera, *Only You Will Recognize the Signal.* Created in collaboration with librettist Rob Handel, and HERE's Founding Artistic Director Kristin Marting, this remarkable piece is set aboard the Grand Crew a luxurious spaceship transporting a group of settlers to a new planet. The passengers are supposed to sleep safely in therapeutic hypothermia until their arrival, but there's a computer glitch. They're waking up too soon and, unable to exit their pods, are slowly going insane, requiring more help than the ship's charming but inept computer, BOB, is programmed to give them.

Set in seven ten-minute sequences, the first six of which were originally broadcast live on six separate dates, the entire opera is now available on-demand until February 15th. As I've said previously, Ms. Sankaram is a composer of genius. Her music is stunning, her technical expertize remarkable, no doubt inspired to a great degree by Mr. Handle and the digitally savvy Ms. Marting, with whom she has worked in the past.

This is an opera, in the grandest sense of the word, a mature art speaking with a modern voice of science fiction marvels that are changing our world. Absolutely first rate in every sense, Kamala Sankaram and her team should be composing for the Metropolitan Opera. **HAPPY FACE PLUS.**

PERFORMANCE INFORMATION

- World premiere of complete work: December 17th, 2020
- Available online through February 15th, 2021
- Tickets: here.org/shows/only-you-will-recognize-the-signal/

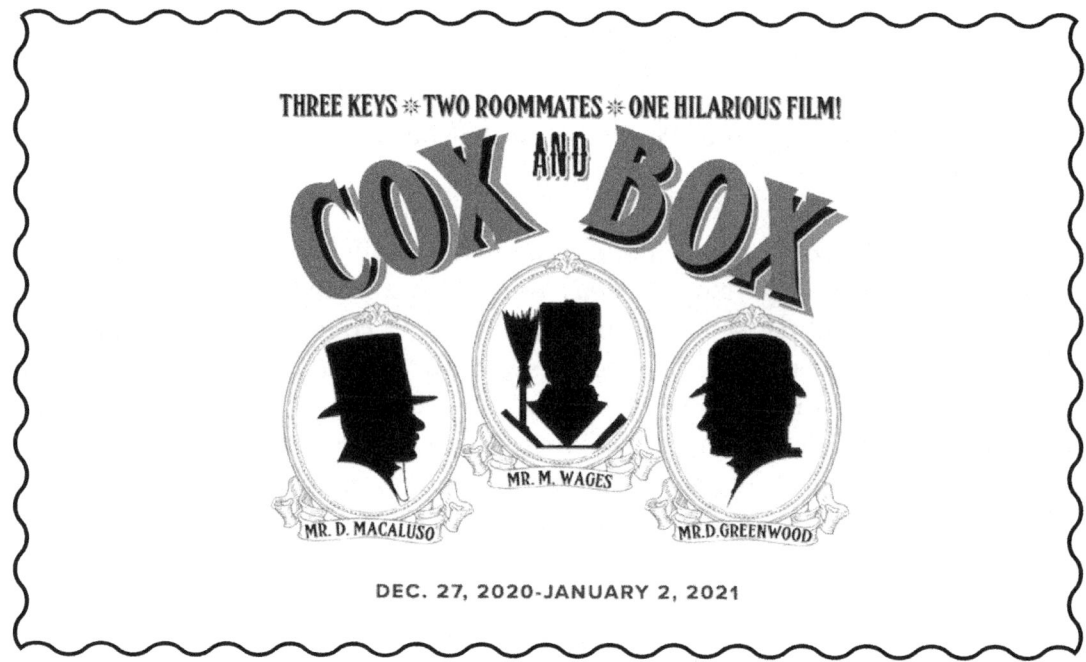

THREE KEYS ✳ TWO ROOMMATES ✳ ONE HILARIOUS FILM!

COX AND BOX

MR. D. MACALUSO

MR. M. WAGES

MR. D. GREENWOOD

DEC. 27, 2020-JANUARY 2, 2021

Cox and Box
Reviewed online by Eva Heinemann & Jan Ewing December 27th, 2020

- Presented by the **New York Gilbert & Sullivan Players (NYGASP)**
- Arthur Sullivan: Composer
- F. C. Burnand: Librettist
- Based on a farce by John Maddison Morton
- Fully staged and filmed at South Orange Performing Arts Center

CAST AND CREATIVES

- Daniel Greenwood: Box
- David Macaluso: Cox/Creative Producer
- Matthew Wages: Bouncer/Director/Set Design

PRODUCTION STAFF

- Danny Bristoll: Director of Photography
- Elizabeth Hastings: Music Director
- David Wannen: Executive Producer
- Joshua Strone: Production Stage Manager
- Laura Sudduth: Assistant Stage Manager
- Albert Bergeret: Technical Director
- Benjamin Weill: Lighting Design

- Rob Cruz: Sound Engineer, TD SOPAC
- Camillo Estrada: COVID-19 Safety Compliance Officer
- Shuhan Xie: Master Camera Operator
- Danny Bristoll: Photos
- Press: Katz PR

Eva Heinemann

Before Sullivan met Gilbert, he penned his first comic operetta with F. C. Burnand. It was called *Cox and Box*.

This extremely silly plot where Bouncer (Matthew Wages) an ex-military man and duplicitous landlord rents the same room to two different tenants: Cox (David Macaluso) who works in the daytime as a hatter, and Box (Daniel Greenwood) who is a printer who works at night.

Coincidences abound, mistaken meats fly out the window, and "Rataplan" is the answer to everything.

If the plot wasn't ridiculous enough, the script is chock-a-block with slyly filled G&S references. *Titwillow* cracked me up.

To add some gravitas to the merriment is the glorious singing of NYGASP regulars: Daniel Greenwood (Box), David Macaluso (Cox and Creative Producer), and Matthew Wages (Bouncer and Director).

I enjoyed this immensely. **MAJOR GENERAL HAPPY FACE**

Jan Ewing

Eva and I agree that **NYGASP** might be the best G&S company in the world. Under the astute direction of company founder, Albert Bergeret (Technical Director this time), their full productions are a delight, with an excellent (standing) orchestra, superb musicianship, and a well-schooled understanding of the theatrical styles created almost singlehandedly by W. S. Gilbert, many of which are still in use today.

Cox and Box, is a short, comic opera written by Bernand and Sullivan in 1866. Bernand, you say? Where is Gilbert? As it happens, Sullivan composed this piece for a private club, **The Moray Minstrels**, an informal gathering of notable men involved in London society and the arts, five years before he and Gilbert ever met. Based on a successful farce written in 1847 by John Maddison Morton, it was adapted for the musical stage by F. C. Bernand, a well-known Victorian playwright, who is, today, remembered only for this piece. It's interesting to note, however, that Gilbert actually reviewed *Cox and Box* for the *Royal Gallery of Illustration* on the 18th of May, 1867. He liked it, but said that Sullivan's music was too "classy" for the ridiculous plot.

The story concerns a landlord who rents a room to two complete strangers, one who works at night and one who works during the day. When one of them has the day off, they accidentally meet each other and, predictably, run amok.

The **New York Gilbert & Sullivan Players** have done a splendid job bringing this excellent piece to life. Originally conceived for three actors and piano, it actually contains up-to-date themes of unintentional social distancing, while allowing audiences to enjoy a fully staged work. This is the third iteration of this production from creative producer David Macaluso and Music Director Elizabeth Hastings, with the film being brought to life by director Matthew Wages, whose vision is thoroughly in-line with situational comedy and 21st Century sensibilities.

Beautifully sung, and presented with a remarkable understanding of the vaudeville style, this thoroughly delightful piece runs through January 2nd, with a special New Year's Eva gala being presented on December 31st @ 8pm. Check the company's website (see below) for tickets.

This Victorian musical is funny, tuneful, and suitable for all ages, and Eva's **MAJOR GENERAL HAPPY FACE** could not be more appropriate. :-)

AVAILABILITY

- December 30th @ 2:30pm
- New Year's Eve Special: December 31st @ 8:00pm
- January 2nd @ 2:30pm
- Tickets: https://nygasp.org/

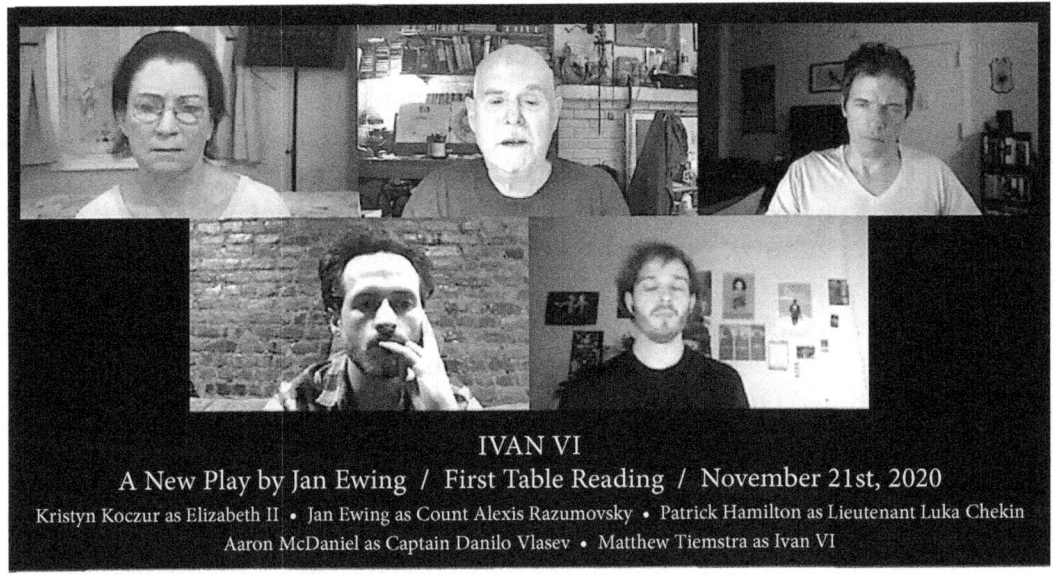

IVAN VI
A New Play by Jan Ewing / First Table Reading / November 21st, 2020
Kristyn Koczur as Elizabeth II • Jan Ewing as Count Alexis Razumovsky • Patrick Hamilton as Lieutenant Luka Chekin
Aaron McDaniel as Captain Danilo Vlasev • Matthew Tiemstra as Ivan VI

Lessons Learned during thc Pandemic
An essay by William J. Cataldi

BACKGROUND

2020 was a trying, scary time for every human being on the planet. Beset with lockdowns and prohibitions designed to keep us safe, we struggled to maintain a minimal existence. Many New Yorkers fled to rural locations, most businesses had to function virtually, and essential workers toiled to keep supply lines flowing. Meanwhile, thousands of victims died alone in ICUs all over the country. Family and friends could only contact one another via social media and video chat. If we hadn't had computers and the Internet, American casualties would likely have numbered in the multi-millions. No one could imagine what life would be like under the thumb of Republicans doing everything in their power to encourage the death toll to increase, and prolong the pandemic. Often, it seemed a losing battle.

March 7, 2020, my beloved partner Jan Ewing (author of this book), went to his last live performance. Theater shuttered completely in the days following. We thought, "It'll last a few months, then we'll be back to normal." Live theater had become an integral part of our lives. **HI! DRAMA** was the vortex of a theater-loving family of critics, producers, actors, directors, etc. I write this at the start of 2021, while I, myself, am in quarantine after a positive test result, and no one knows how much longer it will be before we can return to stage and auditorium. One would think a *pall of doom* clouds everyone involved in theater who remained in New York waiting for a future that still hasn't come. Many were forced to flee the city, no longer able to live with zero income. But that's not what happened to us.

By late May/June, we were being invited to watch casual readings of new plays in the nascent Zoom format. Zoom had been invented for face-to-face business meetings, but many theater companies saw it as a medium suited to readings, albeit awkwardly. The audience could watch from home, camara and microphone muted, and the actors could read from home, coordinated by an unseen director. The first such reading I saw was **Fresh Fruit Festival**'s *PartiTime*, a new play by Gregory Marlow. The medium was troubled, my review reflected that, but everyone was thinking *what if*?

Even before June, **Irish Repertory Theater** was streaming filmed performances. Other companies were advancing with Zoom in fits and starts. But later in June, in time for **National Queer Theater**'s annual *Criminal Queerness Festival, Mosque-4Mosque* and *She He Me* blew me away. The actors weren't just reading, they had rehearsed. Despite the Zoom boxes in which the individual characters had to live, they were interacting with one another. These were actual *live* performances of new plays that transcended the format, involving me in an imaginary world, as if I were watching it on stage. By July everyone began to understand that low-cost, fabulous Zoom-productions could liberate New York theater from its chains.

THE RESURRECTION OF THE RADIO PLAY

Contemporary folks are unlikely to have much experience with radio at all, much less radio plays. Everyone knows what radio is, but in Jan Ewing's childhood, radio was omnipresent. For much of that childhood, there wasn't any television. Radio play listeners typically sat in a room and listened to the parts spoken by actors with original music and frequent sound effects to flesh out the action. The listener stared, while his or her actual vision dissolved into an imaginary world, which replaced the actual world. The listener "saw" the play, as if the actors were performing it in front of them on stage or film, in their mind's eye.

Don't ask me for specifics, but I have heard from various sources that studies of brain activity, comparing radio listeners to television watchers, showed a far more intense activity on the part of radio listeners. Television is passive. Radio is active, causing multiple parts of the brain to "light up," as they become engaged in the listening. This is crucial: radio requires the participation of the listener. Zoom-productions resurrected this active engagement, this participation of the viewer, by creating the play in the imagination of the viewer.

By mid-summer, **Face to Face Films** had found the holy grail of Zoom work. Their series of new and original plays, fully-formed and acted by broad, multi-dimensional actors, would last until the end of the year. The Zoom boxes in which the actors found themselves were simple and nondescript. Of course, all this evolved from the requirement that people during the pandemic stay away from one another. I'll never forget Alex Commito's and Vivien Cardone's performances of George and Martha in *Who's Afraid of Virginia Woolf?* in October. We could only see their faces. They were miles from one another. Yet Zoom brought them together in the crucible of my imagination. I could see their material interaction, as well as their emotional and psychological reaction. I could see their moral inter-action, and their spiritual decrepitude. I watched everything in my mind's eye, with nothing but these brilliant actors' faces and words to go by.

This and many other **Face to Face** productions proved to be the height, the *Renaissance of Zoom* theater work. The fact that they did it repeatedly, showed everyone exactly what could be done with the medium. As with every aesthetic cul-mination, there was a falling off, a mannered phase, an afterward. Other companies took the medium in more fanciful directions, employing special effects, graphic design, and ultimately, expensive techniques to augment the acting, and make it seem that we were watching pandemic era films. **Irish Repertory Company**'s *Meet Me in St. Louis* brought Zoom to the level of artificial cinema. Even though the actors were alone in different states, the effects-team spent a lot of time and money making it look like they were dancing together, kissing, and fully interacting on three-dimensional sets.

ART WITH RESTRAINTS

Mr. Ewing was the first to point out to me that artists frequently face restraints, and indeed, oftentimes the more restraints there are, the better. The computer seems to have done little to improve and to speed up word processing, because secretaries now waste lots of time with page design and font choice. As I have lived with Mr. Ewing's thought, and watched it in action for decades, I have become a big advocate for restraints in art. I am not a fan of big budget films and Broadway theater. I have seen so much fine art produced with little or no money that compares favorably with expensive, polished art, that I now believe most art budgets are wasted money.

Zoom production budgets have no line-item for real estate, the biggest expense for most theatrical productions in New York. Therefore, they are extraordinarily cheap to create, even when the staff is paid. But, despite all of the potential obstacles, we may have had a front-row seat for the inception of a new form of radio play. Certainly, live theater, when it returns, will still be a major preoccupation of theater lovers, but I can't now imagine living in a world without access to wonderful productions, both live and recorded, in the Zoom format. (For one thing, you can eat in the "theater" and even go to the bathroom whenever you have to.)

Zoom productions offer companies a unique, low-cost opportunity to show off their capabilities. Also, the low entry costs for new companies, willing to offer Zoom productions as their primary focus, at least at first, will encourage much new talent to develop. Just as YouTube made many young people famous on a shoe-string, playwrights, actors, directors and impromptu theater companies from all over the country and the world, might now become well-known with Zoom productions archived on YouTube.

Once again, the "restrictions" placed on the creative process by the Zoom format might be just the ticket to encourage growth in the industry, focusing attention on new, low-budget projects, and sapping attention away from wealthy companies and corporations. Regardless, we hope Zoom productions are here to stay, not to replace live theater, but to exist alongside live theater.

All crises, all tragedies, have a silver lining. They usually leave the people who survive better off morally, spiritually, emotionally, psychologically, than they were before the crisis hit. We at **Ewing Reviewing** hope that more good will come from the COVID crisis than bad (and a lot of bad came from it). The theater industry will survive, and hopefully, be more resilient than ever. We hope the brilliant Zoom productions we saw this year will bring about an entire new approach to theater that will not disappear when the virus disappears. We were there when . . . .

—pup

Index

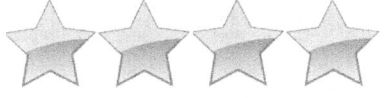
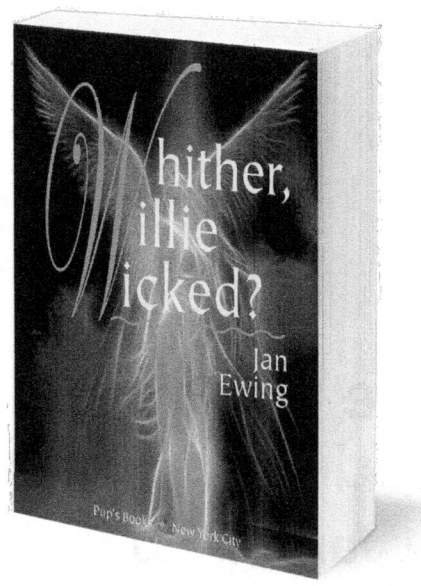

*"The raw intelligence
of this incredible child will
come into your heart."*

- Nan Willow, Amazon Review

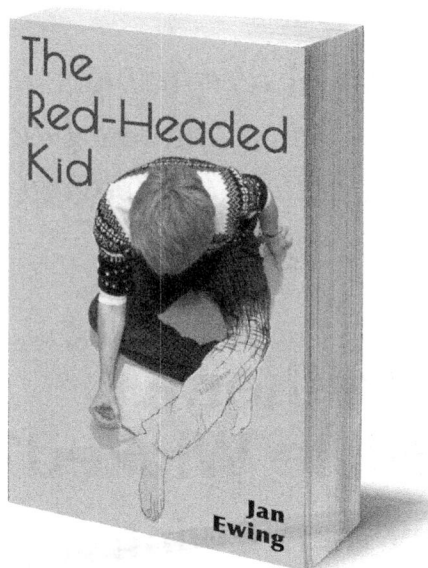

The
Red-Headed Kid
by Jan Ewing

In the 1940s, when the Red-Headed Kid is born, sex is a subject that is not discussed. Men who openly want sex are perverts. Woman who like sex are whores and homosexuals are social pariahs. But, beneath the surface things are not what they seem. Kinsey has begun to ask questions that have never before been asked, and, as the fifties commence, the subject begins to come out of the closet. No one is supposed to do it yet, but at least the world is beginning to openly admit it exists.

Then, the sixties storm in. Margaret Sanger legitimizes birth control, finally freeing women from the threat of unwanted pregnancy and all hell breaks loose. Over the following years, the Kid experiences every bit of the sexual revolution: starting in the forties, when sex isn't mentioned; through the fifties, when there isn't any; into the sixties and seventies, when it never stops; until the eighties, when it morphs into a fatal disease.

The world turns upside down, intercourse is no longer the point. Players direct their sexual energy into elaborate games; dressing up and enacting detailed erotic scenarios in which the sex goes on forever and pornography sets the standard. It is a moment of untrammeled freedom, of a sort that might never be seen again.

☆☆☆☆☆ AN AMAZINGLY GOOD AUTHOR COMING OVER THE HORIZON!
Nan Willow, Amazon Review, January 18, 2014
The raw intelligence of this incredible child will come into your heart. Got to read it and read it again. True prose. And he can actually spell. Doesn't get any better. Mr. Ewing has had an amazing life. When finished, find the books he wrote in the '70s. Watch for Jan's sequel and all his other great works coming to you through Amazon.

☆☆☆☆☆ RED-HEADED, BUT NOT RED-FACED
Win Gould, Amazon Review February 16, 2014
Jan has written with honesty, with clarity, and with humanity of the early years of the Red-Headed Kid. I, being of the author's age, particularly enjoyed our life parallels and divergences. It's fascinating seeing how his mind works, where he goes with his sexuality, his music, and beyond.

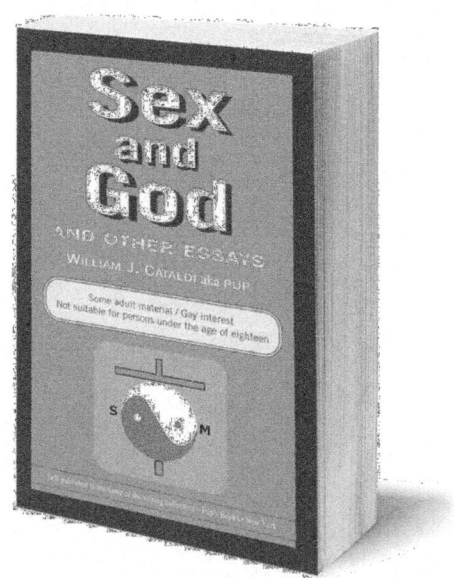

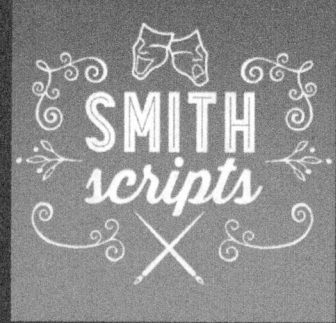

Made in the USA
Middletown, DE
20 March 2022

62975702R00124